Performance Dashboards

Measuring, Monitoring, and Managing Your Business

WAYNE W. ECKERSON

WILEY

John Wiley & Sons, Inc.

For general information on our other products and services, or technical support, please contact our Customer Care Department within the United States at 800-762-2974, outside the United States at 317-572-3993 or fax 317-572-4002.

Wiley also publishes its books in a variety of electronic formats. Some content that appears in print may not be available in electronic books.

For more information about Wiley products, visit our Web site at http://www.wiley.com.

Library of Congress Cataloging-in-Publication Data:

Eckerson, Wayne W., 1958–
    Performance dashboards: measuring, monitoring, and managing your business / Wayne W. Eckerson.
        p.   cm.
    Includes index.
    ISBN-13: 978-0-471-72417-9 (cloth)
    ISBN-10: 0-471-72417-3 (cloth), ISBN: 0-471-77863-X (Custom Edition)
    1. Management—Evaluation.   2. Organizational effectiveness—Evaluation.
    I. Title.
    HD31.E294 2006
    658.4′013—dc22   2005011800

Printed in the United States of America.

10 9 8 7 6 5 4 3 2 1

To my parents,
Homer and Sally,
who made everything possible.

Contents

Foreword

Two adages help us to understand the power of performance dashboards. The first is: "You cannot manage what you do not measure." When managers do not know how their work units and subordinates are functioning compared with previous performance, goals, and benchmarks, it is difficult to reward superior achievement or take corrective action when performance fails to meet expectations. The second adage is: "What gets watched, gets done." When workers know the metrics used for their evaluation, they will strive to perform well on those measurements.

Effective managers have always at least implicitly understood these adages and have had systems and methods for assessing how their organizations are doing. Even before computer-based systems, many executives had their staffs prepare briefing books to keep a close tab on organizational performance. The critical success factor concept, which is directly related to today's key performance indicators (KPIs), was designed to identify the goals and activities that need to be monitored most closely. Executive information systems, which focus on tracking key metrics important to senior management, are the most immediate precursors to today's performance dashboards.

Performance dashboards integrate much of what has been learned about how computer-based systems can help in the effective management of organizations. For example, the most powerful systems are linked to company objectives. Performance dashboards also benefit from technology advances. An early problem with executive information systems was that the data required were often not readily available; considerable human effort was needed to acquire, analyze, and then enter the data into the system. Data warehouses have now made the sourcing of data much less of a problem. Also, the technology vendors have developed packages that, in the best cases, sit on top of powerful business intelligence platforms providing analysis capabilities beyond the building of simple variance charts.

Despite the growing popularity of performance dashboards, considerable confusion still exists. Common questions include: "What is the difference between dashboards and scorecards?" "Must dashboards be implemented top down, or can they be built bottom up?" Then there are important questions about how to build them successfully, such as: "How should I determine how many and what KPIs to include?" "Are there any political obstacles that I am likely to encounter, and how can I resolve them?"

Wayne Eckerson has written a wonderful book that clears up much of the confusion about performance dashboards, addresses the most important issues, and provides answers to the most critical questions. It is not surprising that Wayne has written such a great book. He combines the conceptualization and writing skills that he honed as a research analyst, the survey data that he has collected in his position as Director of Research and Services for The Data Warehousing Institute, and case studies and examples from hundreds of companies that he has consulted with and interviewed over the years. As a result, the book is wonderfully "textured" and is a "must read" for anyone who wants to understand performance dashboards fully. Whether you are an executive wanting to learn about dashboards, an IT professional who needs to understand how to implement dashboards better, or a college student preparing for a career armed with the latest and best thinking about how to improve organizational performance, you will benefit from reading Wayne's book.

Hugh J. Watson
Terry College of Business
University of Georgia

Preface

A PATH TO PURSUE

False Starts

The original focus of this book was business performance management (BPM). Tim Burgard, my editor at John Wiley & Sons, had read an in-depth report that I wrote on the topic in 2003 and asked whether I would be interested in turning it into a book geared to business professionals. Other than the normal reservations one might have about undertaking a book project in addition to a full-time job, I was not particularly thrilled about exploring BPM in greater depth.

My initial research showed that BPM meant different things to different people. It was a broad, catch-all category of applications and technologies, including everything from financial consolidation and reporting tools to planning, budgeting, and forecasting applications to dashboards and scorecards, among other things. BPM seemed to reflect whatever vendors had in their product portfolios at the time rather than representing a distinct and compelling discipline in itself.

Conceptually, however, most people seem to agree that the purpose of BPM is to *focus* organizations on things that really matter. Too many organizations spread their energies and resources far and wide and consequently never make much progress towards achieving their strategic objectives. The theory behind BPM is that organizations need to identify the key activities that contribute most to their success and make sure they do them well. In short, the purpose of BPM is to help organizations become more focused, aligned, and effective.

Dashboards and Scorecards

Thus, in the spirit of BPM, I decided to cast off BPM as a book topic and *focus* on something more tangible and concrete that organizations could use to implement the *discipline* of BPM. At the time, I did not know any companies that had implemented a BPM solution—whatever that might be—but I did notice that many companies were rolling out dashboards and scorecards. These applications seemed to resonate with workers up and down the organizational hierarchy, from boardrooms to shop floors to customers and suppliers. Better yet, dashboards and scorecards helped companies implement the principles of BPM better than any of the other so-called BPM applications or technologies I saw in the marketplace. Now, here was a topic worth exploring!

As I investigated dashboards and scorecards, I encountered much of the same definitional fuzziness as I did with BPM, albeit on a smaller scale. Every "dashboard" I saw looked and functioned differently and served different purposes. Some looked like reporting portals or electronic briefing books, while others contained mostly text and hand-entered data, and still others featured graphical dials and meters that flickered with real-time data.

The only clarity in the field came from the Balanced Scorecard community, which has well-defined principles and a maturing methodology to help organizations create, display, and manage performance data. However, since there were already many good books about Balanced Scorecards that covered both theory and practice and were written by distinguished consultants and professors, I did not see how I could add much value there!

Nevertheless, I knew that organizations were putting a great deal of energy into building dashboards and scorecards using business intelligence (BI) and data integration tools and technologies—two areas that I have been researching and speaking about for the past ten years. I figured that I could add value by identifying the common threads among these initiatives, create a framework to clarify the discussion about their use, and synthesize best practices for designing, building, and growing these systems from organizations that have already done it. The result is this book.

THE PUZZLE OF PERFORMANCE DASHBOARDS

It took many hours of thought, dozens of interviews, and thousands of words to piece together the puzzle of dashboards and scorecards in a way that provides a clear and complete picture without distorting current perceptions that people have about these systems. In highly abridged form, what I came up with is this: dashboards and scorecards are part of a larger performance management system—which I call a performance dashboard—that enables organizations to measure, monitor, and manage business performance more effectively.

A performance dashboard is more than just a screen with fancy performance graphics on it: it is a full-fledged business information system that is built on a business intelligence and data integration infrastructure. A performance dashboard is very different from plain dashboards or scorecards. The latter are simply visual display mechanisms to deliver performance information in a user-friendly way whereas performance dashboards knit together the data, applications, and rules that drive what users see on their screens.z

Three Applications

To flesh out this skeletal definition a tad more, I came to realize that a performance dashboard is actually three applications in one, woven together in a seamless fashion: 1) a monitoring application, 2) an analysis application, and 3) a management application.

The *monitoring application* conveys critical information at a glance using timely and relevant data, usually with graphical elements; the *analysis application* lets users analyze and explore performance data across multiple dimensions and at different levels of detail to get at the root cause of problems and issues; the *management application* fosters communication among executives, managers, and staff and gives executives continuous feedback across a range of critical activities, enabling them to "steer" their organizations in the right direction.

Three Layers

When I looked at the data that performance dashboards display, I discovered that they let users navigate through three layers or views of information: 1) a summarized graphical view, 2) a multidimensional view, and 3) a detailed or operational view. Users can access the performance dashboard at any of these layers, but most start at the summarized graphical view and drill down along fairly predefined pathways through the multidimensional and detailed views.

This layered approach meets the information and analysis needs of a majority of individuals in an organization who are not number crunchers by training and only want to use information as a tool to perform their jobs, not as a profession in itself. Performance dashboards conform to the natural sequence in which these users want to interact with information. First, they want to monitor key metrics for exceptions; then, they want to explore and analyze information that sheds light on the exceptions and reveals hidden trends and issues; and finally, they want to examine detailed data and reports to identify root causes of problems and take action to remedy the situation.

The New Face of Business Intelligence

In many respects, performance dashboards are the new face of business intelligence. They transform business intelligence from a set of tools used primarily by business analysts and power users to a means of delivering actionable information to everyone in an enterprise. Thus, performance dashboards fulfill the promise of business intelligence to help organizations leverage information to increase corporate agility, optimize performance, and achieve strategic objectives.

Three Types

The final thing I discovered about performance dashboards after talking to many companies is that that there are three types—operational, tactical, and strategic—that are distinguished largely by the degree to which they use the three types of applications listed above (i.e. monitoring, analysis, and management.)

Operational dashboards track core operational processes and emphasize monitoring more than analysis or management; *tactical dashboards* track departmental processes and projects and emphasize analysis more than monitoring or management; and *strategic dashboards* monitor the execution of strategic objectives and emphasize management more than monitoring or analysis. An organization can and should have multiple versions of each type of performance dashboard, but they should integrate them using consistent definitions and rules for shared and related metrics.

Success Factors

It is one thing to know what a performance dashboard is and another to implement one successfully. In the course of interviewing people at organizations that have deployed performance dashboards (regardless of what they call them), I discovered many critical success factors. On a macro level, the keys to success are: 1) get proper sponsorship and resources for the project, 2) create the right metrics and standardize their meaning, 3) design a compelling graphical user interface, and 4) plan ahead to ensure end-user adoption and drive organizational change.

Beyond these major success factors, I discovered dozens of tips and techniques that often spell the difference between a successful project and a mediocre one. This book does not pretend to provide a step-by-step methodology for implementing a performance dashboard or a comprehensive list of critical success factors; instead, like a good performance metric, it provides reasonable guidance for the road ahead.

NAVIGATING THIS BOOK

Who Should Read This Book

This book is geared to business and technical managers who oversee performance management projects or who have been recently appointed to create or overhaul an organization's performance management system, including information systems and corporate policies and procedures. These managers generally have deep knowledge of their business and suitable experience managing information technology projects. Most are prime candidates to become Chief Performance Officers.

At the same time, business executives can benefit by reading this book. Although it covers the technical underpinnings of performance management and dives into technical detail at points, the book tries to convey technical concepts in plain English. Conversely, technologists will find value in this book because it provides an overview of performance management concepts and a technical framework for implementing them. In addition, Balanced Scorecard professionals will find the book helps them understand how Balanced Scorecards relate to and can be integrated with other types of performance dashboards in their organizations.

Skim, Drill, and Examine

To help you get the most out of the next 250+ pages, let me tell you how I have approached writing the text. First, I know that business people are busy. If you are like me, you rarely get to read an article or report from beginning to end, let alone a book, unless you are on a plane or vacation. You really just want the prescriptions, the key takeaways that you can apply at work tomorrow, next week, or next month.

To accommodate your needs, I have tried to make the book as easy as possible to skim while staying within the publisher's constraints. For example, I have made liberal use of headings, lead-ins, exhibits, captions, and sidebars so they serve as visual guideposts to the content. Glance at these markers as you flip through the pages, and if you spy something that catches your interest, drill down and read the text for a while. (Does this sound like a performance dashboard in book form? I hope so. The concept is universally applicable!)

Sections in the Book

The book is also divided into three sections. Part One, "The Landscape for Performance Dashboards," provides the framework and context for understanding performance dashboards. Chapter 1 defines performance dashboards and describes their primary characteristics. Chapter 2 provides background on BPM, which contributes the conceptual underpinnings for performance dashboards and represents the broader commercial market for related products and services. Chapter 3 explains business intelligence, which contributes the analytical and technical foundation upon which performance dashboards rest. Chapter 4 provides an organizational readiness assessment for organizations preparing to implement a performance dashboard, and Chapter 5 offers a technical readiness assessment based on a BI Maturity Model that I developed in 2004 and has been well received by BI professionals and their business counterparts.

Part Two, entitled "Performance Dashboards in Action," adds flesh to the conceptual framework defined in Part One by profiling each type of dashboard system using an in-depth case study with plenty of screenshots to help you differentiate between types. Chapter 6 provides an overview of each type of dashboard and compares and contrasts the three types at a conceptual level. Chapter 7 examines operational dashboards using Quicken Loans as a case study. Chapter 8 looks at tactical dashboards by profiling a Key Business Indicator (KBI) portal developed by International Truck and Engine Corporation. Chapter 9 examines strategic dashboards by examining a Balanced Scorecard application developed by Hewlett Packard Co.'s Technology Solutions Group.

Part Three is titled "Critical Success Factors: Tips from the Trenches." This section synthesizes recommendations and guidance from dozens of performance dashboard projects that I've researched. Chapter 10 discusses how to launch a performance dashboard project. Chapter 11 discusses how to create effective metrics, which are the backbone of any dashboard system. Chapter 12 switches to the visual design and examines how to create powerful dashboard screens that communicate relevant facts quickly and concisely. Chapter 13 describes several approaches to integrating or linking multiple dashboard systems, whereas Chapter 14 tackles the thorny topic of how to establish an effective partnership between business and the information technology (IT) department, which is required to deliver a long-lasting, high-value dashboard system. Chapter 15 closes with advice on how to ensure end-user adoption and use a performance dashboard as an agent of organizational change.

Feedback Please!

As someone who works for an educational organization, I know that the best learning occurs not in classrooms but in group discussions and individual conversations. Once you finish reading (or skimming) this book, I hope that you take the time to send me your thoughts. Ideas do not stop evolving once they are put on paper. This book is not my final word on the subject; there is always more to learn! Undoubtedly, there are numerous perspectives I did not cover and nuances I overlooked. Please help me write the next edition; send your thoughts to weckerson@tdwi.org. Happy reading!

Acknowledgments

Although this book focuses on an emerging area of interest to the business community, much of the content was shaped over the course of the past ten years, which I have spent as an analyst, consultant, and educator in the field of business intelligence, which provides the analytical and technical foundation for performance dashboards. Much of what I learned during this period was the result of conversations with hundreds of people who generously shared their time, insights, and camaraderie. Although they are too numerous to mention by name, they include faculty members at The Data Warehousing Institute and my fellow BI professionals at Fortune 1000 companies, consultancies, analyst firms, and vendors. I am eternally grateful to them.

I would like to acknowledge a number of people who contributed directly to the creation of this book. I am indebted to Tim Burgard, my editor at John Wiley & Sons, who approached me with the initial idea and guided me through the process. Special recognition goes to the individuals whose projects I profiled in Part Two and whose experiences and insights helped shape the remainder: Martin Summerhayes of Hewlett Packard, Jim Rappé of International Truck and Engine Corporation, and Eric Lofstrom of Quicken Loans. They spent countless hours with me on the phone and in person answering endless questions and dutifully responding to my every request. This book would not have been possible without their cooperation and enduring patience.

The stories of many other people whom I interviewed were equally compelling, but time, space, or confidentiality prevented me from delving deeper. I would like to thank Viraj Gandhi at Paradigm Management, Doug Smith in the City Administrator's office at the District of Columbia, John Lochrie and Ripley Maddock at Direct Energy Essential Home Services, Kevin Lam at TELUS, Ryan Uda at Cisco Systems, Inc., John Monczewski at Booz Allen Hamilton, Dave Donkin at Absa Bank Ltd., Klaus Detemple at Deutsche Börse, Chris Gentry at

CCC Information Services Inc., Larry Fox, Todd Klessner, Deb Masdea, Alicia Acebo, Mike Grillo, Greg Jones, Christopher Soong, and Preetam Basil, among others.

Next, I would like to commend the many people who reviewed all or portions of the book and kept me from veering too far afield from my task at hand. Their advice provided desperately needed perspective, nuances, and insights. Professors Hugh Watson and Barbara Wixom provided considerable encouragement and gave me constructive feedback on how to approach the assignment and shape the content. Stephen Few generously shared his rich intellectual capital, advising me on visual design principles in general and on techniques for creating effective dashboard screens in particular. Chapter 12 would not have been possible without his input. Bill Balberg, president of Insightformation, Inc., offered many ways to align my ideas with those circulating in the Balanced Scorecard community and was indefatigable in reviewing my text. Neil Raden pointed out numerous areas for improvement; Colin White helped with the framework, taxonomy, and evaluation criteria; Cindi Howson provided input on evaluation criteria; and my good friend Jim Nowicki provided the all-important business user perspective. I would also like to thank Larissa DeCarlo of Hyperion Solutions, Diaz Nesamoney of Celequest, Tracy Shouldice of Cognos, Rebecca Adams of Business Objects, and Doug Cogswell of ADVIZOR Solutions, Inc. for putting me in touch with customers and providing screen shots upon request.

Going back a few years, I would like to pay tribute to my colleagues and friends at *Network World Magazine* who taught me how to think logically and write clearly and succinctly, as well as Patricia Seybold, whose quiet trust gave me the confidence I needed to acquire a strong professional voice in an industry filled with very smart people.

Also, I would like to thank Peter Quinn and Ellen Hobbs, my managers at The Data Warehousing Institute and 101communications, respectively, who for some strange reason encouraged me in this pursuit and made allowances to ensure I could finish on time. I also appreciate the support and patience of my colleagues at The Data Warehousing Institute, including Meighan Berberich, Michelle Edwards, and Eric Kavanagh, who lent their time and expertise to help market the book, and especially Denelle Hanlon, who always provided encouragement at the right moments. Last, but not least, I thank my wife Christina and my children, Harry and Olivia, who gallantly tolerated the long hours I spent in front of the computer at home when I should have been doing things with them.

PART ONE

The Landscape for
Performance Dashboards

CHAPTER 1

What Are Performance Dashboards?

THE CONTEXT FOR PERFORMANCE DASHBOARDS

The Power of Focus

Executives in Training

This summer I found my 11-year-old son, Harry, and his best pal, Jake, kneeling side by side in our driveway, peering intensely at the pavement. As I walked over to inspect this curious sight, I saw little puffs of smoke rising from their huddle. Each had a magnifying glass and was using it to set fire to clumps of dry grass as well as a few unfortunate ants who had wandered into their makeshift science experiment.

In this boyhood rite of passage, Harry and Jake learned an important lesson that escapes the attention of many organizations today: the power of focus. Light rays normally radiate harmlessly in all directions, bouncing off objects in the atmosphere and the earth's surface. The boys had discovered, however, that if they focused light rays onto a single point using a magnifying glass, they could generate enough energy to burn just about anything and keep themselves entertained for hours!

By the time Harry and Jake enter the business world (if they do), they will probably have forgotten this simple lesson. They will have become steeped in corporate cultures that excel at losing focus and dissipating energy far and wide. Most organizations have multiple business units, divisions, and departments, each with their own products, strategies, processes, applications, and systems to support them. A good portion of these activities are redundant at best and conflicting at worst. The organization as a whole spins off in multiple directions at once without a clear strategy. Changes in leadership, mergers, acquisitions, and reorganizations amplify the chaos.

Organizational Magnifying Glass

To rectify this problem, companies need an "organizational magnifying glass"— something that focuses the work of employees so everyone is going in the same direction (see Exhibit 1.1). Strong leaders do this. However, even the voice of a charismatic executive is sometimes drowned out by organizational inertia.

Strong leaders need more than just the force of their personality and experience to focus an organization. They need an information system that helps them clearly and concisely communicate key strategies and goals to all employees on a personal basis every day. The system should focus workers on tasks and activities that best advance the organization's strategies and goals. It should measure performance, reward positive contributions, and align efforts so that workers in every group and level of the organization are marching together toward the same destination.

Performance Management System

In short, what organizations really need is a *performance dashboard* that translates the organization's strategy into objectives, metrics, initiatives, and tasks customized to each group and individual in the organization. A performance dashboard is really a performance management system. It communicates strategic

---

EXHIBIT 1.1   ORGANIZATIONAL MAGNIFYING GLASS

Companies need an "organizational magnifying glass" that focuses the energies and activities of employees on a clear, unambiguous set of goals and objectives laid out in the corporate strategy.

objectives and enables business people to measure, monitor, and manage the key activities and processes needed to achieve their goals.

To work this magic, a performance dashboard provides three main sets of functionality, which I will describe in more detail later. Briefly, a performance dashboard lets business people:

- **Monitor** critical business processes and activities using metrics of business performance that trigger alerts when potential problems arise.

- **Analyze** the root cause of problems by exploring relevant and timely information from multiple perspectives and at various levels of detail.

- **Manage** people and processes to improve decisions, optimize performance, and steer the organization in the right direction.

Agent of Organizational Change

A performance dashboard is a powerful agent of organizational change. When deployed properly, it can transform an under-performing organization into a high flier. Like a magnifying glass, a performance dashboard can focus organizations on the key things it needs to do to succeed. It provides executives, managers, and workers with timely and relevant information so they can measure, monitor, and manage their progress toward achieving key strategic objectives.

One of the more popular types of performance dashboards today is the Balanced Scorecard, which adheres to a specific methodology for aligning organizations with corporate strategy. A Balanced Scorecard is a strategic application, but as we shall soon see, there are other types of performance dashboards that optimize operational and tactical processes that drive organizations on a weekly, daily, or even hourly basis.

Historical Context

Executive Dashboards and Cockpits

Although dashboards have long been a fixture in automobiles and other vehicles, business, government, and non-profit organizations have only recently adopted the concept. The trend started among executives who became enamored with the idea of having an "executive dashboard" or "executive cockpit" with which to drive their companies from their boardroom perches. These executive information systems (EIS) actually date back to the 1980s, but they never gained much traction, because the systems were geared to so few people in each company and were built on mainframes or minicomputers that made them costly to customize and maintain.

In the past 20 years, information technology has advanced at a rapid clip. Mainframes and minicomputers largely gave way to client/server systems, which in turn were supplanted by the Web as the preeminent platform for running applications and delivering information. Along the way, the economy turned global, squeezing revenues and profits and increasing competition for ever-more demanding customers. Executives responded by reengineering processes, improving quality, and cutting costs, but these efforts have only provided short-term relief, not lasting value.

Convergence

During the 1990s, organizations began experimenting with ways to give business users direct and timely access to critical information, an emerging field known as business intelligence. At the same time, executives started turning to new performance management disciplines, such as Balanced Scorecards, Six Sigma, Economic Value Added, and Activity-Based Costing, to harness the power of information to optimize performance and deliver greater value to the business.

These initiatives convinced many executives that they could gain lasting competitive advantage by empowering employees to work proactively and make better decisions by giving them relevant, actionable information. Essentially, executives recognized that the EIS of the 1980s was a good idea but too narrowly focused; everyone, not just executives, needed an EIS. Fortunately, executives did not have to wait long for a solution. At the dawn of the 21st century, business intelligence converged with performance management to create the performance dashboard.

Market Trends

This convergence has created a flood of interest in performance dashboards since the year 2000. A study by The Data Warehousing Institute (TDWI) in 2004 showed that most organizations (51 percent) already use a dashboard or scorecard and that another 17 percent are currently developing one. The same study showed that almost one-third of organizations that already have a dashboard or scorecard use it as their *primary* application for reporting and analysis of data (see Exhibit 1.2).

Benefits

The reason so many organizations are implementing performance dashboards is a practical one: they offer a panoply of benefits to everyone in an organization, from executives to managers to staff. Here is a condensed list of benefits:

- **Communicate Strategy.** Performance dashboards translate corporate strategy into measures, targets, and initiatives that are customized to each

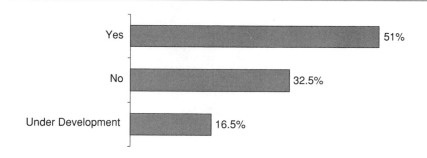

| EXHIBIT 1.2 | DOES YOUR ORGANIZATION USE A DASHBOARD OR SCORECARD? |

Yes 51%

No 32.5%

Under Development 16.5%

A majority of organizations have already deployed dashboards or scorecards, and many are in the process of building them. Data based on 473 responses to a survey of BI professionals by The Data Warehousing Institute.

Source: Wayne Eckerson, "Strategies for Developing Analytic Applications" (*TDWI Report Series*, The Data Warehousing Institute, 2005).

group in an organization and sometimes to every individual. Each morning when business people log into the performance dashboard, they get a clear picture of the organization's strategic objectives and what they need to do in their areas to achieve these goals.

- **Refine Strategy.** Executives use performance dashboards like a steering wheel to fine-tune corporate strategy as they go along. Instead of veering drastically from one direction to another in response to internal issues or industry events, executives can use performance dashboards to make a series of minor course corrections along the way to their destination (see Exhibit 1.3).

- **Increase Visibility.** Performance dashboards give executives and managers greater visibility into daily operations and future performance by collecting relevant data in a timely fashion and forecasting trends based on past activity. This helps companies close their financial books faster at the end of each month and avoid being surprised by unforeseen problems that might affect bottom-line results.

- **Increase Coordination.** By publishing performance data broadly, performance dashboards encourage members of different departments, such as finance and operations, to begin working more closely together. They also foster a healthy dialogue between managers and staff about performance results and forecasts and make it easier for managers to conduct more frequent and constructive performance reviews.

EXHIBIT 1.3	CHARTING A COURSE WITH A PERFORMANCE DASHBOARD

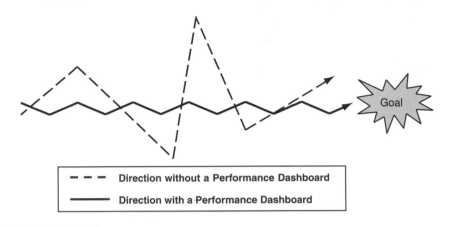

- - - Direction without a Performance Dashboard

——— Direction with a Performance Dashboard

A performance dashboard enables executives to chart a steady course to their destination by making a series of fine-tuned course corrections instead of veering dramatically from one direction to another in response to internal or industry events.

- **Increase Motivation.** It has been said that "what gets measured, gets done." By publicizing performance measures and results, performance dashboards increase the motivation of business people to excel in the areas being measured. Performance dashboards compel people to work harder out of pride and desire for extra pay when compensation is tied to performance results.

- **Give a Consistent View of the Business.** Performance dashboards consolidate and integrate corporate information using common definitions, rules, and metrics. This creates a single version of business information that everyone in the organization uses, avoiding conflicts among managers and analysts about whose version of the data is "right."

- **Reduce Costs and Redundancy.** By consolidating and standardizing information, performance dashboards eliminate the need for redundant silos of information that undermine a single version of business information. A single performance dashboard can help an organization shut down dozens, if not hundreds, of independent reporting systems, spreadmarts, data marts, and data warehouses.

- **Empower Users.** Performance dashboards empower users by giving them self-service access to information and eliminating their reliance on the IT department to create custom reports. Through layered delivery of information, structured navigation paths, and guided analysis, performance dashboards make it easy for average business people to access, analyze, and act on information.

- **Deliver Actionable Information.** Performance dashboards provide actionable information—data delivered in a timely fashion that lets users take action to fix a problem, help a customer, or capitalize on a new opportunity before it is too late. A performance dashboard prevents users from wasting hours or days searching for the right information or report.

In short, performance dashboards deliver the right information to the right users at the right time to optimize decisions, enhance efficiency, and accelerate bottom-line results.

Pretenders to the Throne

Although many organizations have implemented dashboards and scorecards, not all have succeeded. In most cases, organizations have been tantalized by glitzy graphical interfaces and have failed to build a solid foundation by applying sound performance management principles and implementing appropriate business intelligence and data integration technologies and processes. Here are the common symptoms of less than successful solutions:

- **Too Flat.** Many organizations create performance management systems, especially tactical and strategic dashboards, using Microsoft Excel, Microsoft PowerPoint, and advanced charting packages. Although these applications often look fancy, they generally do not provide enough data or analytical capabilities to let users explore the root cause of problems highlighted in the graphical indicators.

- **Too Manual.** In addition, some organizations rely too heavily on manual methods to update performance dashboards that contain sizable amounts of information. Highly skilled business analysts spend several days a week collecting and massaging this information instead of analyzing it. The majority of performance dashboards automate the collection and delivery of information, ensuring a sustainable solution over the long term.

- **Too Isolated.** Some performance dashboards source data from a single system or appeal to a very small audience. As a result, they provide a narrow or parochial view of the business, not an enterprise view. In addition, these dashboards often contain data and metrics that do not align with the rest of the organization, leading to confusion and chaos.

In the end, performance dashboards are only as effective as the organizations they seek to measure. Organizations without central control or coordination will deploy a haphazard jumble of non-integrated performance dashboards. However, organizations that have a clear strategy, a positive culture, and a strong information infrastructure can deliver performance management systems that make a dramatic impact on performance.

COMPOSITION OF PERFORMANCE DASHBOARDS

Definition

Every performance dashboard looks and functions differently. People use many different terms to describe performance dashboards, including portal, BI tool, and analytical application. Each of these contributes to a performance dashboard but is not a performance dashboard by itself. Here is my definition:

A performance dashboard is a multilayered application built on a business intelligence and data integration infrastructure that enables organizations to measure, monitor, and manage business performance more effectively.

This definition conveys the idea that a performance dashboard is more than just a screen populated with fancy performance graphics: it is a full-fledged business information system designed to help organizations optimize performance and achieve strategic objectives. An equivalent, and perhaps better, term is *performance management system*, which conveys the idea that it is a system designed to manage business performance. However, since the title of this book uses the term performance dashboards, I will stick with that term on most occasions, although I feel that the two are interchangeable.

Build or Buy

A common question is whether it is better to build or buy a performance dashboard. During the past several years, many software vendors have shipped dashboard or scorecard solutions. Many qualify as performance dashboards, and some do not. Until recently, most companies built their own performance dashboards or started with a vendor tool and customized it extensively to meet their needs.

Most of the companies profiled in this book built performance dashboards using a mix of custom code and BI tools running on standard corporate infrastructure components (i.e., databases, servers, storage systems). However, organizations that have deployed performance management systems within the past two years have frequently used commercial, off-the-shelf products, sometimes customizing them extensively and, in other cases, minimally.

Whether you plan to build or buy a performance dashboard, it makes sense to create a list of criteria against which you can evaluate your solution. The appendix at the end of this book provides a comprehensive set of evaluation criteria.

Context

The Big Picture: Business Performance Management

Before we dive into the details, let us step back and examine the context for performance dashboards from a business perspective. A performance dashboard plays a pivotal role in an emerging discipline called business performance management (BPM). As we will see in Chapter 2, BPM consists of a series of processes and applications designed to optimize the execution of business strategy. BPM provides a framework that takes the long-standing task of *measuring performance* to the next level, that of *managing performance.* BPM provides the business context in which performance dashboards operate (see Exhibit 1.4).

BPM uses many different tools to help organizations manage performance better, ranging from financial consolidation and reporting tools to planning, budgeting, and forecasting applications to dashboards and scorecards. However, the most important tool in the BPM portfolio is a performance dashboard, because it enables executives to communicate strategic objectives and then measure and monitor the organization's progress toward achieving those objectives. In essence, a performance dashboard helps organizations execute their strategy.

EXHIBIT 1.4   THE CONTEXT FOR PERFORMANCE DASHBOARDS

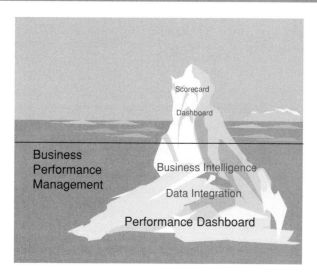

Like an ocean surrounding an iceberg, business performance management (BPM) provides the business context for performance dashboards, which are layered applications built on a business intelligence and data integration infrastructure (i.e., the base of the iceberg). The most visible elements of a performance dashboard are the scorecard and dashboard screens, which display performance using leading, lagging, and diagnostic metrics.

Three Applications

Moving from context to composition, the first thing one notices about a performance dashboard is that it contains three applications woven together in a seamless fashion. Each application provides a specific set of functionality delivered through a variety of means. Technically speaking, the applications are not necessarily distinct programs (although sometimes they are), but sets of related functionality built on an information infrastructure designed to fulfill user requirements to monitor, analyze, and manage performance (see Exhibit 1.5).

1. Monitoring

A performance dashboard enables users to monitor performance against metrics aligned to corporate strategy. At an operational level, users monitor core processes that drive the business on a day-to-day basis, such as sales, shipping, or manufacturing. At a tactical or strategic level, users monitor their progress toward achieving short- and long-term goals.

In general, organizations use *dashboards* to monitor operational processes and *scorecards* to monitor tactical and strategic goals. Dashboards and scorecards are visual display mechanisms within a performance management system that convey critical performance information at a glance. They are the lens through which users view and interact with performance data, but they are not the entire system in themselves. Although dashboards and scorecards share many features and people use the terms interchangeably, they have unique characteristics (see Spotlight 1.1).

EXHIBIT 1.5	PERFORMANCE DASHBOARD APPLICATIONS		
	Monitoring	**Analysis**	**Management**
Purpose	Convey information at a glance	Let users analyze exception conditions	Improve alignment coordination and collaboration
Components	Dashboard Scorecard BI portal Right-time data Alerts Agents	Multidimensional analysis Time-series analysis Reporting Scenario modeling Statistical modeling	Meetings Strategy maps Annotation Workflow Usage monitoring Auditing

A performance dashboard consists of three applications—monitoring, analysis, and management—that deliver related sets of functionality and consist of multiple components.

SPOTLIGHT 1.1   "DASHBOARDS VERSUS SCORECARDS"

Dashboards and scorecards are visual display mechanisms within a performance management system that convey critical performance information at a glance. The primary difference between the two is that dashboards monitor the performance of operational processes whereas scorecards chart the progress of tactical and strategic goals (see Exhibit 1.6).

EXHIBIT 1.6   COMPARING FEATURES

	Dashboard	Scorecard
Purpose	Measures performance	Charts progress
Users	Supervisors, specialists	Executives, managers, staff
Updates	Right-time feeds	Periodic snapshots
Data	Events	Summaries
Display	Visual graphs, raw data	Visual graphs, text comments

Dashboards. Dashboards are more like automobile dashboards. They let operational specialists and their supervisors monitor events generated by key business processes. But unlike automobiles, most business dashboards do not display events in "real time" as they occur; they display them in "right time" as users need to view them. This could be every second, minute, hour, day, week, or month depending on the business process, its volatility, and how critical it is to the business. However, most elements on a dashboard are updated on an intra-day basis, with latency measured in either in minutes or hours.

Dashboards often display performance visually, using charts or simple graphs, such as gauges and meters. However, dashboard graphs are often updated in place, causing the graphs to "flicker" or change dynamically. Ironically, people who monitor operational processes often find the visual glitz distracting and prefer to view the data in its original form, as numbers or text, perhaps accompanied by visual graphs.

Scorecards. Scorecards, on the other hand, look more like performance charts used to track progress toward achieving goals. Scorecards usually display monthly snapshots of summarized data for business executives who track strategic and long-term objectives, or daily and weekly snapshots of data for managers who need to chart the progress of their group or project toward achieving goals. In both cases, the data are fairly summarized so users can view their performance status at a glance.

Like dashboards, scorecards also make use of charts and visual graphs to indicate performance state, trends, and variance against goals. The higher up the users are in the organization, the more they prefer to see performance encoded visually. However, most scorecards also contain (or should contain) a great deal of textual commentary that interprets performance results, describes actions taken, and forecasts future results.

Summary. In the end, it does not really matter whether you use the term dashboard or scorecard as long as the tool helps to focus users and organizations on what really matters. Both dashboards and scorecards need to display critical performance information on a single screen so users can monitor results at a glance.

A monitoring application also delivers information to users in "right time"—usually within minutes or hours depending on the volatility of information and decision making requirements—so they can take steps to fix a problem or exploit an opportunity. We cover "right time" information delivery in Chapter 7. Other key elements of a monitoring application are alerts, which notify users when events exceed predefined thresholds of performance, and agents, which automate the responses to well-known exception conditions, such as ordering new stock when inventory falls below predefined levels.

2. Analysis

The analysis portion of a performance dashboard lets users explore large volumes of historical performance data across many dimensions and down to minute detail. The application enables users to evaluate the origins of exception conditions highlighted by the monitoring application and identify the root cause of a problem or issue. The analysis application leverages a variety of BI technologies, including on-line analytical processing (OLAP), parameterized reporting, query and reporting, and statistical modeling, and relies heavily on a data integration and data warehousing infrastructure to prepare and deliver information in an intuitive, timely, and reliable fashion. Chapter 3 describes the various types of BI and data integration tools in depth.

3. Management

A performance dashboard typically embeds a variety of management and collaboration capabilities into the monitoring and analysis applications. The management features support a variety of business processes, both formal and informal, that guide the way users communicate and share performance information. Their purpose is to help executives steer the organization in the right direction, foster improved coordination among business units and groups, and engender better communication among managers, analysts, and staff.

A key management application is performance review meetings. These can be quarterly strategy sessions, monthly operational meetings, individual performance review sessions, or ad hoc conversations between managers and their direct reports. Performance dashboards facilitate these dialogues using strategy maps at the executive level, workflow applications at the team level, and document-based annotations at the individual level. Usage monitoring features track end-user adoption of the performance dashboard and logs changes made to the system for audit and control purposes.

Three Layers

Besides containing three applications, a performance dashboard consists of three views or layers of information. Just as a cook peels layers of an onion, a performance dashboard lets users peel back layers of information to get to the root cause of a problem. Each successive layer provides additional details, views, and perspectives that enable users to understand a problem better and identify the steps they need to take to address it.

This layered approach gives users self-service access to information and conforms to the natural sequence in which users want to handle that information: 1) monitor, 2) analyze, and 3) examine. That is, most business users first want to monitor key metrics for exceptions; then explore and analyze information that sheds light on those exceptions; and finally, examine detailed reports and data before taking action. By starting at high-level views of information and working down, this layered approach helps users get to the root cause of issues quickly and intuitively (see Exhibit 1.7).

EXHIBIT 1.7   PERFORMANCE DASHBOARD LAYERS

Users

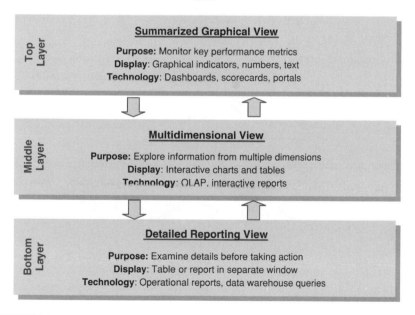

A performance dashboard delivers information to users in layers as they need it. The top layer graphically displays exception conditions; the middle layer lets users explore or "slice and dice" data from multiple dimensions; and the bottom layer lets users examine individual transactions and operational reports.

Here are the three layers:

1. **Summarized Graphical View.** The top layer provides a summarized view, usually graphical, of the status of key performance metrics and exception conditions. When performance exceeds thresholds applied to each metric, the dashboard or scorecard interface alerts users to the exception condition. These exceptions can be in the form of alerts that pop up on users' screens or arrive via e-mail, pager, or another channel. More commonly, the software changes the color or shape of a symbol or graph associated with the metric. In essence, this layer is where users monitor information. The dashboard, scorecard, or portal interface essentially becomes a graphical exception report.

2. **Multidimensional View.** This middle layer provides the data behind the graphical metrics and alerts. Using multidimensional analysis tools, users navigate the data by dimensions (e.g., customer, geography, or time) and hierarchies (e.g., country, region, or city). More colloquially, these point-and-click tools let users "slice and dice," "drill down or up," or "pivot" the data to view exceptions and trends from any perspective they want. The tools let users apply complex calculations to the data, perform "what-if" analyses, and switch between tables and charts. There are many technologies that support multidimensional analysis. Chief among them are online analytical processing (OLAP), parameterized reporting, and advanced visualization tools.

3. **Detailed Reporting View.** The bottom layer lets users view detailed reports and transaction records, such as invoices, shipments, or trades. Users often need such data to understand the root cause of a problem, such as a decline in sales due to missing or incomplete orders or a salesperson who has been sick. This layer either connects users to existing operational reports or dynamically queries a data warehouse or operational system to obtain the appropriate records. The resulting report or query results are then usually displayed in a separate window, which users can view or print.

Navigating the Layers

Users can access the performance dashboard at any of these three layers, but most start at the summarized graphical layer and drill down along fairly predefined pathways as far as they need or want to go. Many BI tools force users to start at the middle or bottom layers, which makes them difficult to use. Most users find the middle multidimensional layer too complex and the bottom reporting layer too detailed. Only business analysts and operational specialists find it easy to navigate these bottom two layers.

This layered approach to delivering performance information meets the needs of most users in an organization. These "casual" users do not crunch numbers and information for a living; they simply want to monitor and manage the key processes for which they are responsible. They only "casually" use information, perhaps checking a performance dashboard or reports once or twice a day or week, depending on their role and responsibilities.

As a result, performance dashboards, with their layers of information, meet the long-standing mantra of these types of casual users: "Give me all the data I want, but only what I really need, and only when I really need it." In other words, casual users do not want to view information except when there is an out-of-bounds condition, and then they want to view all pertinent data but they do not want to spend precious time looking for it. Performance dashboards meet the requirements of casual users perfectly.

Transparent Navigation

The goal for performance dashboards is to make the transition between the three layers transparent to users. This is challenging since most performance dashboards today use different technologies and tools to support each layer. This gives each layer its own distinctive look and feel, making the performance dashboard more challenging to use than it should be.

Fortunately, some vendors are beginning to blend their monitoring, analysis, and reporting tools—which comprise the three layers in effect—to offer a more homogenous navigation experience for users. In addition, home-grown solutions arc building the various components in each layer using a standard programming framework (i.e., .NET or Java) to simplify navigation and ease of use. In the future, performance dashboards will be designed as a single application running against a robust BI infrastructure rather than a combination of disparate applications and components cobbled together from various tools and systems.

Three Types of Performance Dashboards

The last thing you need to know about performance dashboards is that there are three major types: operational, tactical, and strategic. Each type of performance dashboard emphasizes the three layers and applications described above to different degrees (see Exhibit 1.8).

1. **Operational dashboards** monitor core operational processes and are used primarily by front-line workers and their supervisors who deal directly with customers or manage the creation or delivery of the organization's products and services. Operational dashboards primarily deliver detailed information that is only lightly summarized. For example, an online Web merchant may track transactions at the product level rather

EXHIBIT 1.8   THREE TYPES OF PERFORMANCE DASHBOARDS

	Operational	Tactical	Strategic
Purpose	Monitor operations	Measure progress	Execute strategy
Users	Supervisors, specialists	Managers, analysts	Executives, managers, staff
Scope	Operational	Departmental	Enterprise
Information	Detailed	Detailed/summary	Detailed/summary
Updates	Intra-day	Daily/weekly	Monthly/quarterly
Emphasis	Monitoring	Analysis	Management

There are three types of performance dashboards. Operational dashboards emphasize monitoring more than analysis or management; tactical dashboards emphasize analysis more than monitoring or management; and strategic dashboards emphasize management more than monitoring or analysis.

than the customer level. In addition, most metrics in an operational dashboard are updated on an intra-day basis, ranging from minutes to hours, depending on the application. As a result, operational dashboards emphasize monitoring more than analysis and management. Chapter 7 profiles an operational dashboard from Quicken Loans that monitors the calling activity and sales performance of hundreds of loan consultants working in a huge call center at corporate headquarters.

2. **Tactical dashboards** track departmental processes and projects that are of interest to a segment of the organization or a limited group of people. Managers and business analysts use tactical dashboards to compare performance of their areas or projects, to budget plans, forecasts, or last period's results. For example, a project to reduce the number of errors in a customer database might use a tactical dashboard to display, monitor, and analyze progress during the previous 12 months toward achieving 99.9 percent defect-free customer data by 2007. Tactical dashboards are usually updated daily or weekly with both detailed and summary data. They tend to emphasis analysis more than monitoring or management. Chapter 8 profiles a tactical dashboard used by the International Truck and Engine Corporation to monitor financial and operational performance across several business units.

3. **Strategic dashboards** monitor the execution of strategic objectives and are frequently implemented using a Balanced Scorecard approach, although Total Quality Management, Six Sigma, and other methodologies are used as well. The goal of a strategic dashboard is to align the organization around

strategic objectives and get every group marching in the same direction. To do this, organizations roll out customized scorecards to every group in the organization and sometimes to every individual as well. These "cascading" scorecards, which are usually updated weekly or monthly, give executives a powerful tool to communicate strategy, gain visibility into operations, and identify the key drivers of performance and business value. Strategic dashboards emphasize management more than monitoring and analysis. Chapter 9 profiles a strategic dashboard created by Hewlett Packard's Technology Solutions Group that uses a Balanced Scorecard approach.

Integrating Performance Dashboards

An organization can have multiple versions of each type of performance dashboard. More than likely, each department will have its own operational, tactical, and strategic dashboard. At a minimum, all performance management systems should be logically integrated using a common set of metrics and rules that are populated with data from a common BI and data integration infrastructure. In reality, however, most performance management systems are built separately using unique metrics and rules and different BI and data integration platforms. Although each performance dashboard provides value, collectively they create information chaos. Chapter 13 discusses how to integrate disparate performance dashboards.

PERFORMANCE MANAGEMENT ARCHITECTURE

A performance management system consists of both a business architecture and a technical architecture. Exhibit 1.9 shows the components of these two architectures and how they relate. The linchpin that ties the two architectures together is the metrics that define leading, lagging, and diagnostic measures of business performance. On the business side, the metrics embody the organization's strategy and tactics. On the technical side, the metrics contain rules that define what data to collect and when and how they should be aggregated, filtered, and calculated. The metrics are the means by which organizations measure, monitor, and manage the effectiveness of their strategy and tactics to satisfy key stakeholders.

No organization needs to implement all the components in both architectures. In fact, organizations tend to pick and choose components at each level that best meet the organization's needs. However, it is imperative that organizations choose at least one component in each layer; otherwise things break down. Without a complete and harmonized business and technical architecture, the business would fail to deliver a coherent strategy, workable plans, and accurate metrics, and the technical team would fail to deliver a viable information system.

EXHIBIT I.9   PERFORMANCE MANAGEMENT ARCHITECTURE

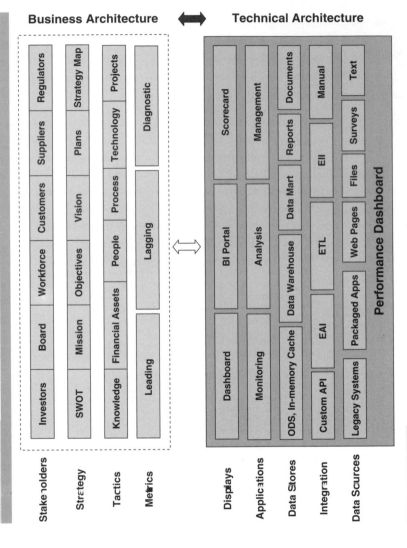

A performance management system consists of a business architecture, represented by stakeholders, strategy, tactics, and metrics, and a technical architecture represented by a performance dashboard, which consists of several layers of components. To deliver a performance management solution, the business and IT department must partner closely.

Business Architecture

Stakeholders

By drilling down into the business architecture, one sees that each organization serves many different stakeholders—the investors, board of directors, workforce, customers, suppliers, and regulators—each of whom has a different perspective or view of the organization and wants to see different information. For instance, investors want to see the financial valuation of the organization, the staff wants to see a process view, and customers want to see the value of their accounts or the products and services they have purchased, bid on, or returned.

Strategy

Executives then devise a strategy to meet the needs of those stakeholders. The strategy may start with a strengths, weaknesses, opportunities, and threats (SWOT) analysis, a strategy map, or some other strategy formulation technique. Ultimately, executives create a mission statement, strategic objectives, a vision, values, and long-term plans and goals. (We will discuss strategy in more detail in Chapter 4.)

Tactics

Executives then throw the strategy "over the wall" to managers and supervisors who implement the strategy using a variety of resources—knowledge, money, people, processes, and technology. The upshot is that managers create projects, initiatives, and annual plans or budgets that try to nudge the organization toward its strategic objectives.

Metrics

Executives and managers then translate the strategy and plans into metrics. Strategic dashboards measure initiatives and plans that range from one to five years in scope, whereas tactical dashboards measure initiatives and plans that span several weeks to several months or more. Operational dashboards usually measure daily operations.

There are three major types of metrics: leading, lagging, and diagnostic. In the past, most organizations used lagging indicators, mainly financial metrics, to measure performance and outcomes. However, BPM and Balanced Scorecard methodologies encourage companies to use leading indicators to gain greater visibility into future performance and to manage people, processes, and technology more proactively. We will cover metrics in more detail in Chapter 11.

Technical Architecture

A performance dashboard consists of multiple layers of technology that work together to deliver the information business people need to execute strategy and tactics and meet the needs of stakeholders. The technical architecture consists of interlocking components that must work together seamlessly to deliver business value. Designers should choose the components in each layer that work best to meet the needs of target users.

Display Layer

The metrics are displayed in the top-level screen of a performance dashboard, which can be a dashboard, scorecard, or portal interface. As mentioned earlier, a dashboard is used to monitor operational information and display alerts, whereas scorecards are used to chart progress toward strategic or tactical goals. Portals provide one-stop shopping for all kinds of information, including performance metrics.

Application Layer

The three applications described earlier—monitoring, analysis, and management—reside below the display layer. Application functionality is interwoven with the display, which serves as the opening screen or initial page to the performance dashboard.

Data Store Layer

The application layer gives users access to information, which can be stored in a variety of data stores. Low-latency data stores, including operational data stores and in-memory caches, are ideal for delivering near real-time information to users in operational dashboards. Data warehouses, data marts, and multidimensional databases (MDBs) are best for analyzing historical data in tactical or strategic dashboards and can also be used to store a limited amount of text. In some cases, performance dashboards do not require sophisticated data stores because they do not store large volumes of data (see Spotlight 1.2).

In other cases, performance dashboards pull data directly from source systems to populate metrics, bypassing persistent data stores, like data warehouses, data marts, and multidimensional databases. This approach makes it easy to get a performance dashboard up and running but can bog down the performance of systems that run the business. Organizations should use this virtual dashboard technique judiciously, to supplement information in persistent data stores, not replace them.

SPOTLIGHT 1.2 QUALITY NOT QUANTITY COUNTS

Although performance dashboards can store large volumes of data, this is not a prerequisite for success, especially with strategic dashboards. In fact, some successful strategic dashboards contain only a few gigabytes of data, less than you can store on a single CD ROM.

For instance, Brown & Root, a Halliburton subsidiary that provides marine oil rig construction and services, used a strategic dashboard with small volumes of information to execute a new business strategy that helped turn around the company, from losing money to number one in its niche, with a net income increase of 30 percent. The strategy involved offering high-margin solutions that simultaneously lowered customer costs by integrating offerings from six operating companies in the newly merged firm.

To chart the effectiveness of the strategy, the company used several metrics, none of which required substantial amounts of data, according to Bill Barlberg, president of Insightformation, Inc., a business intelligence and knowledge management consultancy, and a Balanced Scorecard specialist. For example, the company tracked the number of contracts it won that contained integrated solutions involving two or more operating companies. Since the company does a limited number of huge projects each year, the data for these metrics were hand calculated and manually added to the strategic dashboard. Other key metrics included percent of revenue from integrated projects, number of integrated solutions created, and survey results of employee awareness and acceptance of new cultural values.

For strategic dashboards, the quality of information is the key, not the quantity. In some cases, they can deliver significant business value with just a few gigabytes of data, although this is not the norm. As long as a strategic dashboard focuses an organization on what is important, the volume of data is irrelevant.

Integration Layers

To deliver information to users, a performance dashboard must extract it from source systems. An operational dashboard often uses custom application programming interfaces (APIs) or enterprise application integration (EAI) middleware to capture events from source systems, move them across a network, and update a low-latency data store within the performance dashboard in near real time. In addition, they may query data sources directly, as mentioned above, using SQL queries or enterprise information integration (EII) middleware. Both techniques enable developers to populate metrics with data from a variety of sources, including analytical systems (i.e., data warehouses, data marts, multidimensional databases, or ODSs), operational systems, and external sources, including XML-based Web pages and Web services.

Tactical and strategic dashboards generally use extraction, transformation, and loading (ETL) tools to populate analytical data stores, although they also can query sources directly to supplement historical data with real-time updates or external data. Some strategic dashboards are updated manually when they contain small amounts of information or when users need to add commentary. Chapter 3 will discuss data integration technologies in more depth.

Data Sources

Performance dashboard data may come from a wide range of sources. The most voluminous sources of data include legacy systems running on mainframes or minicomputers and newer packaged applications running on relational databases. The most numerous sources, however, include Web pages, Excel files, Access databases, e-mail messages, survey responses, documents, and commentaries, among other things.

Business–IT Partnership

To deliver a successful performance dashboard, the business must work closely with the information technology (IT) department to create metrics that embody strategic objectives and compare performance to plans. Since strategy and plans are constantly changing, these two groups work closely together to create a performance management system that delivers lasting and significant value. Chapter 14 addresses the all-important issue of how to establish a strong partnership between the business and technical teams.

SUMMARY

Definition. Many organizations lack focus. They may devise strategies but not communicate them well to employees, who often work at cross-purposes without clear guidance from above. For organizations to become both efficient and effective, they need to implement a performance management system that translates the organization's strategy into objectives, metrics, initiatives, and tasks customized to each group and individual in the organization. The system can then provide business people with the information they need to measure, monitor, and manage the key activities and processes they need to achieve their goals.

Applications. A performance dashboard consists of applications that *monitor, analyze,* and *manage* performance. The monitoring application is delivered via a dashboard, scorecard, or portal interface. The analysis application is delivered via a business intelligence and data integration infrastructure that provides users with self-service access to the relevant data they need to analyze performance issues in a timely fashion. The management application allows business users to collaborate with other coordinated activities between departments and to optimize performance over the long haul.

Layers. Well-designed performance dashboards let users drill down from graphical views of performance metrics and their status to detailed information, even down to individual transactions in operational systems if required. Performance dashboards are really glorified exception reports that alert users to out-of-bounds conditions and then guide them quickly and effortlessly into an exploration of the root causes of the issue.

Types. There are three types of performance dashboards. Operational dashboards enable front-line workers and supervisors to monitor operational processes that drive the business on a daily basis. Tactical dashboards let managers and business analysts investigate historical trends and issues against large volumes of information from across the enterprise. Strategic dashboards highlight strategic objectives and the activities and tasks users need to accomplish to achieve those objectives. Sometimes strategic dashboards deliver significant value using very little data.

Architecture. A performance dashboard is a multilayered application built on a business intelligence and data integration infrastructure that enables organizations to measure, monitor, and manage business performance more effectively. To accomplish this, business people and technologists must work together. On one hand, business people need to develop coherent strategies and tactics to meet the needs of stakeholders. On the other, they must work with technologists to create effective metrics that measure the status and progress the organization is making with its strategies and tactics. It takes two to tango and build an effective performance dashboard.

CHAPTER 2

The Role of Business Performance Management

THE LANDSCAPE

Understanding Business Performance Management

Setting the Context

Chapter 1 showed that performance dashboards put business performance in context. They provide a visual interface and a set of analytical and management tools to help organizations monitor, analyze, and manage performance better. However, to understand performance dashboards fully, we need to put them in context as well. In this case, the context is an emerging management discipline and technology solution known as business performance management (BPM).

BPM, which was introduced briefly in Chapter 1, is quickly becoming a familiar term in the business world. It is a business strategy that ties together a number of related management disciplines, processes, and tools into a coherent whole. Performance dashboards play a pivotal role in BPM; they represent the most visible face of a BPM initiative.

Confusion Reigns

Unfortunately, there is much confusion about what BPM is—and is not. Much of the confusion stems from the fact that BPM involves multiple processes and applications that organizations have already implemented. These range from strategic planning to financial consolidation and reporting; from planning and budgeting to forecasting and modeling; and from business intelligence and reporting to dashboards and scorecards. When introduced to the concept of BPM, many managers rightfully exclaim, "We've been doing that for years!"

However, most organizations have not pulled these applications and processes together in a cohesive and concerted way—using a common strategic and technical framework to drive all parts of the organization toward a common set of goals and objectives. Today, organizations implement BPM applications and processes in isolation from each other. Each application provides some local benefit but little global value.

Different Acronyms

Confusion also arises because industry experts cannot agree on what to call BPM, let alone how to define it. Although most experts and users prefer the term "business performance management," others use different names. Gartner Group, a leading technology research firm, favors the term "corporate performance management," whereas some leading software vendors prefer "enterprise performance management."

To add to the confusion, most organizations have a performance management process that they use to measure and evaluate employees on objectives defined by human resources and determine bonus payments and compensation. Although BPM encompasses individual performance plans and reviews, it is much broader than this. Finally, many middleware vendors use the term BPM to stand for business *process* management, a related but distinct discipline (see Spotlight 2.1).

SPOTLIGHT 2.1   BPM VERSUS BPM

Like the old "Spy vs. Spy" cartoons in *Mad Magazine*, business *performance* management and business *process* management are distinct but related disciplines. Both seek to optimize business processes, but one approaches the task from the top down and the other from the bottom up.

Business *performance* management is a top-down discipline that helps executives understand what processes are needed to achieve strategic objectives and then measure the effectiveness of those processes to deliver the desired results. Conversely, business *process* management is a bottom-up approach designed to automate and optimize existing business processes using modeling, workflow, and enterprise application integration tools.

Business Process Management

The Gartner Group defines five key elements of a business *process* management system. Translated into business-friendly language, they are[1]:

1. **Graphical modeling tools** that enable business users to define and optimize the flow of information among business processes and the applications that support them.

SPOTLIGHT 2.1   *(CONTINUED)*

2. **An application engine** that executes and manages the flow of information among applications and notifies business people when they must handle certain tasks in the process.

3. **An adaptive system** that adjusts the flow of information in response to various conditions and automatically updates worklists and tasks accordingly.

4. **Monitoring tools** that monitor and manage process and system performance and highlight out-of-bounds conditions.

5. **Analytical tools** that enable users to analyze historical data about process flows.

Most business *process* management vendors started out selling enterprise application integration (EAI) middleware that links applications together in near real time. They have since added process modeling and management tools as well as business intelligence tools and operational dashboards to deliver a complete system.

In addition, most people use the term BPM informally as shorthand for something else. At a conference I attended in 2003, one speaker equated BPM to budgeting, another to financial consolidation, and a third to compliance with the Sarbanes-Oxley Act. In addition, I found attendees who thought BPM meant either financial reporting, scorecarding, or business intelligence.

BPM Definition

In retrospect, these presenters and attendees were both right *and* wrong. Budgeting, scorecarding, and business intelligence are all components of BPM. You cannot do BPM without them. They are not BPM alone, however. BPM is much broader and bigger than any of these individual components (see Spotlight 2.2).

SPOTLIGHT 2.2   BPM COMPONENTS

Business performance management (BPM) is a management framework that contains the following applications and tools, among others, depending on which vendor or consultant you talk to. It is important to know that BPM is not any of these things individually.

- Performance dashboards
- Budgeting or planning
- Financial consolidation
- Financial reporting
- Business intelligence

SPOTLIGHT 2.2   *(CONTINUED)*

- Portals with embedded key performance indicators
- Strategy maps
- Forecasting software
- Modeling tools for planning

To deliver a true BPM solution, organizations must integrate all the above components in a cohesive and seamless way using a common strategic and technical framework.

After much research and some soul searching, I decided to put a stake in the ground and define BPM. My "big picture" definition is: *a series of organizational processes and applications designed to optimize the execution of business strategy.*

Managing the Business

The concepts behind managing a business are straightforward: Executives set strategy and goals, managers develop plans and budgets to achieve the goals, and the staff executes the plans. Then, everyone continuously monitors their progress toward meeting the goals using reports and analytical tools, and they make course corrections as needed to stay on track. However, defining a good strategy and executing it are two different tasks. BPM processes and tools support good management practices and make it easier for executives at all levels to identify, communicate, and monitor key drivers of business value.

Strategy Gap

Ironically, the prospects for BPM are bright because the state of business management in most companies is so poor. The main problem is that there is a huge gap between strategy and execution. Executives spend days or weeks devising well-crafted strategies and then throw them "over the wall" to the rest of the company, hoping and praying that their vision will bear fruit. Usually, nothing much happens. The organization is deaf to the executives' guidance and direction. Inertia reigns supreme.

Broken Budgets

Another problem is that traditional planning and budgeting cycles—based on centuries-old bookkeeping practices—are no longer fast or flexible enough to meet the accelerated pace of business today. Most plans and budgets are simply irrelevant and out of date before they are completed. Most employees view the budget as a mindless hoop to jump through, a corporate rain dance, rather than a real aid to planning and management.

Lack of Focus

Most people think that BPM is simply about improving performance in general, but it is not. BPM is about improving performance *in the right direction.* It is possible for organizations to work efficiently but not effectively. Groups and teams may work long hours with great enthusiasm, but if they develop or refine the wrong processes, products, or services, then all their sweat, blood, and tears will not help the company achieve its strategic goals. BPM is designed to help organizations focus on the few things that really drive business value instead of many things that generate activity but do not contribute to the organization's long-term health or viability (see Spotlight 2.3).

SPOTLIGHT 2.3   INTEGRATED BPM: BOOZ ALLEN HAMILTON

Booz Allen Hamilton, one of the world's leading strategy and technology consulting firms, has developed an integrated scorecarding, planning, and reporting solution that helps align the firm to corporate strategy and provide timely, accurate, consistent, and transparent information to the entire organization.

In 2003, the firm's Global Operations team, which provides infrastructure and business support services to the consulting business units, began building individual scorecards for 75 teams across the business. In 2004, it began to align the key performance indicators in these scorecards to the Global Operations team's five strategic themes and seven overarching strategic initiatives and then cascading the scorecards down the organizational hierarchy. Today, the scorecards measure both strategic and operational measures and have become an integrated part of how the company does business (see Exhibit 2.1 for Booz Allen Hamilton's top-level scorecard).

To align the business further, Booz Allen Hamilton also overhauled its planning and financial reporting systems and integrated them with the scorecards. To ensure integration, the company purchased software for planning, scorecarding, and financial reporting from Hyperion Solutions.

The planning system replaces a cumbersome, largely manual, Excel-based process. Today, the planning system automates the creation and delivery of planning, budgeting, and forecasting templates based on previous history. It standardizes the rules and maintains them in a centralized repository. This has greatly accelerated the planning process, reduced errors, and enabled the company to make changes in the model and automatically update all plans everywhere.

Moreover, the company aligns its plans to strategic objectives and then uses plans to drive measures in the scorecards. "We can take information in the plan and arrive at targets and ranges we want to use in the scorecard itself," says John Monczewski, senior manager of firm-wide financial reporting at Booz Allen Hamilton.

SPOTLIGHT 2.3 *(CONTINUED)*

Although Booz Allen Hamilton was best of breed for time to close its financial books, it needed to accelerate the speed with which it distributed financial reports, which several years ago were primarily paper-based reports compiled by almost 100 analysts who used slightly different metric definitions for common terms. Today, the firm generates interactive financial reports online. By centrally generating online reports, the firm has reduced distribution and printing costs, standardized metrics, and reduced the time to distribute end-of-month financial reports by more than 50 percent.

"We've gone from no idea how to measure strategy and a planning process that was pretty broken to one that is consolidated and efficient with one portal for managing plans, strategy, and performance," says Monczewski.

BPM Benefits

BPM bridges the gap between strategy and execution. According to Brenda Moncla, a consultant at ThinkFast Consulting, this results in three major benefits:

1. **Improves Communication.** BPM provides executives with an effective mechanism for communicating strategy and expectations to managers and staff at all levels of the organization via planning models and performance metrics tied to corporate goals and objectives.

2. **Improves Coordination.** BPM also fosters a two-way exchange of ideas and information, both vertically between levels within an organization and horizontally among business units, departments, and workgroups that manage a shared activity.

3. **Improves Control.** BPM enables staff to adjust plans continuously and fix or improve operations in a timely manner by providing them with up-to-date information about market conditions and the status of operational processes.

Interestingly, organizations gain many of these benefits when they implement performance dashboards, especially strategic dashboards. This demonstrates that performance dashboards play a central role in BPM solutions.

Research shows that most organizations implement BPM solutions for a variety of reasons. The primary ones are to gain greater visibility into the business, execute strategy better, improve process efficiency, react faster to business events, improve strategic planning, and deliver a more consistent view of business information (see Exhibit 2.2).

The desire among executives to gain greater visibility into the operations of their business is fueled in part by the U.S. Sarbanes-Oxley Act of 2002, which

EXHIBIT 2.1 STRATEGIC DASHBOARD HOMEPAGE

GO Team Scorecard Report
February-28, 2005 80%

Booz | Allen | Hamilton

GO Team Operational Measures

Perspective	Measure	Unit	Target	Score	Status
Value	GT Basis Point Var to Target	%	26.07	98.65	●
	GT Budget vs Actual	%	0	100	●
	GT Cost over Firm Cost	%			
	GT Cost over Firm Headcount	%			
	GT DSO	Days	62	100	●
	GT Staff Utilization	Index	12	90.63	●
Delivery	GT Client Value Index	Index	4	100	●
	GT Model Contractor Rating	Index	5	88	●
People Development	GT Diversity Female - Level II and Below	%			
	GT Diversity Female - Level III and IV	%			
	GT Diversity Minority - Level II and Below	%			
	GT Diversity Minority - Level III and IV	%			

GO Team Strategic Measures

Perspective	Measure	Unit	Target	Score	Status
Outreach	GT Develop and roll out an integrated GO Team outreach strategy	%	75	0	■
Delivery	GT Roll out approach to offer world class service across geograph	%	25	100	●
New Capabilities	GT Blue print and launch a GO Team Service Center strategy	%	75	86.67	●
	GT Build a capacity to place and flawlessly execute big bet progra	%	100	93.46	●
People Development	GT Develop and roll out the GO Team Way for client service	%	100	93	●
	GT Develop and roll out the GO Team Way for people developme	%	100	93	●
	GT Develop and roll out the GO Team Way for problem solving	%	100	93	●

The top-level view of Booz Allen Hamilton's strategic dashboard categorizes and maps strategic objectives and indicates its progress using colored stoplight icons on each objective.

EXHIBIT 2.2   WHY IMPLEMENT BPM?

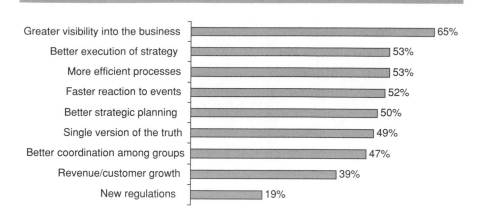

Based on 2004 survey of 635 respondents who have deployed a BPM solution; conducted by The Data Warehousing Institute, 2004.

Source: Wayne Eckerson, "Best Practices in Business Performance Management: Business and Technical Strategies" (*TDWI Report Series*, The Data Warehousing Institute, 2004).

established strict new standards for corporate governance and financial disclosure. In particular, section 409 of the Act calls for organizations to provide real-time disclosure of material events that may affect performance. Combined with heightened competition and the accelerating pace of business today, organizations feel a pressing need to know what is happening in their operations at all times.

The desire to react to events faster and deliver a single version of the truth is also a primary reason why organizations are implementing business intelligence, which will be covered in Chapter 3. Although the respondents in the survey mentioned above are largely BI professionals, nevertheless this demonstrates the central role that business intelligence plays in BPM and, conversely, performance dashboards.

Evolution of Application Packages

The Last Big Market for Business Software?

From a technology perspective, BPM is merely the latest—and perhaps the last— business function that corporations are "automating" with packaged application software. Starting in the 1980s, organizations deployed software packages to integrate and automate back-office operations, such as manufacturing, finance, and human resources. In the 1990s, organizations deployed software packages to support and enhance front-office activities, such as sales, service, and marketing. In the

EXHIBIT 2.3   THE EVOLUTION OF BUSINESS SOFTWARE PACKAGES

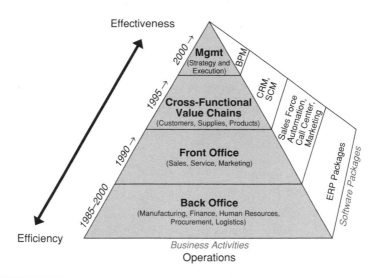

In the past 20 years, companies have employed software packages to integrate and optimize increasingly higher business functions, the latest being business management using BPM solutions.

late 1990s, organizations purchased software packages to optimize cross-functional processes, such as supply chains and customer relationships (see Exhibit 2.3).

Today, one of the last remaining business areas to be automated or fully supported by packaged software is business management. This is the domain of BPM, and it might be the last great untapped market for business software. By virtue of its position at the top of the business pyramid, BPM software holds a commanding view of the rest of the organization, with its processes and activities. Whereas software at lower levels of the business pyramid focuses on increasing the efficiency of business processes, BPM serves as the brains or central nervous system of the entire organization. BPM enables organizations to work more effectively, not just more efficiently, to achieve strategic objectives.

Return on Investment

As a result, BPM has the potential to provide the highest return on investment (ROI) of any business software to date. This is why many vendors are racing to get into the BPM market. Unfortunately, calculating the ROI of BPM is sometimes challenging, because BPM solutions deliver largely intangible benefits, such as better strategies, more alignment, faster access to information, better decisions, and so on. Enlightened executives intuitively understand the value BPM solutions provide, whereas more "bottom-line"–oriented executives may hold off implementing BPM until they see quantifiable ROI.

A FRAMEWORK FOR BPM

Four-Step Process

If BPM optimizes business management, what is the process by which it works? What are its components? What are the technologies required to support it?

BPM is a four-step, closed-loop discipline that turns business strategy into action. The steps are as follows: 1) Strategize, 2) Plan, 3) Monitor/Analyze, and 4) Act/Adjust (see Exhibit 2.4).

The first two steps in the top half of the circle—Strategize and Plan—constitute the "strategy." The last two steps in the bottom half of the circle—Monitor/Analyze and Act/Adjust—"execute" the strategy. Within each step, organizations

EXHIBIT 2.4   BPM FRAMEWORK

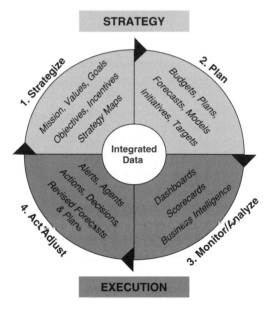

BPM is a four-step process divided equally between strategy and execution. Each step is permitted by the various techniques or technologies shown in the quadrants and supported by a consistent set of integrated data.

use enabling techniques or technologies to support the process. For example, the Plan step uses budgeting, planning, and forecasting software to define initiatives, allocate resources, and establish targets.

When all steps in the BPM process are executed in a concerted manner, they enhance communication, control, and coordination among staff and groups in the organization. In many ways, BPM greases all the parts of the organizational engine to keep it moving in the right direction. The following sections describe the four major steps in the BPM process in more detail.

Step 1: Strategize

Here, executives define key *drivers* of business value and ways to *measure* them. "World class companies focus on value drivers to improve financial performance. They set targets and measures for each driver," says Lawrence Serven, principal at the Buttonwood Group, a management consulting firm in Stamford, CT.

Examples of drivers might be "high customer satisfaction" or "excellent product quality." Measures for these drivers might be "customer satisfaction index" and "number of defects per thousand," respectively. The strategizing process also defines or reaffirms the mission, values, and vision for the organization and sets the goals and objectives to accomplish the mission.

Top executives are not the only ones who can define strategy. Any team of executives or managers in charge of a business unit or department can develop strategies and plans. However, lower level executives must be careful to tie their drivers, measures, and goals to those at the level above them and those of the organization as a whole.

Enablers

Measures of business drivers are called *key performance indicators* (KPIs). KPIs measure how well the organization or individual performs an operational, tactical, or strategic activity that is critical for the current and future success of the organization. KPIs should drive individuals and teams to take action that leads to positive outcomes. As we shall see in Chapter 11, it is not easy to create effective KPIs.

Organizations define drivers, goals, and objectives in strategic planning sessions, which can last several days, weeks, or months. One technique for defining business drivers and KPIs is "strategy mapping," which emanates from a BPM methodology known as Balanced Scorecard. Strategy mapping helps executives define business drivers, objectives, and metrics and map their cause-effect relationships at various levels of an organization. I will discuss strategy maps in more detail in Chapter 9.

Incentives are another key tool that executives use to reinforce value drivers and KPIs. Most companies have systems to evaluate and reward employees for performance, but many of these systems are not tied to strategic objectives and KPIs. Many experts believe that BPM cannot be implemented effectively unless the organization ties performance to compensation.

Step 2: Plan

Next, groups within the organization meet to develop plans to carry out the business strategy and allocate resources. The plans may involve creating new initiatives, projects, and processes, or refining or reaffirming existing ones.

Enablers

The primary planning tool is the *budget or plan*, which allocates resources—people, knowledge, technology, equipment, and money—to carry out the group's goals. The planning process involves breaking down high-level corporate objectives (e.g., "increase market share by 10 percent") into discrete targets and operating models (or scenarios) for every group at each level in the organization. The groups then create projects and processes to meet those targets.

Fixing the Planning Process

Experts agree that planning should be a collaborative process that ties together people across the organization rather than a spreadsheet-driven corporate ritual that imparts little value. Unfortunately, the budgeting process is broken in most organizations. It projects last year's activities onto the coming year and, once approved, is rarely adjusted as circumstances change.

Part of the problem is that most organizations use custom spreadsheets to disseminate and collect data, a process that is cumbersome, error prone, and time consuming. Another pitfall is that many companies do not have a standard planning process or shared definitions for calculating currency conversions or the fully loaded cost of hiring a new worker, for example. If each business unit has a separate planning system, it becomes virtually impossible to align the organization and deliver a consistent view of business activity.

New Web-based planning solutions promise to transform budgeting from a backward looking, static, and labor-intensive process to one that is dynamic, forward-looking, and tied to strategic drivers and objectives. Leading-edge companies are moving away from grueling, bottom-up budgeting to continuous planning with rolling forecasts based on actual performance.

Step 3: Monitor/Analyze

Ideas are a dime a dozen. It is easy to devise strategies and plans. What is difficult is executing them. This requires good people armed with powerful information tools and clear direction from the top. Therefore, the most critical elements of a BPM solution are the tools that let users monitor and analyze performance in a timely manner and take action to improve performance—in other words, a performance dashboard.

Chapter 1 showed that a performance dashboard consists of BI tools for reporting and analyzing information, a data integration infrastructure for collecting and integrating data from diverse sources, data storage systems, such as data warehouses and data marts, and monitoring and management tools. Collectively, these tools and components enable business users to access and analyze information and chart their progress toward achieving strategic objectives and optimizing performance.

Step 4: Act and Adjust

The last part of the BPM process is the most critical. It is the action component. To execute strategy, workers must take action to fix broken processes before they spiral out of control or to exploit new opportunities before they disappear.

Performance dashboards play a key part in the Act/Adjust phase because they alert users to potential problems, and provide them with additional detail and guidance to help them make fast, high-quality decisions. "It's not enough to provide just metrics," says one IT professional. "If the metrics show something is wrong, the first thing users want is more information." For well-known processes, organizations are also implementing *intelligent agents,* which automatically recommend or take action in response to predefined events. For example, one online travel site uses an operational dashboard to alert managers to surges in demand that require expansion of their inventory of airline seats and hotel rooms for sale.

Organizations also need to adjust plans and forecasts to reflect changing market conditions. With centralized, Web-based planning systems, staff can more easily adjust forecasts and models they have built into their plans and budgets. Forward-thinking organizations are using these tools to move to a continuous planning environment. For example, one equipment manufacturer now reforecasts sales eight times a quarter and financials once a quarter after implementing a continuous planning solution. The company now closes its plans up to 90 percent faster using half the staff.

BPM TRENDS

Status

Despite the widespread publicity about BPM, few organizations have deployed BPM solutions, and most have only implemented one or two BPM components, typically budgeting software, performance dashboards, or BI tools. Unfortunately, most companies implement these applications in isolation rather than in an integrated fashion. Vendors are helping to move the BPM market along by evangelizing the value and scope of BPM solutions and offering integrated BPM solutions that comply with the framework described above.

According to research from The Data Warehousing Institute (TDWI), only 13 percent of respondents have implemented a BPM solution. However, another third (33 percent) are under construction or in the planning/design phase, and another third are exploring whether to implement a BPM solution. Only 14 percent have no plans (see Exhibit 2.5). Among the 13 percent of organizations that have deployed BPM, less than a third (21 percent) have had a solution in place for more than two years. Thus, BPM is in its early adopter phase in most organizations.

Scope and Growth

Most organizations that deploy BPM do so on an enterprise basis. These are not necessarily CEO-led initiatives that touch every employee in the organization, rather, many BPM solutions—whether they represent a single component of BPM or the entire framework—are initiated by a business unit, a region, or a department (e.g., typically, finance, operations, or sales). If these initiatives are successful, they quickly spread throughout the enterprise.

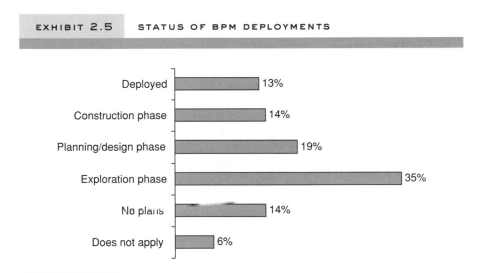

| EXHIBIT 2.5 | STATUS OF BPM DEPLOYMENTS |

Only 13 percent of organizations have deployed a BPM solution, although one-third (33 percent) are in construction or planning/design phases, according to a survey of 796 respondents by The Data Warehousing Institute, 2004.

Source: Wayne Eckerson, "Best Practices in Business Performance Management: Business and Technical Strategies" (*TDWI Report Series*, The Data Warehousing Institute, 2004).

For example, Hewlett Packard Co.'s Technology Solutions Group (TSG), which is profiled in Chapter 9, deployed a strategic dashboard in early 2002 to measure customer service in its European region. The initial solution contained nine metrics and was rolled out in seven weeks to 800 users. Within 18 months, the system grew to support more than 120 metrics and 5,500 registered users in Hewlett Packard TSG worldwide.

Number of Users

Research shows that organizations implementing BPM solutions will experience the same explosive growth as Hewlett Packard TSG. Organizations estimate that the average number of BPM users will jump almost 100 percent, from 404 users to 777 users in 18 months. The median number of users shows an even greater percentage growth, increasing from 50 to 175 in 18 months. The median numbers are more reflective of reality, because a few very large BPM solutions skewed the average numbers (see Exhibit 2.6).

Type of Users

In addition, most BPM solutions support a balanced mix of users: executives (25 percent), midlevel managers (27 percent), business analysts (27 percent), and

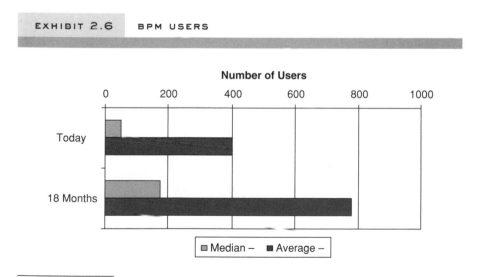

EXHIBIT 2.6   BPM USERS

Most BPM solutions grow exponentially once deployed. Based on a survey of 796 respondents by The Data Warehousing Institute, 2004.

Source: Wayne Eckerson, "Best Practices in Business Performance Management: Business and Technical Strategies" (*TDWI Report Series*, The Data Warehousing Institute, 2004).

operations personnel (29 percent combined), according to research from TDWI. Only five percent said they allow customers and suppliers to participate in a BPM solution. For example, Hewlett Packard TSG initially geared its strategic dashboard to senior executives who wanted a global view of key metrics, but it quickly modified the application to support managers at all levels in the organization, including field offices with perhaps a dozen or fewer employees.

Business Drivers

Given the strategic nature of BPM and its imperative to improve business management, it is not surprising that top executives are the predominant drivers of BPM solutions. Almost half of all solutions (47 percent) have been spearheaded by C-level executives (CEO, CFO, COO), followed by business unit executives (39 percent). Top technical executives (CIO/director of IT) led the initiative in one-third (30 percent) of the cases (see Exhibit 2.7).

Most projects also have more than one executive driver, especially when top executives are leading the charge. Typically, top executives sponsor the project and evangelize its importance to the company, but divisional executives or heads of IT drive the project, especially if it is initiated in a single division or functional area.

EXHIBIT 2.7   BPM DRIVERS

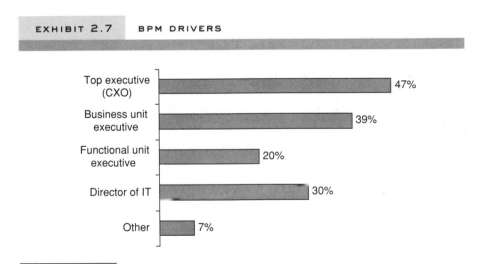

Top executives initiate more BPM solutions than other managers. Percentages don't equal 100% because users could select more than one answer. Based on 360 respondents in a survey conducted by The Data Warehousing Institute, 2004.

Source: Wayne Eckerson, "Best Practices in Business Performance Management: Business and Technical Strategies" (*TDWI Report Series*, The Data Warehousing Institute, 2004).

Strategic Value and Satisfaction

When asked how strategic the BPM project is to executives, most respondents to the TDWI survey said either "very strategic" or "fairly strategic" (86 percent total). An almost equal percentage (81 percent) said the executives were either "very satisfied" or "fairly satisfied" with the BPM solution. More than half (57 percent) said their estimated ROI was "high" or "medium."

Although these data show promising early results for BPM, the jury is still out. Because BPM solutions are still in their early adoptive phase, it will take a few years before we know for sure whether BPM can transform the management of organizations to be more efficient and effective in executing strategy and goals.

SUMMARY

Confusion about BPM. Performance dashboards are part of a larger strategic initiative known as business performance management (BPM). Unfortunately, there is considerable confusion about what BPM is and is not. Part of this confusion stems from the fact that BPM is still in its infancy, both as a management discipline and as an integrated software solution. Confusion also exists because experts call it different things, including corporate performance management and enterprise performance management. Also, many people confuse BPM with business *process* management, which is a distinct, but related, discipline.

Business Management Discipline. In its essence, BPM is about improving business management using software tools to improve execution of business strategy. Given this definition, performance dashboards play a critical role in BPM. Executives translate strategy into metrics and goals, which are displayed in performance dashboards. Performance dashboards are the vehicle by which executives communicate strategy to all employees at every level of the organization. Performance dashboards also align activities of all workers and groups to the strategy so everyone is marching in lock step toward the same destination.

Last Great Software Market. BPM is perhaps the last big market for business software. It sits at the top of the business pyramid, serving as a command and control center for the entire organization. It helps optimize the use of other software packages used to increase the efficiency of business processes at lower levels of the organization.

Four-Step Framework. As a management discipline, BPM prescribes a four-step framework: 1) Strategize, 2) Plan, 3) Monitor and Analyze, and 4) Act and Adjust. The first two steps define an organization's strategy; the last two steps execute the strategy. Performance dashboards support the execution of strategy and enable users to monitor and analyze performance, adjust plans and forecasts, and take action to optimize results.

Rapid Growth. BPM as a management discipline and software applications is still in its infancy. Only a fraction of organizations has deployed a BPM solution, although a large percentage is in the planning or design phase. Those organizations that have deployed BPM solutions—particularly strategic dashboards—report that they expand fast, spreading across departments and business units and adding users at a rapid rate. Most BPM solutions are initiated by chief executives, although business unit heads and IT directors also lead the initiatives.

NOTE

1. Excerpted from a Gartner Group Research Note, "A BPM Taxonomy: Creating Clarity in a Confusing Market," T-18-9669, 29 May 2003 in a white paper "A Closer Look at BPM" (Ultimus, Inc., January 2005).

CHAPTER 3

The Role of Business Intelligence

THE VALUE OF BUSINESS INTELLIGENCE

In Chapter 1, we defined performance dashboards and described their salient characteristics. In Chapter 2, we provided a business context for performance dashboards, showing how they are a critical tool in an emerging business discipline known as business performance management. In this chapter, we provide the technical context for performance dashboards by exploring the business value and composition of business intelligence (BI).

It is important to provide a primer on business intelligence because it is such an integral part of a performance dashboard. Most of the companies profiled in this book built their performance dashboard on top of a BI environment. Without business intelligence, organizations cannot exploit the full potential of a performance dashboard to focus and align people and processes with strategic objectives and make smart, timely decisions. In short, business intelligence is the foundation upon which most performance dashboards grow and flourish.

Origins of Business Intelligence

Early Days

Business intelligence emerged as a distinct discipline in the early 1990s as a way to provide end-users with better access to information for decision making. The initial goal was to give users "self-service" access to information so they did not have to rely on the IT department to create custom reports. By the early 1990s, business intelligence consisted of two nascent segments: data warehousing and desktop query and reporting tools.

Companies began building data warehouses as a way to offload queries from operational systems. Data warehouses became "analytical playgrounds" that let users query all the data they wanted without bogging down the performance of operational systems. At the time, users needed to know SQL, a database query language, to submit queries. So, many prescient vendors began shipping query and reporting tools that hid the SQL language behind a point-and-click Windows interface. Vendors converted these desktop query and reporting tools to the Web in the late 1990s and bundled them with other types of analytical tools to create what are today called "BI suites" or "BI platforms."

The Modern Face of Business Intelligence

Taking a big picture view, business intelligence is an umbrella term that encompasses a raft of data warehousing and data integration technologies as well as query, reporting, and analysis tools (i.e., "BI tools or suites") required to fulfill the promise of giving business users self-service access to information. Performance dashboards represent the latest incarnation of business intelligence; they are built on years of technical and process innovation within the BI field and span both the data management and analytical sides of business intelligence. You could say that performance dashboards are the modern face of business intelligence.

Market Size

Today, business intelligence is big business. Almost every Fortune 2000 company has a data warehouse or some variant. Startup firms that peddled Windows-based query and reporting tools in the early 1990s are now approaching $1 billion in revenues, offer a panoply of products and services, and boast customers around the world. Many software heavyweights, such as Microsoft, Oracle, SAP, and Siebel Systems, have also joined the fray, hoping to take a piece of the BI market's ever expanding pie.

International Data Corporation (IDC), a leading IT market research firm, predicts that the market for BI tools and applications alone will expand from $3.9 billion in 2003 to roughly $5 billion in 2007 with a compound annual growth rate of almost 5 percent, greater than most software market segments in recent years. Adding sales of servers and database management systems used for data warehousing, the BI market exceeds $100 billion annually.

The ROI of Business Intelligence

Case Studies

When done right, business intelligence delivers real value. Organizations in various industries have reaped both tangible and intangible benefits from business intelligence. The Data Warehousing Institute (TDWI) receives more than 100 applications each year to its *Best Practices in Business Intelligence* contest from organizations that can testify to the power of business intelligence to deliver concrete business value. Here are a few examples:

- A major airline estimates that it generated $40 million in new revenue and saved $31 million in costs last year from just four of 35 analytical applications running in its BI environment.

- A major electronics retailer attributes $1.3 million a year in improved assortments and fewer out-of-stock situations to a BI solution. The same solution also saves $2.3 million a year in inventory, a result of more accurate supplier shipments.

- A state department of finance and revenue has closed its tax compliance gap by $10 million a year while optimizing customer satisfaction, thanks to a new BI solution.

If at First You Don't Succeed...

Although these are just a few of many hundreds of successful BI solutions, it would be misleading to suggest that every BI project generates substantial business value. Not everyone succeeds with business intelligence. It takes a considerable amount of money, time, and leadership to deliver real value. Unfortunately, many executives underestimate the commitment that they and their organizations need to make in order to ensure success.

The good news is that most organizations eventually succeed with business intelligence, even if they fail initially. In a recent survey by TDWI, only 18 percent of "stalled" BI projects were canceled outright. The rest were given another chance after restructuring the project with new sponsors, project managers, consultants, or funding levels. With the benefit of hard-earned experience, most teams eventually deliver substantial value.

Tangible and Intangible Benefits

Organizations that deploy BI solutions cite many tangible and intangible benefits. Research shows that most benefits from BI solutions are intangible in nature, which makes them difficult to justify in terms of cost, similar to performance dashboards (see Exhibit 3.1).

Many executives report that they did not foresee the biggest benefits that business intelligence would deliver when they initially approved a project. Consequently, many executives do not insist on a rigorous cost justification.

"Our CEO is the champion of our BI project because he wants to understand what each customer means to our firm in revenue and usage," says Ted Carlson, an energy information consultant at Wisconsin Public Service. "It was difficult to pinpoint the ROI for the project—we primarily justified it as a strategic asset. It

EXHIBIT 3.1 BENEFITS OF BUSINESS INTELLIGENCE

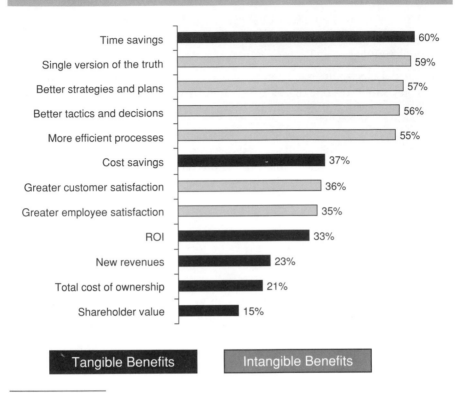

Business intelligence delivers mostly intangible benefits, which is why it is difficult to cost justify. Based on a survey of 510 respondents by The Data Warehousing Institute, 2003.

Source: Wayne Eckerson, "Smart Companies in the 21st Century: The Secrets of Creating Successful BI Solutions" (*TDWI Report Series*, The Data Warehousing Institute, 2003).

has played a big role in attracting and retaining customers and keeping our stock price and credit rating at high levels compared to the rest of the industry."

BUSINESS INTELLIGENCE LANDSCAPE

Conceptual Framework

Business intelligence is often used as a synonym for query, reporting, and analysis tools. However, the term *business intelligence* is broader than a set of software tools. A better definition is as follows:

Business intelligence consists of the processes, tools, and technologies required to turn data into information and information into knowledge and plans that drive effective business activity.

Given this definition, performance dashboards based on a BI infrastructure provide more than just a visual display of performance metrics. They are powerful tools for transforming companies into learning-based organizations that use fact-based decision making to achieve strategic objectives.

One way to think about business intelligence is as a "data refinery." To understand this analogy, think of an oil refinery, which is designed to take a raw material—crude oil—and process it into a multiplicity of products, such as gasoline, jet fuel, kerosene, and lubricants. In the same way, business intelligence takes another raw material—data—and processes it into a multiplicity of information products (see Exhibit 3.2).

The cycle begins when operational systems that "run" the company—such as order entry, shipping, billing, general ledger, and so on—capture business events and turn them into data, the raw material of business intelligence:

EXHIBIT 3.2   THE "DATA REFINERY"

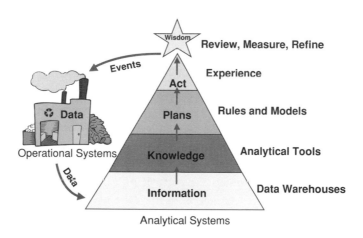

Business intelligence can be thought of as a "data refinery" that processes a raw material—data—into a multiplicity of information products: "Information," which is collected and aggregated by data warehouses; "Knowledge," which is gleaned from query, reporting, and analysis tools; "Plans," which are pieced together from rules, models, and patterns discovered by analytical tools; and "Action," in which business users execute plans that generate events, which starts the cycle over again.

1. **Data to Information.** A data warehouse captures data from one or more operational systems and integrates it at the "atomic" level—the most granular level of data that exists among all systems. For example, a data warehouse might match and merge product data at the SKU level from four operational systems—orders, service, sales, and shipments systems. Integrating data and storing it in a single place transforms data into a new product: *information.*

2. **Information to Knowledge.** Then, users equipped with query, reporting, and analysis tools examine the information and identify trends, patterns, and exceptions in the data. Analytical tools enable users to turn information into a new product: *knowledge.*

3. **Knowledge to Rules.** Armed with these insights, users then create *rules* from the trends and patterns they discover. These rules can be simple— "Order 50 new units whenever inventory falls below 25" or "We expect to sell 1,000 widgets next month based on our past three months of sales and year-to-date comparisons." The rules can also be complex, generated by statistical algorithms or models. For example, statistically generated rules can dynamically configure prices in response to changing market conditions, or optimize freight-hauling schedules in a large carrier network, or determine the best cross-sell opportunities for use in a call center or Web site.

4. **Rules to Action.** Users then create plans that implement the rules. For example, a marketing manager may create a marketing campaign that provides unique offers to customers in six market segments using an optimal combination of marketing collateral and incentives for each customer. The campaign defines what offers to make to each customer segment and the channels (e.g., direct mail or e-mail) through which the offers should be sent. Plans turn rules into *action.*

5. **Feedback Loop.** Once plans are executed, they generate business events that are captured by operational systems, repeating the process. Each time an organization goes through this cycle, it measures, reviews, and refines its plans. This allows users to refine both their mental and statistical models of how the business works and how their decisions affect performance.

This five-step virtuous cycle—in essence, capture, analyze, plan, act, and review—creates a learning organization that can respond flexibly and nimbly to new events in the marketplace.

In many respects, business intelligence is designed to mimic the processes that humans use every day to learn and to make judicious decisions. During our lifetime, we experience millions of events that we assimilate, analyze, and turn into rules, whether consciously or not. Each time we apply a "rule," we get feedback on its validity, which enables us to refine the rules and adapt to changes in our environment. Our "gut instincts" are no more than the unconscious application of rules refined from millions and millions of life experiences. In the same way, business intelligence uses technology to turn millions of business events into models that an organization can use to adapt quickly to changing market conditions.

Common Misconceptions

Some executives make the huge mistake of thinking that there is no difference between BI systems and operational systems. Many executives do not believe they need to spend hundreds of thousands or millions of dollars to create a BI system when their operational systems already generate reports and when business analysts create custom reports in Excel or Access for them.

Eventually, reality catches up with these organizations. They become extremely inefficient in gathering and analyzing data, wasting hundreds of thousands of dollars in man-hours every year. Even worse, they make bad decisions based on incomplete, inconsistent, or inaccurate data, leading to millions of dollars in lost sales. The sad thing is that most organizations do not realize the extent to which they are bleeding themselves dry because of the lack of business intelligence! This is because no accountant or auditor tracks how much money the company loses each day or week or month by not providing timely, consistent data to all workers who need it.

Business Intelligence Is an Adaptable System

The major difference between the two types of systems is that BI systems adapt to the business whereas operational systems structure it. BI systems need to adapt continually to the changing concerns of the business. The questions that business users ask today are different from the ones they will ask tomorrow or next week. In contrast, operational systems impose structure on the business so that a process, such as order taking, is done the same way every time no matter who takes the order. Once designed, operational systems do not change much. The opposite is true for BI systems: the more they change, the more value they provide. In short, whereas operational systems automate processes to improve efficiency, BI systems support decision making to improve effectiveness (see Exhibit 3.3).

So, the real challenge of business intelligence is how to design and manage a system that always changes. In other words, how do you create an adaptive system? This is not easy, which is why many experts say that building a BI system (or a data warehouse) is a "journey, not a destination."

EXHIBIT 3.3   OPERATIONAL SYSTEMS VERSUS BI SYSTEMS

Operational Systems	Business Intelligence
Automate processes	Support decision making
Designed for efficiency	Designed for effectiveness
Structure the business	Adapt to the business
React to events	Anticipate events
Optimized for transactions	Optimized for queries

Types of Data

The dichotomy between operational and BI systems is also evident in the type of information that each manages (see Exhibit 3.4). Operational systems track current transactions (e.g., debits, credits, and current account balance) and keep little history around (i.e., usually only 60 to 90 days of transactions). In contrast, BI systems maintain *years* of detailed transactions culled from multiple operational systems. Moreover, BI systems create new or derived data by summarizing and calculating transaction data to support the metrics that the business uses to track performance.

Operationalizing Business Intelligence

Until recently, BI systems captured transactions by taking periodic "snapshots" of data in an operational system at regular intervals. Now, however, companies want to analyze more timely or "fresher" data to make operational or right-time decisions. For example, store managers who can analyze product sales hourly or daily might change product displays twice a day to optimize revenues by analyzing hourly shopping trends. To support this type of decision making, BI systems are

EXHIBIT 3.4   OPERATIONAL DATA VERSUS BI DATA

Operational Data	BI Data
Current	Historical
Continuously updated	Periodic snapshots
Source specific	Integrated
Application oriented	Subject oriented
Detailed only	Detailed, summarized, and derived

EXHIBIT 3.5   BUSINESS INTELLIGENCE TECHNICAL FRAMEWORK

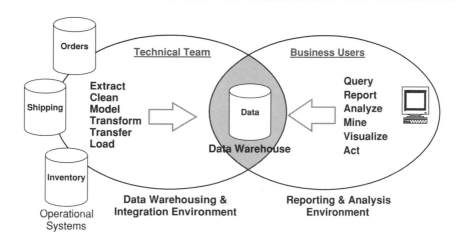

Business intelligence consists of two intersecting environments represented by the ovals above: the data warehousing and integration environment and the reporting and analysis environment.

beginning to adapt the characteristics of operational systems noted in Exhibits 3.4 and 3.5. We will discuss right-time BI in more detail in Chapters 6 and 7.

Technical Framework

Now that we understand the conceptual basis of business intelligence, let us explore the components that comprise a BI environment. The diagram shown in Exhibit 3.5 depicts business intelligence as two intersecting ovals, with operational systems (e.g., orders, shipping, and inventory) off to the left.

Data Warehousing and Data Integration Environment

Data Archaeology

In Exhibit 3.5, the left-hand oval is the data warehousing and integration environment. This is where the technical team spends 60 to 80 percent of its time. Its job is to capture, clean, model, transform, transfer, and load transaction data from one or more operational systems into the data warehouse. These tasks are not easy because operational data is rarely clean, consistent, or easy to integrate. Like archaeologists, the technical team needs to decipher the meaning and validity of thousands of data elements and values in multiple operational systems. It then needs to glue everything back together again into a single coherent "model" of the business, much like a paleontologist might reconstruct a life-size model of a dinosaur from an assortment of bones.

Needless to say, these tasks take a tremendous amount of time and effort. Just as it takes years for a paleontologist to piece together a dinosaur from its relics, it can take months for a technical team to create an initial data warehouse or data mart. This is why most teams start small and incrementally build an enterprise view one subject area at a time. Also, just as paleontologists need expert knowledge of their subject matter, technical teams need a deep understanding of the business they are trying to model. In fact, technical teams cannot do this work themselves. They need business analysts who are intimately familiar with both the business and the data to guide them step by step through the process of gluing the business back together again.

Data Warehouses

Once the data archaeology is complete, the technical team loads the integrated data into a data warehouse, which is usually a relational database designed to handle large numbers of both simple and complex queries. A *simple query* might ask for the customer record for "John Doe," which was pieced together from multiple systems and stored in one row of the data warehouse database. A *complex query* might ask to see the top 10 customers for the previous 12 months who have outstanding credit but declining orders. Whereas simple queries take seconds to execute, complex queries can take many minutes or hours depending on the complexity of the query and the volume of data in the data warehouse.

Data Marts

To improve query performance and narrow the scope of data warehousing projects, technical teams often create subject-specific data warehouses, called data marts. Data marts became popular once it became clear that early data warehousing projects that tried to model and map large portions of the enterprise took years to build, cost millions of dollars, and, not surprisingly, failed to deliver meaningful results. Data marts scale down projects to a realistic scope, allowing technical teams to deliver results within three to six months. Typical data marts are designed to support individual business areas, such as sales, marketing, or accounting.

Most data warehouses are modeled in a highly normalized format, such as third normal form, which minimizes redundancy in the database by dividing data into tables and specifying relationships between them. Third normal form models are commonly used in transactional systems so applications only have to access a single table to make an update instead of multiple tables, increasing application speed and accuracy.

In contrast, most data marts are designed using a star schema model, which arranges relational data so that it is easy and fast to query and quick to load into online analytical processing (OLAP) cubes. Unlike normalized models, a star schema puts all the fact-based information (e.g., the numbers) in a central table surrounded by multiple dimension tables, such as customer, geography, channel, product, which is why it is called a "star" schema. The dimension tables filter the central fact table in response to a user query, such as "I want to see revenues (i.e., a "fact") for the last 12 months (i.e., time dimension) in the Midwest region (i.e., geography dimension), by our top 10 customers (i.e., customer dimension ranked)."

Multilayered Architecture

Today, most companies use a hub-and-spoke architecture to meet users' information needs. This architecture consists of a central data warehouse that feeds information to multiple downstream data marts. In this environment, users query the data marts, which are designed to meet the specific information requirements of a department or workgroup. Only data-savvy business analysts query the data warehouse, which contains a superset of information in the marts.

The use of data marts frees technical teams to design a data warehouse to handle two major tasks: 1) collect and integrate data from multiple systems at the most granular level possible and 2) prepare and distribute data to data marts. The data warehouse never gets rid of data and serves as a perpetual recycling center and staging area. This multitiered architecture enables technical teams to create new data marts quickly by repurposing data already in the warehouse and perhaps extracting new data from operational systems either periodically in a batch process or in near real-time using enterprise information integration (EII) tools. However, not all data warehousing experts believe that a multi-tier architecture is best (see Spotlight 3.1).

SPOTLIGHT 3.1 DATA WAREHOUSING ARCHITECTURES: THE BATTLE OF THE TITANS

The BI community has experienced its share of religious wars over the years. The biggest battle has been waged over how to construct a data warehousing environment.

The Inmon Model. The Inmon model, named after Bill Inmon, a prolific author and respected figure in data warehousing circles, advocates using a "hub-and-spoke" architecture in which a central data warehouse serves as a staging area to collect data from multiple sources systems and then distribute subsets to downstream data marts. In this multitiered approach, users query data marts instead of the data warehouse, which functions more as a staging area and distribution center. The data warehouse contains detailed data whereas the data marts contain mostly summary data.

SPOTLIGHT 3.1 *(CONTINUED)*

The Kimball Model. Another major camp follows the advice of Ralph Kimball, another prolific author and respected figure in the industry. The Kimball model dismisses the need for a data warehouse. Because most users want detailed data, Kimball argues that it is best to store the detailed data in individual data marts and logically connect them using "conformed" dimensions. In essence, Kimball's data warehouse is the sum of all the data marts. To optimize query performance and improve ease of use of the data marts, Kimball popularized a type of data model known as a *star schema* that is widely used today, even among "Inmonites" when creating data marts.

Centralized Data Warehouse Model. Teradata, a division of NCR, advocates using data warehouses without any data marts. This centralized approach gives users unfettered access to all data in the data warehouse instead of restricting them to individual data marts. It also makes it easier to manage and maintain the system because all the data are kept centrally within a single data management platform. However, central data warehouses can become extremely large in terms of the amount of data and number of users they support. To maintain adequate query performance in large central warehouses, organizations need a high-performance, parallel-processing database (such as the one Teradata provides).

Federated or Virtual Approach. The federated approach creates a virtual data warehouse. Instead of consolidating data into a single repository, this approach pulls data together on the fly from multiple source systems, including data warehouses, data marts, operational systems, Web pages, and external systems, among other things. From the user's perspective, however, the data appear to exist in a single system since the federated approach delivers a virtualized view of remote systems. Users aren't aware of the complexity of the data environment, although some complex queries may not run as fast as in a traditional environment.

Although the federated approach does not always scale well, it is a quick and easy way to get a performance dashboard up and running when an organization either does not have a data warehouse or data mart or does not want to wait for the IT department to upgrade an existing one with the right data. An organization can use the technique to populate metrics in a performance dashboard with data from different systems. For instance, it can pull budget data from a planning system, last month's results from the data warehouse, and yesterday's activity from an operational system. Many organizations now prefer the flexibility of the federated approach, and it is one reason for the explosion of performance dashboards today.

Research from TDWI shows that most organizations prefer Inmon's multilayered, "hub and spoke" approach to either a central data warehouse or a Kimball architecture. Interestingly, these approaches are not mutually exclusive. Most organizations create hybrid architectures that blend elements from each. In reality, there is no one right or wrong way to build a data warehouse as long as it meets an organization's information needs.

Operational Data Stores

To confuse matters, many organizations create a specialized data warehouse, known as an *operational data store* (ODS), to support operational applications that require fast access to integrated data. Unlike traditional data warehouses or data marts that store large volumes of historical data and support complex, long-running queries, ODSs do not store more than a few months of data and support quick look-up queries (e.g., customer records.) In addition, users can update records in the ODS but not the data warehouse, which typically appends new information to existing records but never throws anything out in order to keep a true historical record of events.

A good example of an ODS is a customer database that delivers a customer record to a telephone service representative when the customer calls with a question or an order. The customer record contains a history of customer purchases and past interactions with the company culled from multiple customer-facing systems. It may also contain a "score" that informs the customer service representative what products to cross-sell to the customer based on their buying history. (The scores are usually calculated in the data warehouse and passed to the ODS.) In addition, whereas data warehouses are read-only environments, an ODS lets business users edit or delete records on the fly. For example, a service representative can update a customer's address, marital status, or other information within the ODS while on the phone with the customer.

Data Warehousing Tools

To build a data warehousing environment, technical teams must first analyze source systems to see what data they contain and also examine the condition of the data. Often, source systems contain incomplete, missing, or invalid data, which makes it challenging to build a data warehouse. Most teams now use *data profiling tools* to audit and assess the condition of source data and identify relationships among columns and tables. They use *data cleansing tools* to validate and fix known problems in source data as it is loaded into the data warehouse.

Once the team finishes analyzing the data in source systems, it creates a target *data model* for the data warehouse. The model, in effect, is a logical representation of how the business operates in a specific area, such as sales or service. Most technical teams create conceptual, logical, and physical data models using commercially available *data modeling software*, although some data modelers still work entirely by hand.

Data Integration Tools

With a target model in hand and a good understanding of data in source systems, the team is now ready to map source data to the target data warehousing model.

It does this by using *extraction, transformation, and loading (ETL) tools* or by coding transformation logic by hand. ETL programs are the heart and soul of a data warehousing environment because they contain all the rules for gluing data from multiple source systems into a single data store that provides an integrated picture of the business. ETL tools also contain engines that automate the process of extracting source data, transforming and mapping it to the target model, and moving and loading it into the data warehouse.

To support right-time or even real-time updates, a performance management group may also employ high-speed middleware in conjunction with their ETL tools. For example, organizations that use *enterprise application integration (EAI)* to integrate packaged and legacy applications are now pushing data to ETL engines in real time. This "trickle feed" approach replaces traditional batch-loading processes that limit data warehouses to storing historical data only. The combination of EAI and ETL promises to transform data warehouses from stodgy historical archives into active repositories of on-demand information.

Another way to deliver right-time information is to use *enterprise information integration (EII)* middleware. These tools query multiple, distributed data sources, join the results on the fly, and display them to end-users. EII tools, in effect, create a virtual data warehouse or virtual performance dashboard that is dynamically generated transparently to users. However, many EII tools only work well against small volumes of clean, relatively non-volatile data that have well-defined database keys. Most experts agree that EII tools provide a good way to prototype the contents of a proposed data warehouse or performance dashboard or supplement an existing one with right-time or external data.

Lightweight Infrastructure

Not all performance management systems require organizations to build data warehouses and deploy data integration middleware, which can be expensive. Some strategic dashboards succeed without them. However, just because an organization does not want to spend money creating a BI infrastructure does not mean it can succeed without it (see Spotlight 3.2).

SPOTLIGHT 3.2 DO WE REALLY NEED A BI INFRASTRUCTURE?

Some executives who want to deploy a performance dashboard balk at the cost and complexity of creating a BI infrastructure, including data warehouses, data marts, and data integration tools. They question whether these tools and structures are absolutely critical and wonder if there is a shortcut.

SPOTLIGHT 3.2 *(CONTINUED)*

It is true that not all performance management systems require a BI infrastructure. Chapter 1 described a strategic dashboard built by Brown & Root that did not hold much data and thus didn't require a classic BI infrastructure. However, just because an organization does not want to spend money on a BI infrastructure does not mean it can get away without one.

Most operational and tactical dashboards require a BI infrastructure, but strategic dashboards may not need one right away. However, once a company starts cascading scorecards throughout the enterprise and to lower levels of the organization, its information requirements expand substantially and it will need to invest in a BI infrastructure. Lower level scorecards generally require more detailed data than higher level scorecards.

Organizations that put off building a BI infrastructure create problems for themselves in the long run. They usually hit a brick wall once they try to expand the performance dashboard beyond the initial target group of users. Successful projects are cursed with success and the team must support three to four times more data and users than they anticipated. When this happens, the team often quickly slaps together a BI infrastructure that is not reliable, scalable, or aligned with corporate information standards. These makeshift BI infrastructures are costly to maintain and are prime candidates for consolidation into a more standard infrastructure.

A robust BI infrastructure does not have to cost a fortune, and it does not have to be built all at once. Many companies profiled in this book bootstrapped their performance dashboards with little or no money and without making long-term technical compromises at the infrastructure level. Most built the BI infrastructure incrementally along with new applications and functionality requested by users. Some also leveraged existing data warehouses and data marts, accelerating development and avoiding duplication of resources.

Analytical Environment

The right-hand oval in Exhibit 3.5 refers to the reporting and analysis environment, which is the domain of the business users, who use a variety of tools to query, report, analyze, mine, visualize, and, most importantly, act on the data in the data warehousing environment.

Report Design Tools

Report design tools allow power users or developers to craft custom queries and format the results in a standard report layout, such as master-detail reports or pixel-perfect invoices and account statements. A decade or two ago, most standard business reports were hand-written using a programming language, printed on paper, and distributed via snail mail. However, vendors now offer powerful new report design tools that run on a variety of platforms (e.g., Windows, Web, mainframe) and pull data from multiple source systems. The tools now generate online reports that users can interact with by linking to subreports (i.e., "linked reports") or selecting parameters from a drop-down list box (i.e., "parameterized reports"). Many report design tools now use a desktop publishing paradigm that makes it easier for report developers and power users to create custom reports quickly and easily.

The earliest report design tools exhibited many characteristics of modern day data warehouses and data integration tools. They extracted, joined, and massaged data from multiple source systems, placed the data into a large report file, and stored it on a central server. Many financial, management, and regulatory reports are still produced this way. Unfortunately, many executives mistake their 15-year-old production reporting systems for a full-fledged business intelligence environment. They believe that because they spend hundreds of thousands of dollars each year producing standard reports they already "do" business intelligence. It is difficult to convince these executives that they are losing money and a competitive edge by not giving users timely access to relevant information, something that most standard and production reports do not deliver.

Whereas early report design tools created static reports, many now create interactive reports that function similarly to end-user query and reporting tools. For example, parameterized re-ports make users think they are performing ad hoc queries when, in reality, they are simply filtering a preexisting report. A single parameterized report with multiple filters can replace hundreds or thousands of custom reports, liberating end-users from having to request custom reports from the IT department (see Exhibit 3.6).

Query and Reporting Tools

End-user versions of report design tools are known as *query and reporting tools*. These tools provide users with predefined query objects that shield users from having to know SQL or master the complexity of navigating back-end databases and networks. With a semantic layer, end-users simply drag and drop data elements and measures onto a "query panel" and hit the submit button. The results come back in rows and columns (i.e., tabular format) that users can then turn into charts or apply other formatting as needed. Business Objects and Cognos were among the first vendors to deliver end-user query and reporting tools.

Online Analytical Processing Tools

OLAP tools are essentially spreadsheets on steroids. Whereas spreadsheets store data in two dimensions in a file, OLAP tools store data in multiple dimensions in a specialized database (see Exhibit 3.7). The beauty of OLAP tools is that they let users query data the way they think about the business—dimensionally. Whereas

EXHIBIT 3.6   PARAMETERIZED REPORTING

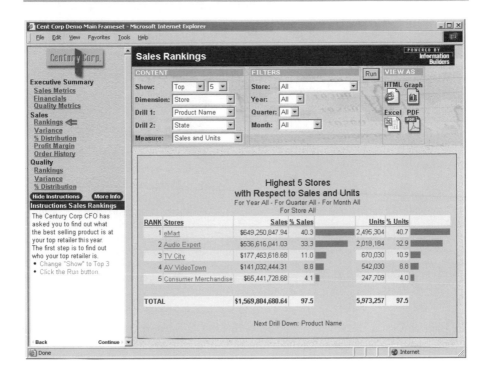

Parameterized reports let users filter an existing report by selecting values from one or more drop-down list boxes, as in the example above. With parameterized reports, users think they are performing "ad hoc queries" when they're really just applying filters to an existing report. Parameterized reports let developers create one report that provides many views or slices of the data.

Source: Courtesy of Information Builders, Inc.

query and reporting tools require users to select tables, rows, and columns—which are the artifacts of databases—OLAP tools let users select measures and dimensions—which are artifacts of the business. A typical OLAP query might be "Let me see net profits by product, by channel, by geography, and by time." Like spreadsheets, OLAP tools let users apply complex calculations to the data and create hierarchies within each dimension. A geography hierarchy might be Region, Country, District, City, or Office. A time hierarchy might be Year, Quarter, Month, Week, or Day.

Unlike spreadsheets, however, OLAP tools hold much more data because they run on a specialized multidimensional database. OLAP tools are fast—they provide split-second response times to most queries, allowing users to "slice and dice"

EXHIBIT 3.7 OLAP CUBE: DIMENSIONAL ANALYSIS

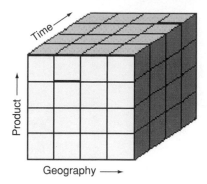

OLAP tools are like spreadsheets on steroids. Whereas spreadsheets store data in two dimensions, OLAP tools store data in multiple dimensions. Users can quickly and easily navigate through dimensions and hierarchies in the cube, hence the term "slice and dice." The diagram above only shows three dimensions, but OLAP cubes can hold dozens of dimensions, each with multiple hierarchies of data.

the data almost at the speed of thought. Interestingly, most users cannot tell the difference between a parameterized report and an OLAP application. Both provide flexible navigation. The major difference is that OLAP users navigate a dimensional database whereas parameterized report users navigate query filters defined by a report designer. Thus parameterized reports are ideal when you want to impose greater structure on user navigation, whereas OLAP is best when you want to give users unfettered access to a predefined set of data.

The traditional downsides of OLAP databases are that they only hold a limited amount of data (but much more than a spreadsheet) and they run on a proprietary database that may not match your company's architecture. Traditionally, OLAP tools take a long time to populate with data because they precalculate results at the intersection of each dimension and each hierarchy. This effectively limits them to storing summary data only. However, in recent years, vendors have made dramatic breakthroughs in OLAP server scalability and calculation performance. Many companies are now considering replacing star schema data marts with OLAP servers because they are equally scalable.

Data Mining Tools

Data mining tools, also known as knowledge discovery in databases (KDD), provide highly specialized tools for statisticians and skilled business analysts. These tools automatically "mine" or discover patterns in the data and generate statistical models and rules. Unlike query, reporting, and analysis tools that require users to start with a hypothesis of trends in the data, data mining tools do not require business users to make such assumptions.

Using sophisticated statistical analysis and data mining techniques, such as neural networks, decision trees, and linear regression, these tools find patterns in the data that might take days or weeks for users to discover on their own, if at all. Some vendors now sell *text mining tools* that discover patterns in documents or text, such as call center conversations, Web forums, or Web pages. Both data and text mining tools turn the patterns into rules or algorithms (i.e., "models") that can be applied to other data to make predictions, classifications, segmentations, recommendations, and forecasts. For example, companies use data mining models to spot fraudulent credit card transactions, anticipate machinery breakdowns, or recommend products to new or existing customers.

The ROI of predictive mining applications is almost five times greater than that of nonpredictive applications using standard query, reporting, and analysis tools, according to research firm IDC. The downside is that data mining applications require high-priced specialists and software that make them almost twice as expensive to set up and maintain as other analytical applications, according to IDC.

Fitting Users to Tools

One Size Does Not Fit All

The five categories of BI tools described above—report design, end-user query and reporting, OLAP, and data mining—deliver different types of functionality for different types of users. To meet user requirements, organizations must purchase multiple BI tools, something most executives are loath to do. For years, executives have made it abundantly clear that they only want to purchase one tool for all users to minimize upfront license fees and downstream maintenance, support, and training costs. The reality, however, is that one size does not fit all when it comes to BI tools.

To date, companies that have purchased a single BI tool for all users pay in the end. Users get frustrated with BI tools that are over- or underpowered for their needs and stop using them. There is a lot of BI shelfware today, representing hundreds of millions of dollars in wasted investments. The beauty of performance dashboards is that they support a broad range of users by incorporating the functionality of a variety of BI tools in a layered fashion that conforms to the way users want to view and manipulate information. Performance dashboards finally give executives a single tool that meets the needs of most users in their organizations.

Outside of performance dashboards, many BI vendors sell integrated suites of BI tools, which meet most users' requirements and minimize the risks of purchasing BI tools, although they generally increase upfront license fees. However, even when purchasing a performance dashboard or BI suite, organizations need to assess user requirements to ensure that they display the right functionality in a performance dashboard or outfit users with the right modules in a BI suite. To do this, organizations need to segment users into categories based on their analytical habits and requirements. Most organizations have between four or eight distinct categories of BI users. Once these profiles are known, organizations can then assign the right BI tool to each type of user.

Exhibit 3.8 provides a simple framework for mapping users to BI tools. The framework divides all users into two categories: 1) *information producers*, who create reports and views for others to view and 2) *information consumers*, who consume those reports and views.

Information Producers

Information producers comprise 20 percent of the total user population and generally use desktop tools to create reports or models. Information producers consist of *statisticians*, who use data mining tools, and *report authors*, who use report

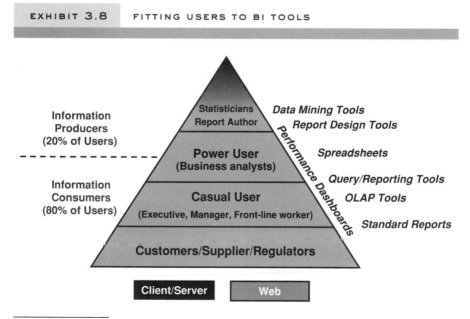

EXHIBIT 3.8   FITTING USERS TO BI TOOLS

This diagram provides a simple framework for classifying types of business intelligence users and fitting them with appropriate BI tools. The beauty of performance dashboards is that they support the broadest range of users by incorporating the functionality of a variety of BI tools in a layered fashion that conforms to the way users want to view and manipulate information.

design or programming tools to create custom reports. Report authors can be IT developers or "power" users—business users who taught themselves how to use a report design tool or were trained by the IT department. Because *power users* both create and consume reports, they straddle the line between information producers and information consumers. The most typical type of power user is a *business analyst*, who uses Microsoft Excel and Microsoft Access to analyze data and build custom reports.

Information Consumers

Most information consumers are *casual users* who regularly view reports but do not crunch numbers or perform detailed trend analysis on a daily basis. Casual users include executives, managers, staff, and external users. This is a large group that is well served by a performance dashboard, which encompasses query and reporting tools, OLAP tools, spreadsheet reports, standard reports, and the output of statistical models. Most of these tools now provide a Web interface to promote ease of use and minimize administration and overhead.

Promise and Reality of BI Tools

When BI tools made their debut in the early 1990s on Windows desktops, there were high expectations that the tools would liberate end-users from their dependency on the IT department to create custom reports. The combination of these tools and newly minted data warehouses caused vendors and pundits to proclaim that the era of "self-service" business intelligence had arrived.

However, reality quickly fell short of promise. It turns out that most users found the tools too difficult to use. Even when the tools migrated from Windows to the Web, simplifying user interfaces and easing installation and maintenance burdens, it was not enough to transform BI tools from specialty software for power users to general-purpose analytical tools for everyone in the organization.

Even power users abused the early generations of BI tools (and still do!). Most use BI software as glorified extraction tools to download huge data sets to their desktops, clogging networks and bogging down query performance for everyone else. These users then dump the data into Microsoft Excel to do their "real" analysis, creating spreadmarts that undermine data consistency and a single view of the business.

New Wave on the Way

However, a new wave of BI tools has arrived: performance dashboards. These next-generation BI tools blend the once distinct worlds of reporting and analysis behind a dashboard or scorecard interface. These tools hit the BI "sweet spot"

EXHIBIT 3.9   BUSINESS INTELLIGENCE "SWEET SPOT"

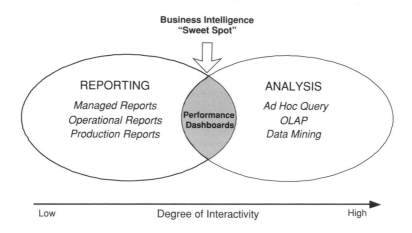

Performance dashboards blend the attributes of reporting and analysis to create a dynamic or "drillable" exception report that meets the needs of 80 percent of your workforce.

by delivering the information and functionality that most users in an organization want and need to do their jobs effectively (see Exhibit 3.9).

The information needs of these users are best summed up in the mantra: "Give me all the data I want, but only the data I really need, and only when I really need it." In other words, most users don't want to spend unnecessary time analyzing data unless there is an exception condition that demands their attention. When that happens, they want immediate access to all relevant information, but in a systematic and structured way so they don't get lost in the data.

Key Features

Performance dashboards support the "user mantra" by providing only the information users need when they need it. Performance dashboards do not overwhelm users with a dizzying array of reports or analytical options; they keep things simple by highlighting anomalies in a graphical interface and giving users the option to investigate the details if they desire.

In essence, performance dashboards are "prettified" exception reports with built-in analytical tools that make it easy and fast for users to examine information about an exception condition. In short, performance dashboards conform to the way users want to work instead of forcing them to conform to the way the tools work.

SUMMARY

Business intelligence is the foundation upon which performance management systems grow and flourish. Without business intelligence, organizations cannot exploit the full potential of a performance dashboard to focus and align people and processes with strategic objectives and optimize performance. Business intelligence consists of a data warehousing environment and a reporting and analysis environment.

Data Warehousing and Integration. Technical teams use a variety of data integration tools to populate a data warehousing environment, including tools that capture data in real time directly from source systems. Although most organizations use a multitiered architecture, there are numerous ways to build a data warehousing environment. The reporting and analysis environment allows end-users to query, report, analyze, mine, and act on data in a data warehousing environment.

Reporting and Analysis. Although there are many reporting and analysis tools, no one tool will fit all users in an enterprise. Organizations need to purchase different tools for different categories of users according to their analytical requirements and abilities. Although every organization classifies users differently, there are two basic categories of users: information producers, who create reports, and information consumers, who consume them. Within these categories are multiple segments, each of which has slightly different requirements and needs. Organizations need to fit BI tools carefully to users; otherwise users will not use the tools.

The New Face of Business Intelligence. Performance dashboards represent the latest incarnation of business intelligence, building on years of technical and process innovation. Performance dashboards meet the information requirements of most casual users by hitting the business intelligence "sweet spot," which blends reporting and analysis capabilities within an intuitive dashboard interface. Performance dashboards deliver on the promise of self-service data access by providing the right data to the right people at the right time to optimize decisions and accelerate results. In short, performance dashboards are the modern face of business intelligence.

CHAPTER 4

Assessing Your Organizational Readiness

READINESS CRITERIA

Performance dashboards cannot take root in a hostile environment. The organization must be ready to accept and nurture a performance dashboard for it to succeed.

Paul Niven, author of *Balanced Scorecard Step by Step: Maximizing Performance and Maintaining Results,* defines seven criteria for evaluating an organization's readiness to implement a Balanced Scorecard. Although Niven created these criteria specifically for Balanced Scorecards (i.e., strategic dashboards), they are equally valid for any kind of performance dashboard.

I have adapted Niven's list and added three criteria to reflect the importance of having a solid business intelligence (BI) infrastructure to support all types of performance dashboards, not just strategic ones. Although some strategic dashboards do not initially require an investment in BI and data integration software, most eventually do, as explained in Chapter 3. Therefore, the following ten criteria are good ways to evaluate an organization's readiness to deploy and sustain a performance management system for the long haul.

To evaluate readiness, ask whether your organization has:

1. A clearly defined strategy

2. Strong, committed sponsorship

3. A clear and urgent need

4. The support of mid-level managers

5. The appropriate scale and scope

6. A strong team and available resources

7. A culture of measurement

8. Alignment between business and IT

9. Trustworthy and available data

10. A solid technical infrastructure

Let us describe each of these criteria in detail and then use them to create an assessment tool to evaluate organizational readiness.

1. A Clearly Defined Strategy

A performance dashboard is a window into an organization's strategy and planning processes, especially a strategic dashboard. If the strategy and planning processes are unclear, unaligned, or uncoordinated, the performance dashboard will be ineffective and short lasting. For example, Hewlett Packard Co.'s Technology Solutions Group (TSG) asks business sponsors a series of questions to ascertain whether their group or unit has a measurable strategy and a culture of measurement before creating scorecards for them (see Spotlight 4.1).

SPOTLIGHT 4.1   STRATEGIC DASHBOARD READINESS ASSESSMENT

Hewlett Packard Co.'s Technology Solutions Group (TSG) has a program office that creates strategic dashboards for its regional groups and other units. When working with a new group, the program office first meets with the sponsoring executives to explain strategic dashboard concepts and discuss their concerns. To assess the group's readiness to use a strategic dashboard approach to manage performance, the program team asks executives to answer the following six questions:

1. **Is the relationship between your strategy and measures clear and obvious?** This question communicates the need to translate strategy into a small number of carefully defined metrics with corresponding objectives, targets, and initiatives. Most companies have hundreds of metrics, most of which they rarely consult and few of which are truly relevant to their mission.

2. **Do you measure outcomes or causes?** This introduces executives to the concept of "leading" and "lagging" indicators and gets them to start thinking about measuring value drivers instead of historical activity.

3. **Is there consensus about the importance of the measurements and objectives?** Do all executives agree that existing metrics accurately define the strategy? If the strategy and vision are vague, the answer is usually "no." Second, do employees agree that the metrics used to evaluate their performance are valid and produce the desired results? Without employee buy-in, a performance management system cannot work.

4. **If you select ten managers at random, how many know whether they are help-ing to achieve the strategy?** Most managers and workers know what tasks they need to do each day, but few know how their work contributes to the company's strategy. This helps executives see that the strategic dashboard is a communica-tions tool that lets employees literally "see" how their work contributes to the strategy and performance of the company.

5. **Is important information easy and readily available for the right people?** It is one thing to measure performance, but it is another thing to empower people with information so they can take action to improve performance. This helps executives assess the state of their information delivery systems and whether they need to be overhauled.

6. **What do you do with the figures you receive?** This can be a gut-wrenching question. A strategic dashboard broadcasts performance results so managers can compare themselves with their peers and no longer hide behind well-scrubbed spreadsheets. Many executives will be threatened by the free flow of performance data required in a successful implementation.

The organization must have a strategy that defines its mission, values, vision, goals, and objectives, as well as metrics for measuring progress toward reaching those objectives. It also needs a planning process that devises new initiatives, refines existing ones, and allocates resources to implement the strategy. The fol-lowing are the major components of a strategy.

Mission

A mission statement communicates the purpose of a business to people both inside and outside the organization. In about 50 words or less, a mission statement describes what the company does, how it differs from the competition, and its broadest goals. It communicates to employees and the outside world the reason for the organization's existence. To define a mission statement, Niven recommends the "Five Why's" technique developed by Collins and Porras.[1] An individual crafts a short description of what the organization does and then a facilitator asks "Why is this important?" five times. Each answer refines the description until it becomes a powerful and pithy encapsulation of the company's mission.

Goals and Objectives

Goals and objectives define the path a business takes to achieve the mission. They state what the company is committed to doing and, more importantly, what it *will not* do. Goals and objectives are the heart of any strategy statement. They should be aligned with the mission statement and disseminated widely. Specifically, goals are the major aims of the company or the broad results it wants to achieve, whereas objectives are the steps it takes to reach each goal. Goals are generally stated without much detail. They are ambitious but realistic, motivating employees, not demoralizing them. Objectives, on the other hand, are more narrowly defined. They specify targets, time frames, and measures for each goal. Objectives are revised regularly as the business changes.

Values

Values reflect the principles and beliefs that guide the way the company does business. Values are shared assumptions about how things should get done. Values are very important in a crisis situation when a new and unique situation confronts the company and it must decide how to act. For example, values helped executives at Johnson & Johnson decide to quickly pull every bottle of Tylenol from retail shelves when several were found to be contaminated with cyanide, an act that cost the company more than $100 million. However, its rapid action to safeguard the lives of the public ultimately garnered tremendous goodwill and public respect, which helped to minimize the impact of its financial losses.

Vision

The vision statement describes where your company wants to go or what it wants to become. It is inspiring, a call to action. Whereas goals represent what a company hopes to achieve in the near term, a vision shows where the company plans to be in 5, 10, or 15 years. The vision represents the company's "stretch" goals. Think of John F. Kennedy's speech, when he called for the country to send a man to the moon by the end of the decade. This challenge galvanized the country, which rose to the task and achieved the seemingly impossible.

Metrics and Targets

A critical part of a strategic planning session that most companies overlook is the task of translating strategy (i.e., mission, goals, objectives, values, and vision) into metrics and targets that can be tracked over time. Without such metrics and targets, companies have no idea how well their strategy is being carried out in the field and cannot make course corrections to stay on track. Chapter 11 goes into detail about how to craft metrics and targets for performance dashboards.

Planning

Planning translates strategy into initiatives at the local level and allocates resources to various groups to carry out the initiatives. When plans and budgets are tied to strategic objectives, the business moves collectively toward the same goals and destination. One way to do this is to reevaluate group and individual plans on a quarterly basis. Such continuous planning gives an organization greater flexibility to adapt to changes and opportunities in the marketplace.

2. Strong, Committed Sponsorship

It is almost an industry cliché to say that strong business leadership is critical to the success of any information management project, including performance dashboards. A committed and involved business sponsor evangelizes the system, secures and sustains funding, navigates political issues, effects cultural change, and helps prioritize projects. Research shows a high correlation between the commitment of a business sponsor and success rates of BI solutions, which include performance dashboards (see Exhibit 4.1).

In fact, what is most interesting is that projects with a "very committed" sponsor are twice as likely to succeed as those with a "fairly committed" sponsor (67 percent versus 30 percent). And almost half (46 percent) of projects with "fairly committed" sponsors—the next level below—are actually struggling. So, sponsors cannot be half-hearted or even three-quarters hearted; they must give it 100 percent if they want a successful project.

The sponsor must also assign a trusted lieutenant to guide the project on a daily basis. These "drivers" or "champions" need to devote at least 50 percent of their time to the project. Like the sponsor, they must be well respected and con-

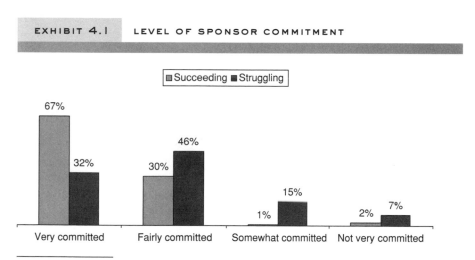

EXHIBIT 4.1   LEVEL OF SPONSOR COMMITMENT

Projects with "very committed" sponsors are more than twice as likely to succeed, whereas projects with "fairly committed" sponsors are more likely to struggle.

Source: Wayne Eckerson, "Smart Companies in the 21st Century: The Secrets of Creating Successful Business Intelligence Solutions" (*TDWI Report Series*, 2003).

EXHIBIT 4.2 DOES YOUR PROJECT HAVE A BUSINESS DRIVER?

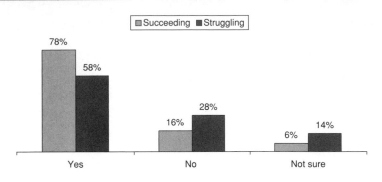

Successful BI projects almost always have a business driver and are more likely to be succeeding than struggling.

Source: Wayne Eckerson, "Smart Companies in the 21st Century: The Secrets of Creating Successful Business Intelligence Solutions" (*TDWI Report Series*, 2003).

nected in the organization, with a direct line to the executive suite. They need to lead interference for the project when it gets bogged down in politics, vendor negotiations, or budget planning. Often, the driver is the person who initiates the idea for the project and sells it to the sponsor, whose influence and credibility are vital to the success of the project.

Although the presence of a business driver does not correlate with success to the degree that having a committed sponsor does, nevertheless most successful projects have a business driver (see Exhibit 4.2).

3. A Clear and Urgent Need

This aspect is almost too elementary to mention, but it plays a pivotal role in whether a performance dashboard project succeeds or not: the sponsoring group must demonstrate a clear and urgent need for a performance management system. If not, the system will not take root. The best performance dashboards address a critical pain in the business that stems from a lack of information and alignment with strategy. Paradoxically, the more pain, the more likely a performance dashboard will flourish. Unless the business is starving for information and a way to monitor and manage business performance, the project will not survive the strong tides and currents that wash many technology projects out to sea.

There are many legitimate reasons to implement a performance dashboard. Perhaps the biggest is that an existing performance management system is ineffective. It tracks lagging measures and has not improved the company's profitability, revenues, or share price. Or perhaps employees hardly notice when the system is updated. Or maybe few managers conduct personal performance reviews on a regular basis, which shows that the company's culture does not value performance measurement or individual accountability.

Other events that often drive organizations to implement a performance dashboard include the following:

- **A New Top Executive.** The company hires a new CEO, CFO, or CIO who is used to running an organization using business performance management techniques and performance dashboards.

- **A New Strategy or Initiative.** Executives need a way to educate the organization about a new strategy or strategic initiative, align everyone's actions to the objectives, and monitor progress toward achieving goals.

- **A Merger or Acquisition.** A company must align two incompatible sets of strategies, cultures, values, and goals and get everyone marching in the same direction quickly.

- **A Business Crisis.** There are many events that can put an organization into crisis mode, requiring laser-like focus for the company to survive the calamity: a new competitor or market-transforming technology, an economic downturn, a natural disaster, financial mismanagement, or criminal wrongdoing, and so on.

- **Organizational Restructuring.** Executives who reorganize groups and divisions to improve productivity or competitiveness need to explain their rationale and monitor the effectiveness of the move.

- **Confusion over Data.** Executives can become exasperated by the lack of consistent data, which prevents them from getting a clear picture of the organization at any given moment.

- **Core Systems Overhaul.** An organization that replaces multiple legacy systems with a packaged business application needs to monitor the progress of the project and measure the return on investment.

- **New Regulations.** New regulations, such as the Sarbanes-Oxley Act or the Basel Accord, may force organizations to change their strategy or revamp core processes.

Coaches frequently motivate players with the maxim "There is no gain without pain." However, with performance dashboards, it is better to say, "There is no project without pain." Find a group with strategic or informational pain, and you have found a good place to implement a performance dashboard.

4. The Support of Mid-Level Managers

Successful performance dashboards solutions need the support of mid-level managers to succeed. This group determines the success or failure of a performance dashboard more than any other. These managers translate strategic goals and objectives into initiatives, metrics, and budgets to govern their areas. Their words and actions signal whether their staff should take executive edicts seriously or not. If they are unwilling partners—or worse, active saboteurs—the project cannot succeed. It is critical to win the support of mid-level managers because they know how the company operates on a day-to-day basis and can provide a healthy "reality check" to senior executives. Mid-level managers often know which metrics will work and which will not, what data are available to populate metrics, and to what level in the organization it makes sense to deploy scorecards.

"They generally know the best sources of information, the biggest issues, and the best workarounds. We also use these mid-level managers as advocates back into the organization, both up and down and across, to help communicate the program, benefits, and what people will be able to use," says Martin Summerhayes, program manager in Hewlett Packard TSG. Unfortunately, mid-level managers can also be the ones most threatened by a performance dashboard. They are used to massaging and spinning numbers to present themselves and their group in the best possible light to executives higher up in the organization. A performance dashboard undercuts their ability to do this, leaving them feeling exposed and vulnerable. A performance dashboard broadcasts their performance to everyone through an unfiltered lens. They may feel they have to scramble and compete for budget dollars, resources, and promotions like never before and aren't happy about it.

It takes considerable effort and political savvy to win the hearts and minds of mid-level managers. Executives have to educate these managers about how the program benefits them personally as well as their group, and they have to quell unfounded fears. Executives identify key individuals who can make or break a project and communicate with them early and often. If appropriate, executives should invite the most pivotal managers to sit on the steering committee that oversees the project. The managers may see this as an honor and view the project more favorably as a result; at the very least, it gives executives a good way to keep an eye on key managers and make sure they have a positive attitude toward the project.

5. The Appropriate Scale and Scope

Most people assume a performance dashboard is always implemented on an enterprise scale starting with the executive suite, but this is not always true. Sometimes, it is better to implement a performance dashboard in a business unit, region, or department that is highly receptive to it. If the initial project succeeds, it will spread quickly throughout the organization. However, if executives try to force-fit a performance management system into an organization or business unit that is not ready for it, the tool will not gain the momentum it needs to expand throughout the enterprise.

When deploying a strategic dashboard (i.e., Balanced Scorecard) in a business unit or group, Niven recommends selecting a unit that conducts business across an entire value chain of activities. In other words, the business unit should have a "strategy, defined customers, specific processes, operations, and administration." Selecting a unit with a narrow, functional focus will produce a strategic dashboard with narrow, functionally focused metrics that will not be readily transferable elsewhere in the organization.

6. A Strong Team and Available Resources

To succeed, an organization needs business and technical people with the right skills who are willing and available to work on the project.

On the business side, the sponsor and driver must allocate enough time and attention to nurture the project through its entire life cycle. They also must stick around for the duration of the project or garner sufficient consensus and momentum so the project can continue without them. Successful projects have business people who are skilled at selling, funding, prioritizing, and completing projects as well as communicating requirements, managing risk, and accepting responsibility for the outcomes (see Exhibit 4.3).

On the technical side, successful projects have technical teams with strong technical and project management skills. Successful technical teams score especially well on the "soft issues," such as the ability to communicate technical issues

EXHIBIT 4.3   BUSINESS TEAM CAPABILITIES

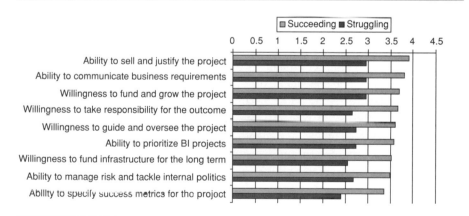

Business teams that can sell, manage, and develop the project further are more likely to deliver successful solutions. (Chart based on a 5-point rating scale, with 1 being "poor" and 5 being "excellent.")

Source: Wayne Eckerson, "Smart Companies in the 21st Century: The Secrets of Creating Successful Business Intelligence Solutions" (*TDWI Report Series*, 2003).

EXHIBIT 4.4   TECHNICAL TEAM CAPABILITIES

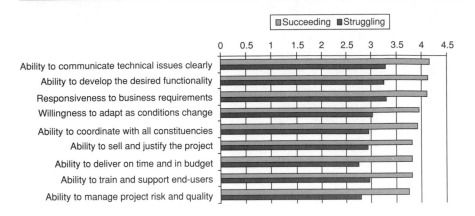

Technical teams that work well with the business and exhibit strong technical skills are more likely to deliver successful solutions. (Chart based on a 5-point rating scale, with 1 being "poor" and 5 being "excellent.")

Source: Wayne Eckerson, "Smart Companies in the 21st Century: The Secrets of Creating Successful Business Intelligence Solutions" (*TDWI Report Series,* 2003).

clearly, respond to business requirements, and develop desired functionality (see Exhibit 4.4).

If the needed resources do not exist in-house, the organization must be willing to bring in outside consultants and contractors. However, they need to put in place a plan to transfer consultants' knowledge and skills to in-house workers so the company is not dependent on the consultants. Organizations with successful solutions rely heavily on management consultants to help formulate strategy and metrics, develop project plans, and implement change management programs; they use technical consultants largely to assist with application development, architectural design, product installation, requirements gathering, and application integration (see Exhibit 4.5).

7. A Culture of Measurement

Does the business already have a culture of managing through performance measures? If not, even the strongest desire may not be enough to overcome organizational inertia. At a bare minimum, does it compare performance with plan or forecasts? Does it hold individuals and groups accountable for performance? Does it conduct individual performance reviews using objective data?

EXHIBIT 4.5   CONSULTANT SERVICES USED BY SUCCESSFUL BI
PROJECT TEAMS

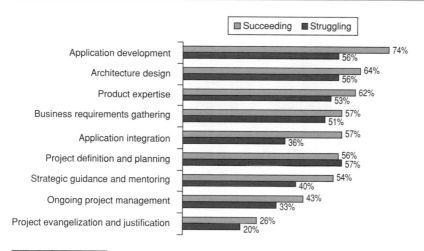

Legend: ☐ Succeeding ■ Struggling

Category	Succeeding	Struggling
Application development	74%	56%
Architecture design	64%	56%
Product expertise	62%	53%
Business requirements gathering	57%	51%
Application integration	57%	36%
Project definition and planning	56%	57%
Strategic guidance and mentoring	54%	40%
Ongoing project management	43%	33%
Project evangelization and justification	26%	20%

Companies with successful BI solutions rely on consultants more than companies with struggling
BI solutions in all areas, but especially application development, application integration, and
strategic guidance and monitoring.

Similarly, the organization should have a history of using information and data
to make decisions. If the organization relies primarily on intuition, it will struggle to succeed (see Exhibit 4.6).

"Our company used to make decisions on gut feel," says a director of business
information and analysis at a major U.S. manufacturer, "but now our executives
believe strongly that fact-based decision making gives us a competitive advantage.
Executives now ask 'Where are the data to back up this decision?' and they expect
sales people to use information to close deals, not just rely on the strength of their
client relationships. And it's working!"

Performance dashboards work best in a corporate culture that encourages
users to share information. They cannot flourish if executives tightly control
information to insulate themselves from the rest of the company; or if managers
use information as a political weapon to protect their turf; or if users are penal-
ized for sharing information with colleagues. In contrast, organizations whose
employees share information "very openly" are five times more likely to have a
successful solution than those whose employees do not (17 percent to 3 percent).
Organizations whose employees do not share information openly are five times
more likely to struggle (23 percent to 4 percent) (see Exhibit 4.7).

EXHIBIT 4.6   HOW ARE DECISIONS MADE?

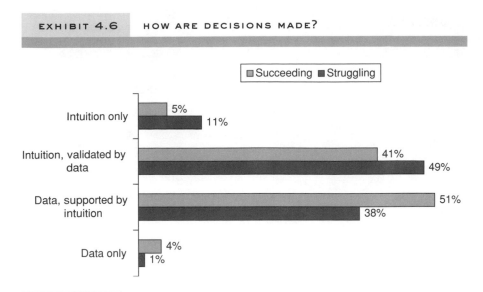

Organizations that rely on data to validate intuition and make decisions are more likely to succeed.

Source: Wayne Eckerson, "Smart Companies in the 21st Century: The Secrets of Creating Successful Business Intelligence Solutions" (*TDWI Report Series*, 2003).

EXHIBIT 4.7   HOW OPENLY DO USERS SHARE DATA?

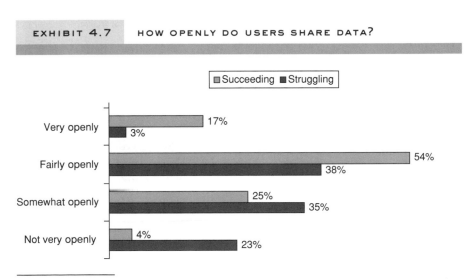

Organizations in which users share data openly are more likely to succeed with BI projects, such as performance dashboards.

Source: Wayne Eckerson, "Smart Companies in the 21st Century: The Secrets of Creating Successful Business Intelligence Solutions" (*TDWI Report Series*, 2003).

8. Alignment between Business and IT

The degree of alignment between the business and the technical team also determines the readiness of an organization to adopt a performance dashboard. That is because performance dashboards are adaptive systems that continually change as the business changes. Performance dashboards require a great deal of ongoing interaction between the business user and the technical team to define new requirements, metrics, and targets and refine old ones. If the relationship between business and technical groups is tense and both groups eye one another with distrust and sarcasm, then the chances that a performance dashboard will succeed are minimal. We will discuss business-IT relationships in detail in Chapter 14.

Like sponsorship, there is no middle ground with alignment. Teams that are "very aligned" are almost five times more likely to succeed, whereas teams that are only "fairly aligned" struggle a whopping 46 percent of the time. The key to guaranteeing success is to achieve total alignment between the business and technical sides of the team (see Exhibit 4.8).

So what does a "very aligned" team look like? First of all, it has an actively involved business sponsor or driver. Second, it is a team—not two or more disparate groups with different leaders, objectives, and cultures. "We sit side by side with business people and report into the same leadership," says a senior technology manager who helps run the BI team at a telecommunications firm. "The only difference is that we specialize in the data and they specialize in the business processes."

EXHIBIT 4.8   HOW ALIGNED IS THE BUSINESS AND IT?

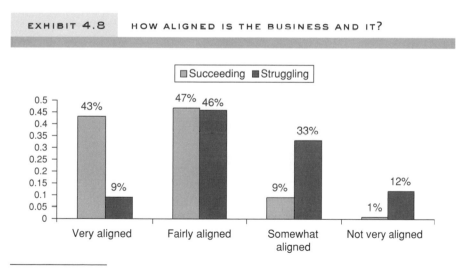

When business and technical teams are "very" aligned, a project is almost five times more likely to succeed than fail. Teams that are only "fairly" aligned are as likely to fail as succeed.

Source: Wayne Eckerson, "Smart Companies in the 21st Century: The Secrets of Creating Successful Business Intelligence Solutions" (*TDWI Report Series*, 2003).

9. Trustworthy and Available Data

Does the organization have the right data to populate metrics in a performance dashboard? Although it is unlikely that data exist for all measures, a new initiative should supply data for most of the metrics under consideration. It is also critical that someone evaluate the condition of the data. Nothing can damage the credibility of a project faster than launching a performance dashboard with inaccurate and untrustworthy data.

Because data are at the heart of most performance management systems, organizations need to treat data as a vital corporate asset, as important as other assets, such as buildings, people, and cash. Companies whose executives view data as a corporate asset are six times more likely to be successful than those whose executives do not (31 percent versus 5 percent). Companies with executives who do not view data as an asset are between two and three times more likely to struggle with BI projects (see Exhibit 4.9).

10. A Solid Technical Infrastructure

To generate data for performance dashboard metrics, companies often must either overhaul operational systems and processes or establish a BI infrastructure

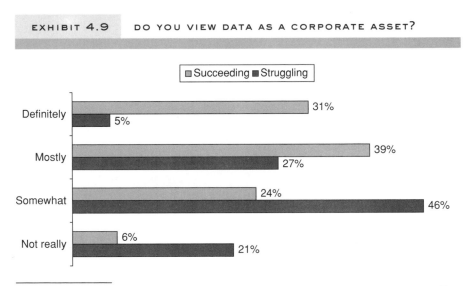

EXHIBIT 4.9   DO YOU VIEW DATA AS A CORPORATE ASSET?

Companies that perceive data as a corporate asset are more likely to succeed with BI projects like performance dashboards.

Source: Wayne Eckerson, "Smart Companies in the 21st Century: The Secrets of Creating Successful Business Intelligence Solutions" (*TDWI Report Series,* 2003).

that delivers high-quality data, or both. However, not all performance dashboards require a robust technical infrastructure to initiate a project. Strategic dashboards, in particular, can often start by using manual processes to capture and disseminate key data elements (see Spotlight 4.2).

SPOTLIGHT 4.2   GROWING INTO A BI INFRASTRUCTURE

Balanced Scorecard consultants argue that organizations should not delay a strategic dashboard project because they lack the requisite data or a robust BI infrastructure. Bill Barberg, president of Insightformation, Inc., describes a hypothetical scenario:

Suppose that the executives at a mid-sized manufacturing company that recently acquired several plants, each with its own IT systems, create a strategy to become a low-cost producer. One "causal driver" in this strategy involves driving scrap and rework to levels significantly below the industry average. Unfortunately, the company does not have good data to measure scrap and rework processes, and the data that exist are spread across many operational systems with different database fields and definitions. Few of the systems track why things are scrapped and do not reflect labor costs associated with the process. In addition, there are no industry benchmarks against which they can compare their performance.

The executives quickly realize that it might take several years to overhaul the company's operational systems and processes to capture the information they need and then create a BI solution to analyze, aggregate, and accurately track detailed scrap and rework information across the company. Rather than delay the Balanced Scorecard project until they have a solid technical foundation, the executives decide to forge ahead and make do with less than perfect information.

Barberg says the executives made the right choice. Even a set of rough monthly measures for scrap calculated by hand provides direction and, more importantly, communicates a powerful message about what the company needs to focus on to succeed. The scorecard motivates managers and staff to take positive steps to reduce scrap, and these behaviors can be reinforced through additional objectives and monthly scorecard review meetings.

To track progress against its strategic objectives regarding scrap, executives can assign a business analyst to create a spreadsheet report that merges and standardizes data collected by hand at each plant with relevant operational data. At the very least, the analyst can summarize monthly results in the Balanced Scorecard and attach the report. However, if the scorecard software has simple aggregation or roll-up capabilities, it can also show trends for each plant.

Meanwhile, with a clear understanding of the type of information that is needed, the company can work on a parallel track to upgrade its operational systems to capture data required for the Balanced Scorecard and implement an activity-based costing system to allocate labor cost to scrap. The company can also implement reporting and analysis tools that deliver a standardized view of scorecard metrics, Barberg says.

Although the company would have benefited from having integrated operational systems and a robust BI infrastructure to start, it can reap some benefits without them. Eventually, it can upgrade its technical infrastructure to further increase the value the project delivers, says Barberg.

EXHIBIT 4.10   WILLINGNESS TO FUND INFRASTRUCTURE

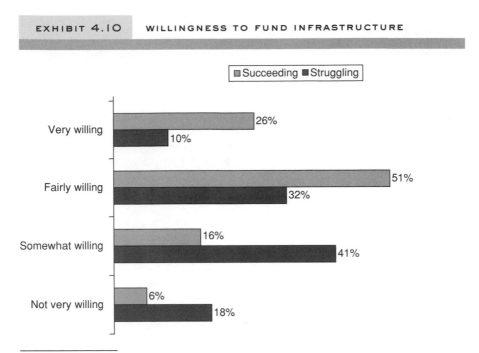

Organizations that are "very willing" or "fairly willing" to fund a BI infrastructure are more likely to succeed with BI projects than those that don't.

Source: Wayne Eckerson, "Smart Companies in the 21st Century: The Secrets of Creating Successful Business Intelligence Solutions" (*TDWI Report Series*, 2003).

The BI infrastructure consists of the BI environment (data warehouses, data marts, and analytical tools), the technical platform (servers, storage, networks), and the people to feed and maintain the environment. Organizations that are very willing or fairly willing to fund a BI infrastructure are more likely to succeed than those that are not. We will discuss what a robust BI infrastructure looks like and how to get there in the next chapter (see Exhibit 4.10).

Readiness Worksheet

Using the above criteria, organizations can assess their readiness to implement a performance dashboard as a whole or identify the best business unit or group to start with. Exhibit 4.11 adapts Niven's readiness assessment tool to an evaluation of a performance dashboard project within a business unit of a larger company.

To use the tool, assign a percentage weight to each criterion based on its importance to your organization. The weights should add up to 100 percent. Then, score the organization (or a group within it) on its ability to support each crite-

EXHIBIT 4.11   BUSINESS UNIT READINESS ASSESSMENT

Criteria	Score	Weight	Total Points	Rationale
Strategy	10	15%	1.5	This unit has recently completed a new strategic plan for the next five years.
Sponsorship	9	15%	1.35	The new unit president used a strategic dashboard at two other organizations.
Clear need	5	10%	0.5	This group has performed well and may not see the need for this tool to sustain future efforts.
Midmanager support	7	5%	0.35	Young, energetic management group willing to experiment with new approaches.
Appropriate scope	8	5%	0.4	This unit produces, markets, and sells a distinct set of products.
A strong team	4	5%	0.2	The unit has talented staff who are already overextended so the unit will have difficulty finding resources for this project.
Culture of measurement	7	15%	1.05	Despite the unit's success, it has not used performance measurement systems in the past.
Business–IT alignment	5	15%	0.75	The unit has its own IT team, but it has lost staff since corporate IT declared its intentions to subsume the group.
Trustworthy and available data	4	5%	0.2	Many customer metrics (i.e., loyalty) have no data source, and customer data are spread across many systems.
Solid BI infrastructure	5	10%	0.5	The unit primarily runs on spreadsheets maintained by many people, although it wants to purchase a BI tool.
TOTAL	64	100%	7.3	

Overall Assessment: This unit scores a very high 7.3 out of 10 and is a good candidate for the performance management system but poses a few potential risks. The data, resource, and alignment issues, while not insignificant, are mitigated by the strong leadership of the unit president, and the creation of a new strategic plan. Early education initiatives within this unit could focus on the value of the system as a means of sustaining results for the long term. This may reduce skepticism surrounding the implementation based on the past success of the unit.

Source: Adapted from Paul R. Niven, Balanced Scorecard Step By Step: Maximizing Performance and Maintaining Results (John Wiley & Sons, Inc.), 2002, page 46.

rion, using a value from one to ten. Then, for each criterion, multiply the score by the weight to obtain points. Add up all the points for each criterion to get a total score. Because the maximum number of points that can be scored is ten, an organization (or group) that scores between seven and ten points is a good candidate for a performance dashboard. An organization (or group) that scores between four and six points poses significant risk, and a group that scores below four points should not attempt the project (see Exhibit 4.11).

Evaluating a business unit or department against the ten criteria above provides a great way to assess the readiness of an organization to implement a performance dashboard.

SUMMARY

Not all companies are ready to implement a performance dashboard. Organizations need strong leadership, a receptive culture, and a robust technical environment.

You can assess your organization's readiness to implement a performance dashboard by asking the following questions:

- Does your organization have a clear, coherent strategy with well-defined goals, objectives, and measures?
- Is there a high-level executive who strongly believes in the project and is willing to spend time evangelizing and nurturing the project?
- Does the organization have a demonstrated need for the system? How much is it suffering from an inability to track and measure performance?
- How willing are mid-level managers to support the project? Will the open sharing of performance results threaten their positions and their hold on power?
- Does the group have sufficient scope so that the implementation can be adapted by other groups in the organization?
- Does the group have business and technical people with proper skills and experience to deliver a successful project?
- Does the group already have a culture of measurement and make decisions by fact instead of intuition?
- How aligned are the business and technical teams? Do they have a good working relationship and trust one another?
- Do data exist to populate the measures? How clean, valid, and complete are the data?
- Does the group have a solid technical infrastructure that generates the required data and delivers it to users in a format that is easy to monitor and analyze?

These ten questions can help executives determine the best place to implement a performance dashboard as well as understand better the risks the project poses and the obstacles they will need to overcome.

NOTE

1. James C. Collins and Jerry I. Porras, "Building Your Company's Vision," *Harvard Business Review*, September–October 65–77 (1996), as referenced in Paul Niven, *Balanced Scorecard Step by Step: Maximizing Performance and Maintaining Results* (Hoboken, NJ: John Wiley & Sons, Inc., 2002), p. 74.

CHAPTER **5**

Assessing Your
Technical Readiness

BUSINESS INTELLIGENCE MATURITY MODEL

The Big Picture

In the previous chapter, we discussed ten criteria for evaluating the readiness of an organization to implement a performance dashboard. This chapter focuses more specifically on evaluating an organization's technical readiness. Without a strong technical foundation—especially in business intelligence (BI)—most performance dashboards will not survive long. They will be crushed by the weight of cumbersome and costly data-gathering processes, inaccurate and untrustworthy data, poor performance, and antiquated functionality.

Like organizational readiness, technical readiness does not happen overnight. It takes years to build a robust BI infrastructure and develop the internal skills and talent necessary to support an effective performance management system. During the past several years, many organizations that initiated performance dashboards became disillusioned when they could not automate the solution or populate its metrics with valid, accurate data.

I've created a BI Maturity Model to help organizations understand the maturity of their BI infrastructures and, by extension, their readiness to build and sustain a performance management system. The six-stage BI Maturity Model shows the trajectory that most organizations follow when evolving their BI environments from low-value, cost-center operations to high-value, strategic utilities that drive market share. The model provides organizations with a "big picture" view of where their BI environment is today, where it needs to go, and how to get it there.

The model shows that performance dashboards are best deployed once organizations reach Stage 4 or later. At this level of maturity, organizations can quickly deploy performance dashboards without having to make significant investments to create or rearchitect a BI environment. In Stage 5, organizations are ready to cascade strategic dashboards throughout the enterprise and link them (logically at least) to operational and tactical dashboards. In short, it takes a reasonable amount of BI maturity for organizations to deploy a performance dashboard successfully.

Six Stages

Exhibit 5.1 shows that the BI Maturity Model consists of six stages: Prenatal, Infant, Child, Teenager, Adult, and Sage. As an organization moves through successive stages, business value increases as data become more consolidated and logically integrated within fewer analytic structures.

The BI Maturity Model is shaped in a bell curve to indicate that most organizations today have reached Stages 3 and 4. Only a few are still stuck in the first two stages or have advanced to highly mature implementations in Stages 5 and 6. Because business intelligence originated as a distinct discipline in the early 1990s, it is no surprise that after a decade or so most organizations have reached "BI adolescence" and are suffering all the requisite growing pains (see Spotlight 5.1).

EXHIBIT 5.1   BI MATURITY MODEL

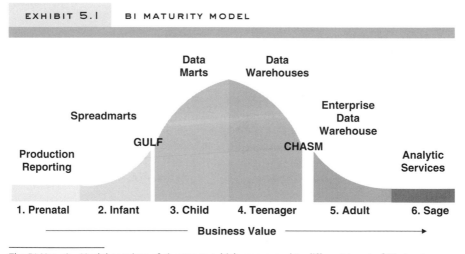

The BI Maturity Model consists of six stages, which correspond to different types of BI structures.

SPOTLIGHT 5.1 SYMPTOMS OF BI ADOLESCENCE

Most organizations today are in the adolescent phase of business intelligence. If you remember correctly from your youth, adolescence is both an exciting and a painful time, full of change, transition, and surprises. The same is true for companies that reach adolescence in business intelligence. Every step forward is tentative, and more setbacks are experienced than victories. The key to getting through this stressful period is to stay focused on the future and the value that awaits those who persevere while taking one step at a time in the present. Here are a few symptoms that signify that your organization is square in the middle of BI adolescence.

- The BI team moves perpetually from one crisis to the next.
- The BI program manager has to explain continually why the BI budget should not be cut.
- Usage of the BI environment peaked several months after deployment and continues to decline.
- The BI manager has to evangelize continuously the value of the BI environment to executives and business users.
- The number of spreadmarts, independent data marts, and other data warehouses with redundant data keeps increasing instead of decreasing.
- Users keep asking the IT department to create custom reports even though the organization recently purchased a "self-service" BI tool.
- Executives still believe BI is a tool, not a strategic information resource to drive the organization in the right direction.

Managing a BI environment in its adolescence is painful. Perhaps the only comforting thought is that most companies are also experiencing the same growing pains. Like your organization, they spend more time reacting to problems than proactively solving them and put more effort into putting out fires than delivering lasting business value. In short, most organizations are stuck in the Chasm, halfway between adolescence and adulthood.

The BI Maturity Model defines each stage using a number of characteristics, such as scope, analytic structure, executive perceptions, types of analytics, stewardship, funding, technology platform, change management, and administration (for which we borrow concepts from the Software Engineering Institute's Capability Maturity Model). This book will focus only on a few of these characteristics.

Organizations evolve at different rates through these six stages and may exhibit characteristics of multiple stages at a given time. Thus organizations should not expect to move cleanly and precisely from one stage to the next.

Although it is possible to skip stages, it is unlikely. Organizations must learn critical lessons at each stage before they can move to the next. Organizations that feel compelled to "catch up" and skip stages will encounter problems that eventually bog down the project. Organizations that successfully skip stages must have strong senior leadership, considerable funding, and experts with considerable BI experience to guide the project to a successful completion.

More likely, an organization will regress and slip backward in the evolutionary cycle. Often, the cause is beyond the project team's control: a merger, acquisition, new executive leadership, changing economic or competitive circumstances, or new regulations. Here, the plans are put aside to address the new issues. This makes many BI professionals feel like "Sisyphus," the ancient Greek condemned to roll a huge stone perpetually up a hill in Hades only to have it roll down again upon nearing the top.

Sticking Points

Although a few companies skip stages, and more regress, almost every organization gets stuck at two points in the life cycle. These are represented in the model as the "Gulf" and the "Chasm." Most BI initiatives stall here. They have one foot stuck in the previous stage while the other is reaching out to the next, and they are unable to make a clean leap beyond. As a result, many never fully reach the other side and reap the benefits therein.

The Gulf

The primary way to cross the Gulf is to change executive perceptions. Executives must recognize that they need more than a production reporting system to make timely, effective decisions and that the dozens of spreadsheets and desktop databases (i.e., spreadmarts) that run the business undermine productivity and effectiveness. Once they recognize this, they need to mandate and fund a BI initiative to move the organization off the old systems and onto the new ones that empower users to access, analyze, and act on information.

The Chasm

The Chasm is deeper and wider than the Gulf and harder to cross. There are several reasons:

- **Perceptions.** Executives fail to transform their view of BI from a tool for power users to an enterprise resource for all users and that is critical to the mission of the company.
- **Ownership.** Divisional or departmental managers resist turning over their successful BI initiatives, including performance dashboards, to a corporate group so the systems can be scaled up and out and disseminated to the rest of the organization.

- **Consolidation.** Organizations fail to stem the proliferation of analytical silos by consolidating them into a standard BI environment that delivers a consistent view of the business.

- **Self-Service.** Organizations fail to shift their emphasis from building data warehouses to empowering users with BI tools, such as performance dashboards, that foster self-service access to information.

- **Mental Silos.** The organization fails to break down end-users' mental silos for accessing information in a BI environment and show them how to perform cross-departmental analyses that lead to deep insights about how to optimize performance.

The following is a brief description of each stage and its major characteristics.

Prenatal Stage: Production Reporting

Most established organizations have production reporting systems generating standard reports that are usually printed and distributed to large numbers of employees on a regular basis, usually weekly, monthly, or quarterly. Because programmers hand-code the reports, it can take several days or weeks to produce a new or custom report. This creates a backlog of requests that the IT department can never get ahead of, as well as many frustrated users who cannot obtain timely information to do their jobs.

Consequently, many users take matters into their own hands, especially business analysts who know their way around corporate information systems and whose job is to crunch numbers on behalf of executives and managers. These individuals circumvent the IT department by extracting data directly from source systems and loading the information into spreadsheets or desktop databases. This gives rise to an abundance of spreadmarts, which is the hallmark of Stage 2.

Infant Stage: Spreadmarts

Spreadmarts are spreadsheets or desktop databases that function like data marts. Each spreadmart contains a unique set of data, metrics, and rules that do not align with other analytical systems in the organization. An organization afflicted with spreadmarts has no consistent view of the business and no single version of truth from which every employee can work.

Spreadmarts ultimately wreak havoc on organizations. They bleed organizations dry, often without the organizations knowing it. Users spend inordinate amounts of time collecting and integrating data, becoming, in effect, "human data warehouses." Executive meetings dissolve into chaos as managers argue about whose data are right rather than making effective decisions. This phenomenon is known as "dueling spreadmarts."

Spreadmarts are difficult to eradicate—because they are ubiquitous, cheap, and easy to use. Many users, especially business analysts and financial managers, cannot function without spreadsheets. Spreadsheets give them a high degree of local control at extremely low cost, which undermines departmental, divisional, or enterprise standards. As a result, spreadmarts proliferate like weeds—organizations have dozens, if not hundreds or thousands of these pernicious analytical structures.

Research shows that organizations on average have 28.5 spreadmarts. However, the reality is that most organizations have no idea how many spreadmarts they have, and many have given up trying to control their proliferation. Although spreadmarts are difficult to eradicate, there are remedies for curing this "disease" before it poisons the entire organization (see Spotlight 5.2).

SPOTLIGHT 5.2   STRATEGIES FOR ERADICATING SPREADMARTS

Spreadmarts are renegade spreadsheets and desktop databases that contain vital pieces of corporate data needed to run the business. However, because they are created by individuals at different times using different data sources and rules for defining metrics, they create a fractured view of the enterprise. Without centrally defined metrics and a single version of corporate information, organizations cannot compete effectively.

Today, spreadmarts are the bane of workers in IT departments, who cannot control their proliferation, and the nemesis of CEOs, who cannot gain an accurate view of the enterprise because of them. Here are five strategies—the five "Cs"—for eradicating spreadmarts:

1. **Coercion.** Have the CEO mandate the proper use of spreadsheets and desktop databases. By itself, this strategy rarely works because it is difficult to enforce. In fact, coercion usually makes the problem worse. Users go underground, managing their divisions and departments with clandestine spreadmarts that run parallel to "official" systems. The old adage "What you resist, persists" applies to spreadmarts. However, without a strong executive mandate, users are often reluctant to change their analytical habits. So, it's best to use this tactic in conjunction with one or more of the approaches below.

2. **Conversion.** This strategy involves selling the benefits of the organization's standard BI environment. The key is to make sure the BI environment provides at least 150 percent the value of spreadmarts (which is sometimes difficult!). The key selling points are:

   ○ **Saves Time.** The BI tool collects and integrates the data (via a data warehouse) so you no longer have to perform these functions

   ○ **Improves Data Quality.** The BI tool provides cleaner and more accurate data than any spreadmart (thanks to the data warehouse).

- **Provides Deeper Insights.** The BI tool lets you analyze data across more systems and subject areas, leading to deeper, career-enhancing insights.

- **Offers Comparable Functionality.** The BI tool provides the same analytical functions and features as the spreadmart, such as briefing books, charting, report manipulation, "what-if" modeling, and offline usage.

- **Offers Additional Functionality.** The BI tool supports additional functions, such as the ability to schedule, share, or annotate reports, collaborate with colleagues, and easily publish reports to a portal.

- **Offers Support.** The BI tool and data warehouse are supported by the IT department so you do not have to worry when something breaks.

3. **Co-existence.** This strategy turns Excel into a full-fledged client to a BI server. Rather than force users to switch tools, let them use Excel to access data and reports on the BI server. This gives them all the spreadsheet features they know and love and lets the organization manage critical data and reports in the standard way. This is perhaps the best option when used in conjunction with number two above. Ironically, this option will expand the use of Excel for BI while minimizing or eliminating the use of Excel as a spreadmart.

   There are two ways to make Excel a BI client. In a tightly controlled environment, Excel users access predefined reports that are rendered in Excel on the server. In a more open environment, Excel users query back-end systems using a semantic layer—a set of predefined query objects defined by the IT department that govern access to data in source systems. Most leading BI vendors now support both methods of integrating with Excel.

4. **Co-option.** The fourth strategy takes the approach: "If you can't beat them, join them." This strategy automates spreadmarts by running them on a central server maintained and managed by IT. IT does not change the data access methods, processes, or rules set up by spreadmart users, it just maintains them on their behalf, freeing up users to spend more time analyzing data and less time collecting and massaging it. Gradually, over time, the IT department can transfer the spreadmarts to a more standard environment. Several BI vendors, such as Compassoft and Meta5, now offer co-option tools.

5. **Cower.** The last strategy is a variation of the first. Sarbanes Oxley regulations in the United States provide the IT department with a huge stick to enforce data management standards across the organization. Because most top executives would prefer to stay out of jail, it often does not take much to convince them to support an enterprise architecture that standardizes the use of tools and data to deliver key financial reports, among other things.

Whatever strategy you use to deliver a single version of the truth, the key is to be patient. Analytical habits do not change overnight. With a heavy dose of patience, strong communications skills, and a robust BI environment, you should be able to control the proliferation of spreadmarts.

EXHIBIT 5.2　　CROSSING THE GULF: THE SPREADMART DILEMMA

	Prenatal	Infant	Child	Teenager	Adult	Sage
Scope	System	Individual	Department	Division	Enterprise	Inter-Enterprise
Funding	IT	H.R.	Dept. Budget	Div. Budget	IT/Bus.	Self-funding
Team	IT	Analyst	Dept. IT	Div. IT	Corp. IT	BI Business Unit
Governance	IT	CEO	BI Project Mgr	BI Program Mgr	BI Stewardship Team	BI Unit Execs
		Local control "Think Local, Resist Global"		"Negotiate & Consolidate"	"Plan Global, Act Local"	
Flexibility/ Standards		Enterprise Standards				
Architecture	Mgmt Reporting	Spreadmarts	Data Marts	Data Warehouses	Enterprise DW	Analytical Services

Like invasive weeds, spreadmarts are difficult to eradicate. They provide a high degree of local control at low cost, which undermines departmental, divisional, or enterprise standards. This is why many organizations have a difficult time crossing the gulf and reaping the full benefits of the Child and Teenager stages. Enterprise standards start to gain the upper hand (as they should) in the Teenager stage and then grow in parallel with local control in the final two stages, as the BI environment becomes extremely flexible and responsive to new and changing user requirements.

Although organizations afflicted with spreadmarts may build data marts and data warehouses and appear to enter Stages Three and Four, they do not get very far. Spreadmarts sap the vitality of those structures and prevent organizations from reaping their benefits. To cross the Gulf from the Infant to Child stage, spreadmart users must sacrifice their autonomy and individual views of the business and adopt departmental or divisional standards for design, delivery, and definition of data and information. Most users do not relinquish local control and their spreadmarts without a fight, which is why the Gulf is so difficult to cross! (See Exhibit 5.2.)

Child Stage: Data Marts

In the Child stage, departments recognize the need to empower all knowledge workers with timely information and insight, not just business analysts and executives, who are the primary beneficiaries of spreadmarts. Departmental leaders fund the development of data marts, assign project managers to oversee the initiatives, and purchase BI tools so users can access and analyze data in the marts.

A data mart is a shared, analytic structure that generally supports a single business process or department, such as sales, marketing, or finance. The departmental team gathers information requirements and tailors the data mart to meet the needs of the members in its group. A data mart requires members of a department to consolidate or replace multiple spreadmarts and negotiate data definitions and rules to ensure data consistency throughout the department.

Unfortunately, data marts often fall prey to the same problems that afflict spreadmarts. Each data mart supports unique definitions and rules and extracts data directly from source systems. Although these so-called "independent" data marts do a great job of supporting local needs, their data cannot be aggregated to support cross-departmental analysis. What is needed is a mechanism to integrate data marts without jeopardizing local autonomy. This is the hallmark of the Teenager stage.

Also, most companies purchase more BI licenses than they need. They do not realize that many BI tools are geared to "power" users who are technically literate and conversant with the company's databases and access methods. These power users comprise less than 20 percent of all knowledge workers. Thus, the payoff from BI in this stage is low, with minimal to nonexistent return on investment (ROI) although the company may reap significant intangible benefits (see Exhibit 5.3).

EXHIBIT 5.3   THE ROI OF BUSINESS INTELLIGENCE

	Prenatal	Infant	Child	Teenager	Adult	Sage
Type of System	Financial System	Executive System	Analytical System	Monitoring System	Strategic System	Business Service
Analytics	Paper Report	Briefing Book	Interactive Report	Dashboards	Cascading Scorecards	Embedded BI
Executive Perception	"Cost Center"	"Inform Executives"	"Empower Workers"	"Monitor Processes"	"Drive the Business"	"Drive the Market"
ROI	Cost / Value				ROI	
Architecture	Mgmt Reporting	Spreadmart	Data Marts	Data Warehouses	Enterprise DW	Analytical Services

The ROI of business intelligence starts to increase dramatically in the Teenager stage as the organization provides users with timely, consistent data delivered in an intuitive fashion using all types of performance dashboards. ROI further escalates in the final two stages as the organization uses the BI environment to rapidly create large numbers of highly valuable analytical applications and insights that drive the business and the market.

Teenager Stage: Data Warehouses

The Teenager Stage begins when a business unit executive recognizes that the proliferation of non-integrated data marts is costing the group considerable sums of money and undermining a single view of operations. The executive calls a halt to the creation of new data marts and consolidates existing marts onto a single data warehousing platform. This consolidation usually happens in concert with something else, such as a strategic initiative to improve customer loyalty or an acquisition, merger, or reorganization.

Value Chain Analysis

Unlike single-subject data marts, a data warehouse encourages deeper levels of analysis. This is because users can now submit queries across functional boundaries, such as finance and operations, and gain new insights not possible when data were confined to departmental subjects. Unfortunately, most users fail to recognize the value of information in the data warehouse and never move beyond their mental silos to conduct cross-departmental analyses and discover highly profitable correlations in the data. BI managers must spend a great deal of time educating users about the full potential the data warehouse offers.

Performance Dashboards

This stage also empowers "casual" users with self-service BI tools, namely operational and tactical dashboards, that enable them to monitor and manage business processes quickly and easily. The performance dashboards provide actionable information to large numbers of individuals with minimal maintenance and administration. Executives value the performance dashboards as a way to improve process efficiency, empower users, and foster fact-based decision making.

Unfortunately, many organizations never advance further than here. They fall headfirst into the Chasm. They do not capitalize on their momentum. They fail to consolidate analytical silos throughout the enterprise, show users the benefit of cross-departmental analyses, or deliver self-service BI tools. Executives continue to view BI as a tactical tool instead of a strategic lever that drives the business and differentiates them from the competition. Departmental executives refuse to work cooperatively with corporate IT to expand successful solutions into enterprise resources.

It takes a lot of energy, vision, and willpower to cross the Chasm and enter into the final two stages of business intelligence.

Adult Stage: Enterprise Data Warehouse

Although a data warehouse delivers many new benefits, it does not solve the problem of analytical silos. Most organizations today have acquired multiple data warehouses through internal development, mergers, or acquisitions. Like spread-marts and independent data marts, divisional data warehouses contain overlapping and inconsistent data, creating barriers to the free flow of information within and between business groups and the value chains they manage.

Integration Machine

In the Adult stage, organizations make a firm commitment to deliver a consistent view of the business. Executives view data as a corporate asset that is as valuable as people, equipment, and cash. They anoint one data warehousing environment as the system of record or build a new one from scratch to service the entire organization. This enterprise data warehouse (EDW) serves as an "integration machine" that the BI team uses to continuously consolidate all other reporting systems, data marts, and data warehouses unto itself. For example, some organizations use an EDW to assimilate acquired companies after a merger or acquisition.

An EDW does not have to be a single centralized data warehouse running on a single database management system. An EDW is a standardized BI environment that can be constructed in many different ways, ranging from a centralized or hub-and-spoke data warehouse to a set of conformed data marts or a federated environment glued together on the fly with EII and other tools and techniques (see Chapter 3 for more information on BI architectures).

In the Adult stage, the EDW serves as a strategic enterprise resource for integrating data and supporting mission-critical applications that drive the business. To manage this resource, executives establish a strong stewardship program. Executives assign business people to "own" critical data elements and appoint committees at all levels to guide the development and expansion of the EDW resource. On the analytical side, the organization starts to cascade strategic dashboards and integrate them with other performance dashboards in the organization. The cascading scorecards align every worker and business process to corporate strategy.

ROI

During the Adult phase, investments in business intelligence really begin to pay off. The ROI comes from delivering actionable information in a consistent fashion to large numbers of users who make better and more timely decisions that increase profits and revenues. The EDW also benefits from economies of scale and a fast-track development process that churns out new applications rapidly, meeting user requirements quickly and efficiently. In addition, users begin to perform profitable cross-departmental analyses and find new and unexpected uses for data in the EDW that developers had not anticipated, leading to a proliferation of profitable analytical applications. This "serendipity of scale" further accelerates ROI. Meanwhile, costs actually decline as the organization eliminates analytical silos and reduces overhead (see Exhibit 5.3).

Sage Stage: BI Services

Once business intelligence becomes a strategic enterprise resource that drives the business with an ever growing panoply of mission-critical applications, you may think the job is done. It may well be! However, there are additional opportunities to increase the strategic value of a BI environment by driving the resource outward and downward.

Interactive Extranets

Many companies today are already opening their data warehouses to customers and suppliers—extending and integrating value chains across organizational boundaries and driving new market opportunities. Next-generation extranet applications will provide customers and suppliers with simple, yet powerful interactive reporting tools to benchmark their activity and performance and compare them with those of other groups across a variety of dimensions. Some companies have already created new business units to sell data warehousing and information analysis services, creating a competitive advantage for themselves and altering the competitive landscape of their industries.

Web Services

At the same time, BI teams are encapsulating data and reporting and analysis functions into Web services that developers—both internal and external to the organization—can use (with proper authorization, of course) to build a raft of new analytical applications. The advent of Web services turns BI into a market-wide utility that can be embedded into any application. With BI services, workers will no longer have to shift contexts to analyze data. The data, information, and insights they need to do their jobs are embedded in the operational applications they use on a daily basis.

Decision Engines

These BI services also make it possible for companies to capitalize fully on their investments in statistical analysis and modeling. They turn statistical models into "decision engines" embedded in internal and external applications. Workers or applications feed information into these engines and receive recommendations instantaneously. For instance, a fraud detection system reviews your credit card transactions and compares them to a statistical model of your past purchasing behavior and spits out a score that indicates the degree to which a given purchase may be fraudulent. Other examples of decision engines are Web recommendation engines and automated loan approval applications (see Exhibit 5.4).

Once an organization enters the Sage stage, its value increases exponentially as its visibility and costs decline. As a Web service, BI becomes a utility that no one thinks about until it stops working. Our economy has commoditized innumerable services in the past: electricity, sewage, water, transportation, and so on. Insights delivered via BI are simply the next in line.

EXHIBIT 5.4   EVOLUTION OF REPORTING AND ANALYSIS

	Prenatal	Infant	Child	Teenager	Adult	Sage
BI Focus	What happened?	What will happen?	Why did it happen?	What is happening?	What should we do?	What can we offer?
BI Output	Information	Plans	Rules	Alerts	Action	Recommendations
Tools	Reports	Forecasts	OLAP	Dashboards	Cascading Scorecards	Statistical Models

Decision Latency

Awareness   Understanding   Actionable Information   Decision Automation

Data Freshness

← Insights →   ← Action →

The first three stages of business intelligence deliver "Insights" using historical data to analyze what happened, why it happened, and to build forecasts. The second three stages deliver "Action" using right-time data to populate performance dashboards and statistical models that automate decision making.

SUMMARY

The BI Maturity Model described in this chapter is a good way to assess an organization's technical readiness to deploy a performance management system. The model shows that performance dashboards are best deployed once organizations reach Stage 4 or later. At this level of maturity, organizations can quickly deploy operational and tactical dashboards without having to make significant upfront investments. In Stage 5, organizations are ready to cascade strategic dashboards throughout the enterprise and link them (logically at least) to operational and tactical dashboards.

Many people who have heard presentations about the BI Maturity Model say it is "therapeutic." They find comfort in knowing that others have encountered the same growing pains they have. Many view the BI Maturity Model as a tool to help them envision the future and the steps needed to get there. They also view it as a perfect way to explain the potential of BI to their business counterparts as well as the investments and persistence required to deliver real value.

PART TWO

Performance Dashboards in Action

CHAPTER 6

Types of Performance Dashboards

DIFFERENTIATING PERFORMANCE DASHBOARDS

Overview

Performance dashboards are becoming pervasive in organizations today. As we saw in Chapter 1, most organizations have already deployed a performance management system of some kind, and one-third use it as their primary analytical application. However, not all performance dashboards are created equal.

Chapter 1 described three types of performance dashboards:

1. **Operational dashboards** enable front-line workers and supervisors to track core operational processes.
2. **Tactical dashboards** help managers and analysts track and analyze departmental activities, processes, and projects.
3. **Strategic dashboards** let executives and staff chart their progress toward achieving strategic objectives.

Application Functionality

As mentioned above, each type of performance dashboard delivers three sets of related functionality—monitoring, analysis, and management—but in different degrees.

Operational dashboards emphasize monitoring functions more than analysis or management functions. Monitoring makes it easy for business users to track key metrics and receive alerts about out-of-bounds conditions. Tactical dashboards emphasize analytical functionality more than monitoring or management features. Analytical functionality enables users to investigate the root causes of problems, issues, or trends. Strategic dashboards emphasize management features more than monitoring or analytical functionality. Management functionality enables executives to manage the execution of business strategy and foster collaboration among managers and staff and improve coordination among business units and departments.

Information Layers

Chapter 1 also showed that each type of performance dashboard contains three layers of information: graphical summarized views that make it easy for users to monitor exceptions; multidimensional views that let users "slice and dice" data; and transactional views that present users with detailed records and reports. However, the layers in each type of performance dashboard vary in thickness.

For example, operational dashboards tend to be "flatter" than both tactical and strategic dashboards because they report information at a transactional or lightly summarized level. There is not much room left to drill down in an operational dashboard. Tactical dashboards, on the other hand, provide the greatest analytical heft, giving users the ability to drill down from highly summarized to highly detailed information and across various dimensions and hierarchies in the data. While many strategic dashboards provide the same depth and breadth of information, some may only provide high-level strategic views based on a thin layer of highly summarized information, at least to start.

Dashboard Components

To understand the differences between the three types of performance dashboards, it is necessary to examine the application components that each uses. Although there are no hard-and-fast rules about component usage, Exhibit 6.1 provides some general guidelines.

Operational Dashboard Components

Operational dashboards use a dashboard interface to monitor operational processes. The dashboards generate alerts that notify users about exception conditions in the processes they are monitoring so they can act quickly to fix a problem or exploit an opportunity. For instance, an alert might notify a dispatcher that a truck is leaving later than scheduled or with half its cargo space unfilled. Agents take alerts one step further by automating actions based on the nature of the

EXHIBIT 6.1   PERFORMANCE DASHBOARD COMPONENTS

	Operational Dashboard	Tactical Dashboard	Strategic Dashboard
Monitoring	Dashboard	BI Portal	Scorecard
Analysis	Statistical models Decision engines	OLAP analysis Interactive reporting Advanced visualization Scenario modeling	Time-series analysis Standard reports
Management	Alerts Agents	Workflow Usage monitoring Auditing	Meetings Annotations Strategy maps

The monitoring, analysis, and management components that most commonly comprise the three types of performance dashboards.

alerts. For instance, an automated agent that detects low sales in the Midwest region last period might query a database to find the contact information for the regional sales manager and send the information via pager to the manager of North American sales.

In general, operational dashboards display information about business events soon after they occur. However, sometimes even real-time information arrives too late for workers to do anything to rectify or improve a situation. For instance, an alert indicating that a truck just left the warehouse half-full does not allow the dispatcher or shipping dock worker to figure out a way to load the truck with additional cargo before it leaves.

Consequently, many operational dashboards apply statistical models to forecast or predict future states. For example, airlines dynamically modify prices for airlines seats by applying yield optimization routines to current bookings. Fraud detection dashboards use decision engines built on predictive models that automatically identify fraudulent transactions and trigger a workflow to validate the results, close the account, and contact the customer.

Tactical Dashboard Components

Tactical dashboards often display results in a business intelligence (BI) portal that contains charts and tables as well as other documents users need in order to monitor a project or process that they manage. These portals are built into most BI tools and usually integrate with commercial portals that many companies use to run their corporate intranets.

Tactical dashboards encourage users to explore information to identify trends and ascertain the root causes of problems or issues. This exploration is done using OLAP (i.e., multidimensional analysis) tools, parameterized reports, query tools, and advanced visualization tools, among other things.

Tactical dashboards also contain modeling tools that let users create plans that contain multiple scenarios. For instance, a pricing scenario might define a rule or hypothesis that says "If we increase prices by X percent, it will cause revenues to decrease by Y percent and profits to stay even." Most business people use Excel to create these scenarios or plans. However, most BI vendors now provide tight integration with Excel to corral such analysis within a centrally managed environment.

Because decisions are not made in a vacuum, tactical dashboards use workflow tools (i.e., primarily e-mail at this point) to allow users to share their findings with colleagues and request approval or action before going further. Usage monitoring and auditing tools help project sponsors and administrators to track user adoption and to audit who creates and edits key financial and performance reports.

Strategic Dashboard Components

Strategic dashboards use a scorecard interface to track performance against strategic objectives. Although they are similar to dashboard interfaces, scorecards generally track progress of groups on a monthly basis rather than a right-time basis. Also, scorecards generally display more metrics across a broader spectrum of the organization than dashboards, especially in corporate scorecards. Performance information in a scorecard interface is usually more summarized than in a dashboard interface.

In the analysis layer, strategic dashboards tend to display data using time-series charts and tables that plot performance over various intervals, such as every week or month for the past year. Strategic dashboard users, especially executives and managers, like to view standard reports along with the scorecard summaries.

Strategic dashboards are useless without meetings between managers and staff to review the results and discuss ways to improve performance. Strategic dashboards facilitate virtual meetings through use of annotations and threaded discussions. Strategy maps help executives work together to examine their assumptions about what drives business value in the organization and to make strategic course corrections as they go.

PERFORMANCE DASHBOARD TRENDS

Purpose

Strategic Dashboards Are Most Popular

Organizations are rapidly implementing all three types of performance dashboards, but the most popular is the strategic dashboard. A survey of organizations that have already implemented a performance dashboard shows that 41 percent have implemented a strategic dashboard, 35 percent have implemented a tactical dashboard, and 23 percent have implemented an operational dashboard, using the definitions contained in this book (see Exhibit 6.2).

The popularity of the strategic dashboard is a testament to its allure in the executive suite. Many top executives gravitate to strategic dashboards like desert travelers to an oasis. They see it as an effective tool for keeping their fingers on the pulse of the organization without getting buried in detail. Credit goes to Harvard Business School professor Robert S. Kaplan and consultant David P. Norton for popularizing the Balanced Scorecard, the most popular type of strategic dashboard today.

| EXHIBIT 6.2 | WHICH BEST DESCRIBES THE PURPOSE OF YOUR DASHBOARD OR SCORECARD? |

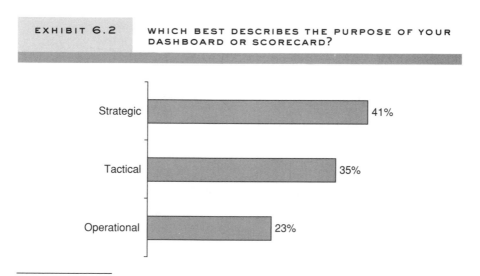

A 2004 survey by The Data Warehousing Institute (TDWI) provided definitions of "strategic," "tactical," and "operational" that are the same as those used in this book. Based on 240 respondents.

Source: Wayne Eckerson, "Development Techniques for Creating Analytic Applications" (*TDWI Report Series*, The Data Warehousing Institute, 2004).

Most Lack a Strong Foundation

Unfortunately, some strategic dashboards are not built on a strong foundation and will vanish quickly. In some cases, this is okay if the strategic dashboard is intended as a short-term management tactic to galvanize the organization around a new strategy or guide it through a challenging period. However, many strategic dashboards are simply not built to provide the depth of information and analysis required to deliver long-term business value.

For example, as soon as business users notice an out-of-bounds condition, the first thing they want to do is explore the cause. Without sufficient information embedded in the performance dashboard, they will become frustrated. They will have to work hard to find answers to their questions. They may have to create a custom report themselves or call someone to do it for them; worse yet, they may not consult information and may make assumptions about the source of the problem or issue. Unless a strategic dashboard helps business users resolve the issues highlighted on the scorecard interface, it will not provide much value.

Recognizing these potential problems with a strategic dashboard, Hewlett Packard Co.'s Technology Solutions Group (TSG) built two distinct systems and linked them together: 1) a scorecard interface called Libra to display performance status of key performance metrics, and 2) a reporting system called Muse that lets users view both interactive and standard reports. Chapter 9 profiles Hewlett Packard TSG's strategic dashboard implementation and provides more information on how they constructed their system to meet business users' needs.

Enterprise Scope

Besides greater popularity, strategic dashboards also have more of an enterprise scope than either tactical or operational dashboards, according to the same survey by TDWI. A slim majority (51 percent) of strategic dashboards have an enterprise scope, whereas only 26 percent of tactical dashboards and 23 percent of operational dashboards have an enterprise scope (see Exhibit 6.3).

Top-Down Deployment

Top-down deployment makes sense because many strategic dashboards are initiated by the CEO to manage strategy better. Kaplan and Norton, the authors of the Balanced Scorecard discipline, encourage organizations to start building strategic dashboards at the CEO level and cascade them to all levels of the organization. However, strategic dashboards can also be initiated at lower levels of the organization, such as a region within a business unit, which is what Hewlett Packard TSG did. If designed properly, these regional or divisional strategic dashboards can spread quickly throughout the enterprise.

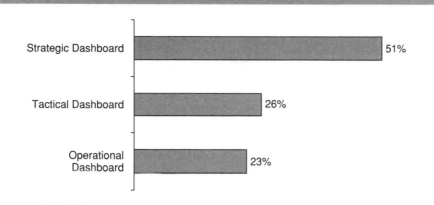

EXHIBIT 6.3   IS YOUR DASHBOARD ENTERPRISE IN SCOPE?

Strategic Dashboard — 51%

Tactical Dashboard — 26%

Operational Dashboard — 23%

Data based on 240 respondents who answered "yes" to the question above.

Source: Wayne Eckerson, "Development Techniques for Creating Analytic Applications" (*TDWI Report Series*, The Data Warehousing Institute, 2004).

Bottom-Up Deployment

Conversely, tactical dashboards are generally deployed from the bottom up. These systems start small, focusing on one department, and spread outward to other departments. Some companies, such as the International Truck and Engine Corporation, have spread their tactical dashboards far and wide, spanning several business units and departments.

Departmental Focus

Operational dashboards almost always focus on a single department or subject area and rarely expand further. Most operational dashboards support specific operational processes that require specific sets of functionality or metrics that do not translate well to other departments. For example, a baking department in a process manufacturing company tracks oven temperatures by displaying a heat map alongside a numerical display. This type of dashboard display does not work well in other departments. However, other departments could create a distinct application using the same underlying infrastructure to meet their requirements.

Number of Active Users

Although strategic dashboards are more enterprise in scale, tactical dashboards support the most active users (i.e., who use the system at least once a week). On

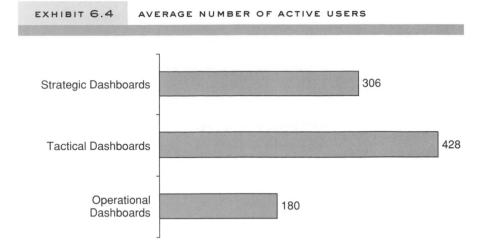

EXHIBIT 6.4   AVERAGE NUMBER OF ACTIVE USERS

Data based on 240 respondents.

Source: Wayne Eckerson, "Development Techniques for Creating Analytic Applications" (*TDWI Report Series*, The Data Warehousing Institute, 2004).

average, tactical dashboards support 428 active users, strategic dashboards 306 active users, and operational dashboards 180 active users (see Exhibit 6.4).

Because tactical dashboards have been around longer than the other types of performance dashboards, it is not surprising that they have a higher number of active users. For the past decade, organizations have been building data warehouses and deploying reporting and analytical tools at the departmental level. Many are now rolling out data warehouses and BI tools on an enterprise scale. Leading-edge companies now report that they have thousands of internal BI users and tens of thousands of external BI users (i.e., customers and suppliers).

In the next five years, the average number of strategic dashboard users will grow significantly as organizations cascade scorecards throughout the organization. Most strategic dashboards today are still in their infancy. Many companies have yet to deliver more than a few downstream versions of the corporate scorecard. Operational dashboards will probably not grow much more than they have already, because their focus is fairly narrow, as mentioned in the paragraphs above.

The rest of this chapter will provide a quick profile of each type of performance dashboard, covering its purpose, architecture, and usage. Each section provides a quick summary of the case study profiles in the next three chapters.

OPERATIONAL DASHBOARDS

Operational dashboards are used by front-line workers and their supervisors to monitor and optimize operational processes. For example, store managers need to monitor inventory to avoid stock outs; dispatchers need to monitor the location, destination, and cargo of trucks to optimize carrying capacity and profits; plant supervisors need to monitor manufacturing quality and yields to meet shipment schedules and quality requirements; and call center managers need to monitor call volumes, call lengths, and resolution outcomes to ensure there are enough agents with the right skills to meet calling demand.

Operational dashboards use components from each layer of the performance management architecture described in Chapter 1. Exhibit 6.5 shows how operational dashboards use right-time infrastructure components and a dashboard interface to monitor business processes using leading and diagnostic metrics designed to achieve goals laid out in operational plans and satisfy the needs of customers, suppliers, and the workforce.

EXHIBIT 6.5   OPERATIONAL DASHBOARD ARCHITECTURE

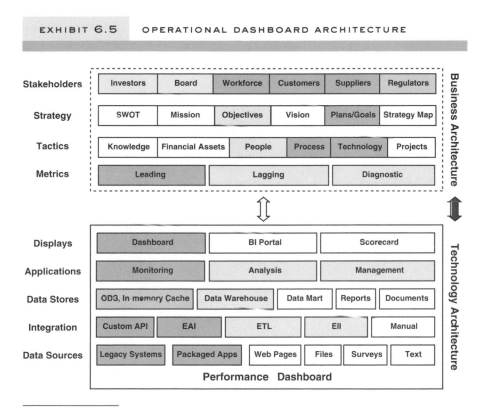

The degree of shading in the rectangles above shows the extent to which a component contributes to the business and technical architecture of an operational dashboard.

For example, Quicken Loans, which is profiled in Chapter 7, uses an operational dashboard to help its mortgage consultants reach their daily quotas for sales and calls and provide optimal service to customers. Mortgage consultants use the operational dashboard in part to check their commissions, whereas managers use it to monitor which mortgage consultants are on track to make their daily quotas using leading indicators of performance. This makes both sales consultants and their managers stakeholders in the system, as indicated in Exhibit 6.5.

Dynamic Updates

Workers use operational dashboards to monitor business events that are captured and displayed on dashboards in seconds, minutes, or hours depending on the nature of the process. Some dashboards "twinkle," that is, data are dynamically refreshed as new events enter the system and are displayed. Others let users decide when to refresh their screens with new data.

In most cases, operational dashboards update data on a continuous basis. Updates either happen as soon as events occur (i.e., real time) or after a suitable lag time (i.e., right time), depending on when users need to see the data to make a decision. Most operational dashboards are updated on an intra-day basis, which is at least two or more times during a 24-hour period. (For more information on the origins of right-time updates, see Spotlight 6.1.)

SPOTLIGHT 6.1   FROM REAL TIME TO RIGHT TIME

Two Interpretations. Technologists use the term *real time* to mean data that are updated instantaneously after an event occurs. Here, the latency between an event and when workers view it on a dashboard is zero. This has given rise to the notion of a "zero latency enterprise", which has gained prominence in some business circles. In actuality, it is difficult, expensive, and often unnecessary to deliver data in real time with zero latency. Most business people do not need to make decisions that rapidly.

Conversely, business people use the term *real time* to mean something that happens quickly. However, how fast is real time to them? Is it a second? A minute? An hour? In the end, the definition of real time varies from business person to business person. For example, airline executives interpret real time as anything that happens within 14 minutes because the airline industry defines "on time" as 14 minutes or less from an aircraft's scheduled arrival or departure, according to Alicia Acebo, a former data warehousing manager at Continental Airlines.

Right Time. Perhaps, a better term to describe the timely delivery of information to decision makers is *right time*. Ultimately, business executives do not care about the degree of latency in a performance dashboard. They simply want the system to deliver the right information to the right people at the right time so they can make optimal business decisions. Right time puts the emphasis on the business value of information, not its latency.

Metrics

Most operational dashboards use diagnostic metrics to measure the output of ongoing processes, such as number of calls per hour by salesperson, oven temperature every minute for the past hour, product defects detected by thousand units, and so on. Operational dashboards often compare these numbers with recent historical data, such as performance during the past several hours, days, or weeks. When performance goes above or below the expected norm, the system triggers an alert. For example, a retail dashboard might alert a store manager when inventory for a particular product has been below target for the previous eight hours (see Exhibit 6.6).

EXHIBIT 6.6   AN OPERATIONAL DASHBOARD WITH ALERT

This operational dashboard dynamically displays an alert indicating that a store is about to run out of a product, which needs to be reordered. The alert overlays a variety of graphical indicators, charts, and tables that adjust dynamically as the dashboard captures new events.

Source: Courtesy of Celequest Corporation, 2004.

Statistical Metrics

In addition, many operational dashboards apply statistical models and algorithms to current events to forecast future activity, optimize results, or identify hard-to-detect patterns. The metrics based on these algorithms help organizations work more proactively. For example, they can help organizations detect fraud as it happens, dynamically optimize pricing in response to sales, or anticipate product or system failures before they happen.

Simple Navigation

Although operational dashboards are not designed for complex analysis, they still make it easy for users to view different perspectives of the data or examine individual transactions or events. For example, a logistics manager who notices that a truck is behind schedule should be able to drill into the operational dashboard to find out the cargo the truck is carrying, the route it is taking to its destination, and the items it is scheduled to pick up when it gets there. This level of detail is critical if workers are going to optimize processes and maximize profitability.

Small Volumes of Data

Because the focus of operational dashboards is on monitoring rather than analysis or management, they usually do not store much information, usually a week or two of data at the most. In some applications, this may be less than a hundred gigabytes—about the amount that many laptop computers store today.

Most operational dashboards store events in an in-memory database or cache to provide exceptionally fast performance in response to user queries. There is no sense in making users wait several minutes for a screen to refresh or a query to return if they are monitoring events in real time. Data that are older than one day are usually transferred to an operational data store, another form of low-latency database designed to deliver small amounts of integrated data at rapid speeds. (See Chapter 3 for a more complete definition of ODS.)

Aliases

Operational dashboards are called many different things. For example, the Gartner Group, a technology research firm based in Stamford, Connecticut, uses the term *business activity monitoring* to describe applications that monitor and measure end-to-end business processes (see Spotlight 6.2). Another alias is *business process management*, a term favored by middleware vendors whose products transmit events in real time across a messaging backbone that interconnects many operational applications.

SPOTLIGHT 6.2 AN ALIAS FOR OPERATIONAL DASHBOARDS

Business activity monitoring (BAM) is a term coined by Gartner Group, a technology research firm, that describes a right-time system enabling organizations to monitor and manage business processes that span multiple systems, departments, and organizations. BAM is basically another label for an operational dashboard.

According to Colin White, president of BI Research in Ashland, Oregon, BAM systems exhibit the following characteristics:

1. **Event-driven processing model** that captures events in real time from multiple systems that comprise an end-to-end business process.

2. **Robust business rules** that let users define alerts, targets, and thresholds for individual performance metrics.

3. **A business-user-friendly dashboard** that updates metrics as events flow through the system and puts metrics into context by relating them to business objectives.

4. **A collaborative workflow system** that lets one set up formal and informal processes by which users can collaborate and discuss results.

Although the Gartner Group and others have given BAM plenty of publicity, most business and technical managers find the term too abstract to comprehend. For example, Diaz Nesamoney, who founded Celequest, a BAM vendor, now pitches his system as an operational dashboard for managing business performance: "Once customers see our operational dashboard, they understand the benefits it offers immediately."

TACTICAL DASHBOARDS

Self-Service Access

The main benefit of a tactical dashboard is that it provides users self-service access to information instead of having to rely on the IT department to create a custom report for them. More importantly, it structures their exploration so they do not get lost in the data and can find what they are looking for quickly.

With freedom to explore information without getting lost, business managers use tactical dashboards to improve their understanding of the processes and activities for which they are accountable. Specifically, they use the systems to measure their progress against predefined goals, forecasts, or targets at the departmental or project level and drill into detailed data if they need to perform further analysis. Because managers do not need real-time information to manage their areas, tactical dashboards are typically updated daily or weekly, frequently enough to give managers and analysts time to absorb and analyze trends and take action.

Architecturally, tactical dashboards are much more "bottom heavy" than operational or strategic dashboards. Exhibit 6.7 shows that tactical dashboards draw from every type of source system imaginable and load the data into a data

EXHIBIT 6.7   TACTICAL DASHBOARD ARCHITECTURE

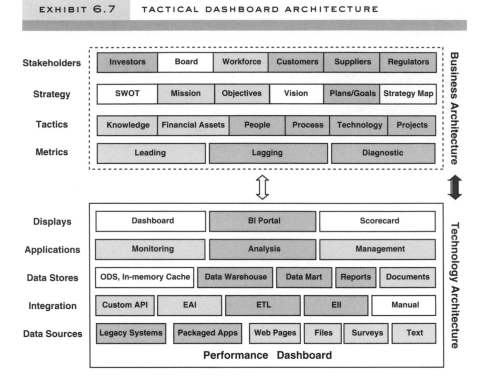

The degree of shading in the rectangles above shows the extent to which a component contributes to the business and architecture of a tactical dashboard.

warehouse, data mart, or multidimensional database primarily using extraction, transformation, and loading tools. A tactical dashboard delivers information through a BI portal that lets users analyze primarily lagging and diagnostic measures using OLAP and other analytical tools to support departmental projects and initiatives. Key stakeholders are investors, who are interested in the financial information that a tactical dashboard can generate, as well as customers and suppliers (see Exhibit 6.7).

For example, the International Truck and Engine Corporation, which is profiled in Chapter 8, uses a tactical dashboard to give financial managers greater visibility into operations and help close their financial books faster at the end of each month. Of course, this makes investors and regulators happier and helps managers take more proactive steps to address costly problems on the factory floor that impact on supplier shipments, which makes suppliers a key stakeholder as well.

A "Reporting Portal"

In truth, a tactical dashboard is really a reporting portal designed for reporting and analysis. Instead of providing users with an endless list of reports like traditional BI tools do, a tactical dashboard displays the most critical metrics that users need to monitor based on their role and security profile. The portal interface lets users arrange these metrics on the screen any way they want, along with other documents, alerts, and files that are important to them. Tactical dashboards provide users with a single place on the Web where they can find all the information they need to do their work.

Analytics for All

Tactical dashboards focus heavily on the middle layer of a performance dashboard, which provides a multidimensional view of information. As we will see in Chapter 8, the ability of novice users to "slice and dice" data starting from high-level graphical views of performance metrics is a hallmark of tactical dashboards.

Unlike traditional BI tools, which have been geared to technically savvy analysts and power users, tactical dashboards make it easy for casual information users to analyze data and find the reports they are looking for. Tactical dashboards give users the option to change perspectives on the data by switching business dimensions, such as product, location, channel, and time, or drilling down in more detail. Users can also modify the formatting of the view or report, take a "snapshot" of it, and send it to colleagues via e-mail or publish it to the dashboard.

Guided Analytics

To assist casual users in getting to the root cause of a problem or deciding what actions to take, many tactical dashboards offer "guided analytics." These are built-in recommendations that show users which reports or views they should look at or what actions they should take based on the context of the information they are examining. These recommendations are generated by veteran analysts and then built into the software so less experienced users can literally follow in their footsteps.

Some guided analytics provide decision trees or other expert systems that guide users to the data they are seeking (see Exhibit 6.8). Other types are more subtle; they are built into the navigational pathways that users follow when drilling down or across dimensions and hierarchies in the data.

Meeting Diverse Analytical Needs

Casual users are not the only ones who use tactical dashboards. Business analysts and power users who spend most of their days analyzing data, crunching num-

EXHIBIT 6.8   GUIDED ANALYSIS

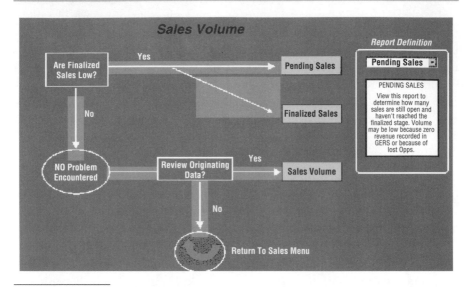

There are many ways to assist casual users to navigate through information or find the right reports. The example above provides a context-sensitive decision tree that helps users identify the most appropriate report to view and launch.

Source: Copyright © 2005 Direct Energy–Essential Home Services. Reprinted with Permission.

bers, and building forecasts also require access to multidimensional views and transactional views of data. Today, power users collect and analyze data largely in Excel spreadsheets and Access databases, which is cumbersome, time consuming, and expensive and creates the dreaded spreadmarts.

If designed properly, tactical dashboards can meet the needs of both casual and power users. The key is to create a BI environment designed to support the information needs of power users and then turn off functionality as needed to avoid overwhelming casual users with too many bells and whistles or pathways to explore. To be honest, not many companies have succeeded in doing this. Companies that have tried to purchase a single BI tool to meet everyone's needs usually end up with a power tool that alienates casual users. The power of performance dashboards is that they tip the balance the other way, in favor of casual users.

BI Vendors Step Up to the Challenge

On a positive note, BI vendors have made tremendous strides in the past few years in delivering flexible, role-based functionality geared to different analytical roles (e.g., authors create reports, managers interact with them, recipients view them). These so-called BI platforms support a range of integrated tools or modules that deliver role-based functionality to every type of user in an organization. Modules that run off the same extensible BI platform are tightly integrated and possess a common look and feel, reducing end-user training, and making it feel like they are using a single BI tool rather than multiple tools.

Analytical Dashboards

Some tactical dashboards are designed for heavy-duty analysis, a subtype called an analytical dashboard. Such dashboards expose rich navigational features that let users explore data by any dimension to any level of detail and provide sophisticated analytical techniques (such as linear regressions for forecasting "what if" analyses for scenario planning) and advanced visualization (see Exhibit 6.9).

EXHIBIT 6.9	TACTICAL DASHBOARD OR "ANALYTICAL DASHBOARD"

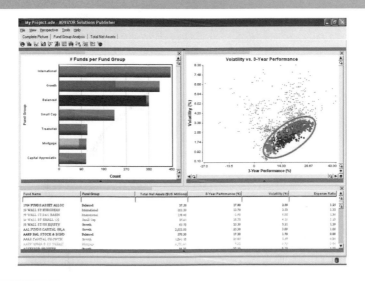

Some tactical dashboards are geared toward power users or business analysts and incorporate more complex navigation, statistical analysis, modeling, or advanced visualization techniques. The dashboard above displays a scatter plot and accompanying bar chart and data sheet. When an analyst highlights selected data points in the scatterplot, the bar chart and data sheet are dynamically updated, making it easier for analysts to identify correlations within the data, among other things.

Source: Courtesy of ADVIZOR Solutions, Inc.

STRATEGIC DASHBOARDS

Executive Favorite

Many organizations are now beginning to implement strategic dashboards to measure and evaluate performance against strategic objectives and goals set by top executives. Ideally, strategic dashboards deploy customized scorecards to every group at every level in the organization, and sometimes to every individual. When deployed in such a hierarchical or "cascading" format, strategic dashboards help align the activities and efforts of all individuals, departments, and divisions in the organization.

Strategic dashboards are currently the tool of choice among executives to ensure that their strategy gets executed in the field. The most popular type of strategic dashboard today is the Balanced Scorecard. Architecturally, a strategic dashboard is top heavy compared with a tactical dashboard (see Exhibit 6.10).

EXHIBIT 6.10   STRATEGIC DASHBOARD ARCHITECTURE

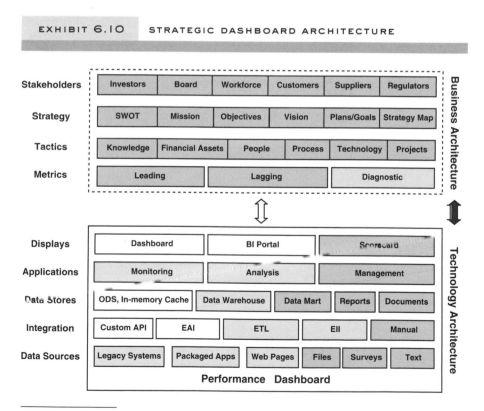

The degree of shading in the rectangles above shows the extent to which a component contributes to the business and architecture of a strategic dashboard.

A strategic dashboard measures, monitors, and manages an organization's strategy, which is designed to support all stakeholders. The strategy is executed using plans and resources and measured primarily, but not exclusively, using leading indicators of performance. These indicators focus executives, managers, and staff on the critical activities needed to optimize future results.

Technically, a strategic dashboard has a lighter-weight architecture than other performance dashboards, at least initially. A CEO who creates a corporate scorecard usually has a business analyst (or several) update it manually with text and numbers from Excel spreadsheets, desktop databases, surveys, and e-mail messages. Eventually, however, the organization will want to cascade unique versions of the corporate scorecard to every group in the enterprise and begin tracking additional metrics. At this point, it needs a more robust infrastructure, including data marts, data warehouses, and data integration tools, to ensure that the performance management system scales to meet user requirements and system loads.

Most strategic dashboards are updated monthly or quarterly, because strategic objectives tend to encapsulate long-range goals. However, the further down that an organization cascades its scorecards, the more frequently it will need to update information in the strategic dashboard system. All cascaded scorecards should run off the same strategic dashboard to avoid creating inconsistent views of enterprise information.

A strategic dashboard uses graphical indicators to compare performance against predefined targets and thresholds and to signal whether performance is trending up or down and how results compare with targets and thresholds. Metrics consist primarily of leading indicators, although many strategic dashboards also incorporate lagging and diagnostic measures (see Exhibit 6.11). Often, a strategic dashboard contains metrics that are qualitative in nature, such as customer satisfaction scores, which may be gleaned from surveys conducted and/or verified by external groups.

Management and Analysis

The first thing users want to do when they see that the performance status of a metric is below target is to find out what is going on. A strategic dashboard needs to let users drill down in more detail or access reports or other documents to understand what is causing the alert or variance. In other words, strategic dashboards are not just scorecards; they are layered performance management systems that let users monitor, analyze, and manage critical activities and optimize performance results.

Management Features

Strategic dashboards also provide many management features to help communicate and execute strategy. Executives use strategy maps to identify and link

EXHIBIT 6.11   STRATEGIC DASHBOARD

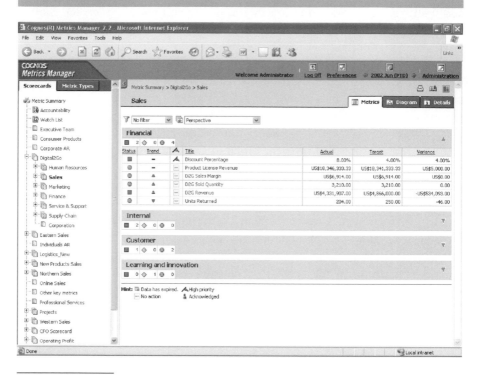

The screenshot above shows a scorecard interface from a Web-based strategic dashboard that groups metrics into four perspectives: Financial, Internal, Customer, and Learning and Innovation. The left panel contains a list of scorecards by region and department; the left side of the center panel graphically displays performance status, trend, and alerts for each metric, whereas the right side shows actual data, targets, and variance between them. Users can view a strategy map diagram, drill into detailed data, or access reports and other documents, such as PowerPoint presentations or spreadsheets, by clicking on tabs in the upper right.

Source: Courtesy of Cognos Corporation.

strategic objectives and test their assumptions about the effectiveness of those objectives and the metrics that measure performance against them to deliver desired results. Strategic dashboards support an array of communications devices to foster greater collaboration among managers and staff and between departments and divisions.

For example, most strategic dashboards let employees attach written commentaries to individual metrics, providing context to results, outlining next steps, or delivering a forecast for the next period. Some strategic dashboards also let users establish workflows in which scorecards are sent to a series of individuals and managers for review and approval. These management features transform a strategic dashboard from a performance measurement system to a performance management system.

SUMMARY

Performance dashboards are here to stay. They provide an intuitive way for users to obtain the information they need in a timely fashion to perform their jobs. There are three basic flavors of dashboards: operational, tactical, and strategic. Operational dashboards monitor business processes at the operational level; tactical dashboards chart the progress of departmental initiatives and projects, enabling users to analyze and forecast trends; strategic dashboards align activity with strategy using scorecards and other performance management techniques.

Today, the most popular, but least mature, of the three types is the strategic dashboard. Executives are deploying strategic dashboards as management tools to align the organization better around strategic objectives. Unfortunately, many strategic dashboards today do not yet provide the depth of integrated information and interactive analysis to deliver long-term business value.

CHAPTER 7

Operational Dashboards in Action:

Quicken Loans, Inc.

*T*he sales floor at Quicken Loans pulses with energy. More than 500 mortgage experts sit at monitors in a large Web call center on the outskirts of Livonia, Michigan. Every representative is talking on the phone with a customer who has contacted the company via phone, e-mail, or the Web while evaluating mortgage programs and interest rates on their computer screens. More than a dozen managers are ready to assist the members of their mortgage team.

Televisions hang from the ceiling every 20 feet, displaying the results of all this activity in a color-coded dashboard. Every two minutes, the monitors show the top 15 mortgage bankers in one of a dozen performance categories. Mortgage bankers and managers periodically glance at the monitors to check their progress toward achieving individual and team milestones.

Rising 10 feet from the center of the sales floor is command central for the Web call center's operations. Operations managers monitor dashboard displays on a half-dozen computer screens and televisions to track the flow of leads, calls, and systems performance in real time and ensure the smooth flow of operations.

BENEFITS OF OPERATIONAL DASHBOARDS

Quicken Loans

The Web call center at Quicken Loans is ground zero for the nation's largest online lender, which closed $12 billion in retail mortgage loans in 2004. Any outage or slow-down in this core operation can cost Quicken Loans millions of dollars an hour. Thus, it is imperative that everyone involved in the process—from mortgage bankers to managers and executives—stay abreast of what is happening on the sales floor from one moment to the next.

To support this fast-paced environment, Quicken Loans two years ago implemented a series of operational dashboards built on a right-time business intelligence (BI) infrastructure. The new system delivers information about a variety of operational processes to executives, managers, and mortgage bankers as quickly as they need it—usually within seconds or minutes. Like many companies, Quicken Loans uses the term "right time" instead of "real time" to describe the delivery of the right data to the right person at the right time to optimize decision making.

"Prior to the new system, we were measuring the business by hand. We needed to accelerate the delivery of information to keep pace with our fast-moving business," says Eric Lofstrom, manager of BI at Quicken Loans. Previously, the company let users run queries and reports directly against its core operational systems, bogging down operational performance and query response times.

In contrast, the new system delivers nearly instantaneous data about leads, channel productivity, and systems performance to more than half of Quicken Loans' 2,500-person workforce. The new performance dashboard and BI infrastructure has improved business efficiency and effectiveness. It gives mortgage operations and marketing managers data about call volumes, revenues, and channel productivity in seconds or minutes, enabling them to work more proactively with mortgage bankers to meet target goals.

The new system has also reduced the time business analysts spend collecting data by 350 man-hours a month and provides a consistent set of metrics and data that everyone in the company uses. More importantly, the system helps align operations with the company's strategy and culture. "At Quicken Loans, we leverage velocity as a competitive weapon. Our new [operational dashboard] helps us meet the needs of our information-hungry corporate culture," says Lofstrom.

The Right-Time Enterprise

Quicken Loans is not alone in exploiting the value of right-time information to optimize operational processes. Many organizations are embracing the notion of doing business faster by accelerating the delivery of information to workers who need it most.

In fact, the right-time enterprise has seeped into mainstream culture, thanks to IBM, which for several years has touted "On Demand Business"™ in television advertisements. Other high-technology firms are marketing the "Zero Latency Enterprise," "Business Process Management," "Business Activity Monitoring," or "Active Data Warehousing" to describe much the same thing (see Spotlight 7.1). Whatever the name, executives now recognize that to make their organizations more nimble, competitive, and profitable, they need to integrate and optimize business processes using right-time information.

SPOTLIGHT 7.1   RIGHT-TIME MONIKERS

The following terms and concepts refer to applications and systems that capture and deliver right-time information in one form or another.

Zero Latency Enterprise (ZLE). Similar to IBM's "On Demand Business"™, a ZLE integrates diverse computer applications and eliminates delays in the propagation of new data throughout an organization, increasing business efficiency and effectiveness. ZLE was first popularized by Compaq (now part of Hewlett Packard) to showcase its high-availability NonStop computers.

Business Process Management. A method for optimizing business processes using a variety of techniques and technologies, most notably EAI software (see Chapter 2).

Business Activity Monitoring. A right-time system that displays performance metrics from multiple systems in an end-to-end process (see Chapter 6).

Active Data Warehousing. Teradata, a division of NCR, uses this term to describe its unique data warehousing platform, which supports queries from both analytical and operational applications without degrading the performance of either one.

An operational dashboard is merely the window through which workers, managers, and even executives can monitor business processes and take action to avert a problem or capitalize on a fleeting opportunity. Operational dashboards sit on top of a right-time BI infrastructure that merges operational and analytical processing into a seamless whole. This new capability is changing the ways companies do business, making them more agile and competitive.

Although operational dashboards can be constructed in many different ways, there are a few indispensable technologies that deliver personalized, actionable information to the right people at the right time. Some of the more prominent technologies, which were described in Chapter 3, are enterprise application integration (EAI), enterprise information integration (EII), active data warehousing, and operational data stores (ODS).

QUICKEN LOANS' DASHBOARDS

No two operational dashboards look or function the same way, but they all help users monitor and analyze information in right time. Quicken Loans uses three types of operational dashboards to optimize Web call center processes. Each style of operational dashboard is designed for a slightly different purpose and audience and supports different degrees of data latency. Most importantly, however, all the dashboards use the same data, which means that everyone is "working from the same version of the truth," says Lofstrom.

1. **The Dashboard "Ticker."** Provides mortgage bankers and managers with real-time information about leads, revenue, and calling data that is updated almost instantaneously.

2. **Kanban Reports.** Provides information about individual performance and is updated every 10 minutes.

3. **Managerial Dashboard.** Provides mortgage operations and marketing managers with trending data that are updated every 30 minutes or so.

The Dashboard "Ticker"

Quicken Loans encourages its 500+ mortgage bankers to place a vertical dashboard on their screens to help them track performance metrics of interest to them. This vertical dashboard resembles a stock ticker that users can populate with both real-time and right-time data and place anywhere on their screen. The real-time data are updated instantaneously after each transaction or event. The right-time data are updated every 10 to 30 minutes depending on the data. Like a stock ticker, users only view the data; they do not interact with it. There are no additional data for users to drill into.

Each dashboard ticker consists of multiple panels that users can populate with data feeds from one or more sources. For example, in Exhibit 7.1, the dashboard ticker consists of three panels. The top panel consists of personal and group metrics that are updated daily from an online analytical processing (OLAP) cube, whereas the bottom two are updated instantaneously via a real time data feed. The bottom panel embeds some simple linear regressions that estimate whether a loan consultant is going to meet daily goals based on his or her activity up to that point in time.

Kanban Dashboard

Quicken Loans' managers use Kanban-style dashboards to track the performance of their team and know when to lend assistance or provide additional training. The Kanban dashboard is a color-coded chart consisting of a dozen or so key performance indicators (KPIs) that are updated every 10 minutes. Like the

EXHIBIT 7.1   DASHBOARD TICKER

User ID:	MyUserName		
Team:	MyTeamName		
Name:	MyName		
Date:	3/30/2005		

Data Source 1			12:30PM
Today			
Measure 1 ◉	1 for	$710,000.00	
Measure 2 ◉	2 for	$186,000.00	
Measure 3 ◉	4 for	$558,100.00	
Measure 4 ◉	3 for	$482,700.00	
MTD			
Measure 5 ◉	43 for	$6,872,275.00	
Measure 6 ◉	42 for	$5,864,275.00	
Measure 7 ◉	44 for	$6,212,775.00	
Measure 8 ◉	43 for	$7,339,800.00	

Data Source 2		12:15PM
Today		
Measure 1		7
Measure 2	◉	24
Measure 3	◉	23
Measure 4	◉	6
Measure 5	◉	4
Measure 6	◉	2
Measure 7		0
Measure 8		8
Measure 9		5
Measure 10		13

Data Source 3		7:30AM
MTD (7 Day Lag)		
Measure 1	◉	40.59 %
Measure 2	◉	14.76 %
Measure 3	◉	14.02 %
Measure 4	◉	12.55 %
Measure 5	◉	6.64 %

This dashboard "ticker" consists of three panels that users can populate with metrics of their choosing. The ticker sits on top of other applications running on their screens and is updated in both real time and right time depending on the metrics chosen. In this case, the top panel is updated every 15 minutes and the bottom two panels are updated instantaneously as events are generated. (The data have been erased intentionally.)

Source: Copyright © 2005 Quicken Loans Inc. Reprinted with Permission.

EXHIBIT 7.2 KANBAN DASHBOARD

Date: 17-Dec-04 ▼

	1,187	855		25	23	21	9	4	8	20
	86	86	1	2	7					
	63	59	3		2	1	1		1	8
	25	25	2	2	1	1			1	
	102	61	3	5						
	52	42	2	3						2
	185	81	3	1						
	195	111	2	1						
	59	57			5	3			4	1
	100	49	3		1					
	99	93	1		3		1			3
	48	43	1		1	5				2
	44	39	3		1		1	1		
	46	45	1	2	1	1				
	28	18		2	1	1	1			4
	74	46						1		

This Kanban-style chart tracks the performance of individual loan consultants every 10 minutes and color codes cells red or green so managers and supervisors can quickly identify individuals who need assistance. (Text has been rubbed out intentionally.)

Source: Copyright © 2005 Quicken Loans Inc. Reprinted with Permission.

dashboard ticker, the Kanban reports are flat displays of data designed for monitoring, not interaction. Kanban is the Japanese term for "signal" that is used to describe a just-in-time manufacturing environment in which materials are dynamically replenished.

As seen in Exhibit 7.2, the Kanban dashboard lists mortgage bankers down the vertical axis and KPIs on the horizontal axis. The KPIs are simple counts with thresholds applied so that managers can quickly see which consultants are on track to meet goals and which are not, by the color-coding of the cells. For example, when a supervisor notices that performance for one loan consultant is dipping into the red zone, the supervisor can provide help as needed.

Quicken Loans also displays a version of this Kanban chart on television monitors spread throughout the floor, as described in the opening scene of this chapter. These Kanban dashboards show the top 15 sales people for each metric, rotating one metric at a time every two-and-a-half minutes. These bare-bones Kanban charts create a friendly, competitive atmosphere as mortgage bankers strive to make the "board."

Managerial Dashboard

Sales, marketing, and operations managers use a standard dashboard to analyze daily and weekly trends on the sales floor. Typically, Quicken Loans updates these types of dashboards every 30 minutes or so. "For the most part, these users are satisfied with a 10 to 30 minute latency," says Lofstrom.

Exhibit 7.3 shows a managerial dashboard that lets sales managers track the flow and mix of sales for the day, among other things. Each metric on the screen can be populated with data from different sources (i.e., OLAP cubes, data warehouse, real-time feed) and updated at different intervals (i.e., instantaneously, every 10 minutes or every 30 minutes). Also, unlike the Kanban dashboards, users can personalize what they see in the managerial dashboard. By clicking on the "content" or "layout" link in the upper right-hand corner, users can select the objects they want to view and where to position them on the dashboard.

Because managers use these dashboards to oversee operational processes, Quicken Loans strives to keep the dashboards as simple as possible. It does not want to overwhelm users with a multitude of options and perspectives that would make it harder for them to obtain the information they need to do their

EXHIBIT 7.3   MANAGERIAL DASHBOARD

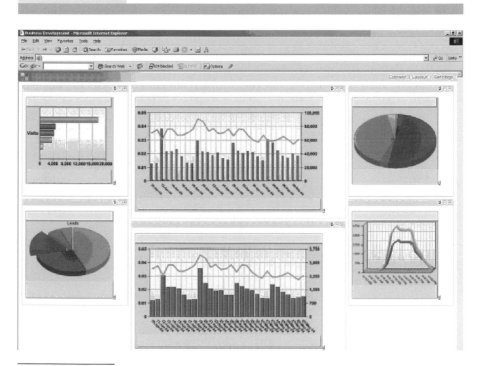

This dashboard shows how a sales or marketing manager might place a variety of metrics on a screen to monitor activity on the sales floor. (Note: the data have been intentionally changed.)

jobs in a timely manner. As a result, most of the objects in the managerial dashboard offer little or no interactivity.

Besides the three types of dashboards described above, Quicken Loans provides traditional reporting and analysis tools to 75 business analysts to explore historical trends and issues. These desktop tools run on the same BI architecture as the dashboards. Quicken Loans created 250 OLAP cubes to support business analysts, who can also query the data warehouse and ODS directly, if they desire. These OLAP cubes generally contain much more data than the OLAP cubes that support the dashboards described above.

QUICKEN LOANS' BI ARCHITECTURE

Quicken Loans developed its right-time operational dashboards on the same BI infrastructure as its reporting and analysis applications. Quicken Loans did not have a BI environment when it started, so it had a clean slate upon which to construct a right-time solution to meet user demand. In contrast, most companies have to retrofit an existing BI environment, which can be costly and cumbersome at best, unless they had the foresight to build right-time capabilities into the BI architecture upfront (see Spotlight 7.2).

SPOTLIGHT 7.2   CONTINENTAL THINKS AHEAD

With a little foresight and the right technology, organizations can deliver right-time capabilities without major surgery to their existing BI infrastructure and at little additional cost. This is exactly what Alicia Acebo did while at Continental Airlines, which proved to be an extremely judicious decision.

"We made our data warehouse real time from day one because I knew users would eventually ask for it," says Acebo, who spent much of her career building online reservation systems. Acebo was aided by the fact that Continental already had an event messaging backbone that connected its reservation system to other online systems in real time and that it used an "active data warehousing" platform from Teradata, a division of NCR, that could accept real-time data feeds.

Anticipating future needs, Acebo's team created a real-time interface between the data warehouse and the event-driven messaging system, even though it still planned load data in batch at nights or on weekends for the foreseeable future.

"After the terrorist attacks on September 11, 2001, our management was ready to move from daily to hourly feeds of the data warehouse. Because we built real-time capabilities into our infrastructure from the start, the whole process took us one week." Subsequently, Continental received recognition from the Federal Bureau of Investigation for its role in tracking down terrorists because of the timeliness of information it provided to the agency.

Architectural Components

Exhibit 7.4 shows how Quicken Loans constructed its BI environment. The architecture has four layers: 1) source systems, 2) application integration, 3) data integration and distribution, and 4) end-user access. This is a classic BI architecture except for the fact that Quicken Loans trickle-feeds the data into the environment one transaction at a time instead of loading the data in batch at night or on the weekend.

Application Integration Layer

Quicken Loans uses EAI software to extract data from source systems in real time. It does this by creating a copy of each event or transaction as it occurs in

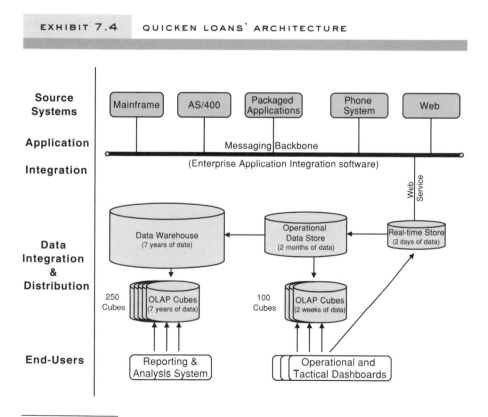

EXHIBIT 7.4   QUICKEN LOANS' ARCHITECTURE

Quicken Loans' BI architecture consists of four layers. The key, however, is a Web service that pulls data off an event-driven messaging backbone and deposits it into a real-time data store that dashboards query at various intervals to update their screens.

the source system and publishing it to a messaging backbone. Any application on the backbone can then "subscribe" to the event or message, grab it off the backbone, and store it locally.

Quicken Loans created a BI Web service that subscribes to the EAI backbone and captures events as they are published, a process known as trickle feeding. The BI Web service is how Quicken Loans moves all operational data into its BI environment. It also created a *real-time data store* to hold events in memory and make them available to other applications in the BI environment, including the dashboard ticker and Quicken Loans' ODS.

Data Integration and Distribution Layer

Like many companies, Quicken Loans distributes data among multiple types of analytical data stores, each of which serves a different analytical task.

The ODS is a data warehouse that has been slimmed down to deliver small volumes of integrated data to operational applications that require subsecond response times. Quicken Loans' ODS holds only two months of data. Its major role is to load OLAP cubes in near real-time and pass new data to the data warehouse, which stores up to seven years of data and is used primarily for in-depth trend analysis, not operational monitoring or analysis.

Once the data are precalculated in the OLAP cubes, users can "slice and dice" the data by dimension and level. This "speed of thought" analysis makes OLAP very attractive to users who want to explore trends and issues in the data. The traditional drawback of OLAP cubes is that they support only summary level data and take a long time to load and calculate. Consequently, most companies have shied away from OLAP cubes to support low-latency analytical applications, such as the one Quicken Loans built.

However, Quicken Loans engineered a way to refresh its OLAP cubes every 15 minutes. It does this in two ways: 1) it keeps a minimum amount of data in these OLAP cubes, usually no more than a few days worth, and it restricts the number of dimensions to seven; and 2) it keeps current data in a separate partition from day-old data and only refreshes the current data. This approach minimizes the amount of data that needs to be refreshed so that the update happens quickly and does not block users from accessing or viewing the data. This is an innovative use of OLAP cubes and helps power Quicken Loans' right-time environment.

End-User Access Layer

Quicken Loans' dashboards generally query the OLAP cubes for data, although they can pull data from the real-time data store, the ODS, or the data warehouse. For example, dashboard tickers query the real-time data store when users want instantaneous updates. Analytical dashboards query the data warehouse when users want to access historical or other data not found in an OLAP cube.

In conclusion, a well-constructed BI environment gives companies a lot of flexibility to meet the broad range of users' analytical requirements at low cost while preserving data consistency. Unfortunately, most companies do not follow Quicken Loans' example. They build different applications to handle different analytical tasks, such as real-time monitoring, "slice and dice" analysis, enterprise reporting, and scorecarding. These analytical "silos" are costly and redundant and make it impossible for the company to ensure that everyone uses the same metrics and data. Quicken Loans shows how it is possible to meet all these analytical needs with a single, integrated BI environment.

CHALLENGES

Many challenges are unique to the deployment of operational dashboards. We have already discussed one major challenge, the need to construct analytical systems to capture and display integrated data in right time. A survey by The Data Warehousing Institute (TDWI) reveals other challenges, including making the business case for right-time analysis, integrating data sources, educating business users about latency issues, and poor-quality data, among other things (see Exhibit 7.5).

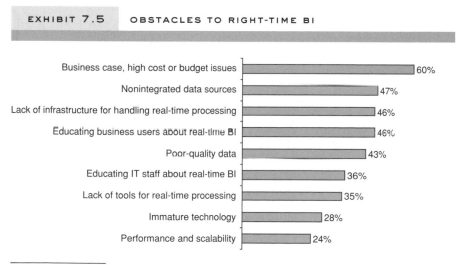

EXHIBIT 7.5	OBSTACLES TO RIGHT-TIME BI

Business case, high cost or budget issues — 60%
Nonintegrated data sources — 47%
Lack of infrastructure for handling real-time processing — 46%
Educating business users about real-time BI — 46%
Poor-quality data — 43%
Educating IT staff about real-time BI — 36%
Lack of tools for real-time processing — 35%
Immature technology — 28%
Performance and scalability — 24%

Data based on responses from 383 data warehousing and business intelligence professionals.

Source: Colin White, "The Real Time Enterprise" (*TDWI Report Series*, The Data Warehousing Institute, 2004).

Increased Costs

Scalability and Availability Requirements

Building a right-time analytical environment from scratch or retrofitting an existing one is not cheap. The primary reason is that users have little tolerance for outages or slow-downs because they depend on these systems to make rapid decisions.

To support right-time requirements, technical teams need to "bullet-proof" the entire information delivery architecture. They need to increase system reliability, availability, and scalability, which adds significantly to hardware, software, and staffing costs.

Specifically, the IT group needs to replace smaller servers with bigger ones to avoid performance slowdowns during peak hours of business activity. They also need to purchase additional servers and software so that if one server crashes, another can automatically pick up its load. As companies purchase additional hardware with greater power and failover capabilities, software license and maintenance costs climb proportionally.

More Staff Required

Right-time systems also stretch technical staff to the limit. It is no longer sufficient to respond to a system problem by the end of a business day. "Because we are publishing new numbers every ten minutes, we have exactly nine minutes to fix a problem before it turns into a crisis," says Quicken Loans' Lofstrom. As a result, Lofstrom has hired additional staff so he can always keep a technical person on call and available to troubleshoot problems within seconds.

Educating Users

Some users often have difficulty adapting to analytical systems that contain right-time information. Many do not like data to change on the screen while they are looking at it, while others do not understand why the transaction they just entered has not shown up on their "real-time" dashboard. Also, many people who manage fast paced processes often forget to check the time and date of information on their screen before making a decision.

To avoid problems, organizations need to teach workers the difference between "real-time" and "right-time" information. Workers need to know that not all metrics and reports are updated as soon as events occur. Some might be refreshed within seconds, but others might take 15 minutes to refresh or more. They also need to remember that sometimes reports and metrics fail to refresh on schedule.

Time Stamps and Labels

In addition, the technical team needs to post the time and date that a screen or report refreshes with the latest data. Users must then learn to check these "time stamps" before jumping to conclusions. To avoid misinterpretation, some technical teams do not refresh screens dynamically. They let users update a report or screen by pushing a "refresh" button. Some even let users choose the time frame for the data they want to view through a drop-down list box.

Finally, the technical team also needs to write clear and unambiguous titles for all dashboard reports and metrics so workers do not confuse one report with another and make a hasty decision based on faulty assumptions. One financial executive likes to say the reports should be labeled in "Forest Gump" style so anyone can understand what they are about.

Prioritizing Requirements

A related challenge is figuring out how fast users really want data to be updated. If asked, most users say they want the most up-to-date information possible. However, what they want and what they really need are often very different. The only way to filter real from perceived requirements is for the technical team to calculate the costs of delivering information at different latency intervals and let users decide what is worth paying for. Attaching dollars and cents to latency requirements often makes the decision straightforward.

"We work with the business, tell them what it would cost to build a real-time system and let them decide whether it's worth it to them," says a BI manager at a telecommunications firm. "So far, they have not been interested in going down that path."

Reengineering Business Processes

There is no point in putting in a right-time BI infrastructure if companies do not reengineer core business processes and systems to exploit the information. For example, it is no use providing store managers with hourly sales data if they can only change prices or shelf displays once a day. If a company deems it critical to their future success to deliver hourly information to store managers, then it must upgrade store systems so managers can exploit the information.

Ultimately, the purpose of an operational dashboard is to empower users to work more proactively and make faster, smarter decisions. Unfortunately, the human part of the right-time dashboard is often the least reliable component. Many workers do not know how to use computers proficiently, or worse yet, interpret data. In addition, most do not want to change their habitual ways of doing things. Any new information system imposes change on an organization.

Companies that underestimate the time and money it takes to change how workers use information are wasting money.

Data Quality

Data quality can also be a problem with operational dashboards. Data that stream into a dashboard often do not receive the same degree of validation and cross-checking as data in a data warehouse and may contain errors. Also, transactions that show up in an operational dashboard may get adjusted afterwards, changing final results. Besides implementing sufficient checks and controls on real-time data feeds, organizations need to educate users about the accuracy and completeness of right-time data.

On the other hand, some organizations report that right-time operations have actually improved the quality and accuracy of their data. This is true when right-time operations eliminate the need for manual reconciliation processes. For example, Continental Airlines knows if it is missing customer information as soon as it closes the doors on a flight, enabling a flight attendant to make a phone call to fill in missing data. Previously, the airline did not recognize missing information until the middle of the night when no one was around to fill in the gaps.

SUMMARY

Benefits. Operational dashboards are growing in popularity as organizations seek to reap the benefits of moving to a right-time environment. Quicken Loans, for example, built a series of right-time dashboards that deliver information to decision makers at all levels of the company as rapidly as they want it—in seconds, minutes, or hours. As a result, decision makers can now intervene more quickly to address problems that may otherwise cost the company revenues.

Dashboard Types. Quicken Loans has created different styles of dashboards to support different analytical needs. A dashboard ticker enables mortgage bankers to track their performance in real time and other metrics on an hourly or daily basis. A Kanban dashboard provides sales managers with a way to oversee the performance of an entire team of mortgage bankers. Managerial dashboards provide daily and weekly trend and performance information that sales, marketing, and operations managers use to optimize their functional areas.

Architecture. The best way to build a real-time BI environment to support operational dashboards is to trickle-feed data into it via an event-driven messaging backbone supplied by EAI vendors. Showing an innovative streak, Quicken Loans developed a Web Service to capture events from its messaging backbone and store them in a real-time data store that dashboards can query for real-time data. It also partitioned OLAP cubes so that it could update them every 15 to 30 minutes without bringing them offline.

Challenges. Despite the many benefits that operational dashboards can bring, there are many challenges. These systems increase staffing requirements and systems costs because they require higher levels of scalability and systems availability. Users also need to be trained about the nature of right-time data, its level of accuracy and completeness, and how to interpret and act on the results. The IT staff can help by clearly time stamping and labeling all dashboard screens and metrics.

Finally, executives should recognize the degree to which a right-time analytical system can change the way people and processes work. They need to devise a change management strategy that ensures the adoption of the new systems and processes and positions the company to compete more effectively in an increasingly fast-paced business climate.

CHAPTER 8

Tactical Dashboards in Action:
International Truck and Engine Corp.

*E*arly one morning, a plant manager enters his office, plunks down a steaming cup of coffee, and logs on to the company's business intelligence (BI) portal to review the performance of the previous two shifts. Last week, the manager customized the BI portal to display the key metrics, reports, alerts, and links to Web sites that he needs to monitor the plant's progress toward meeting monthly budget and planning goals.

The first thing the manager notices is an alert indicating a higher than normal rate of rejected parts during the previous night's shift. He clicks on the alert and views a table and chart that display the number of rejects by part number and shows that the guilty culprit is a hose clamp, which was rejected at twice its normal rate. The view also contains comments from a line supervisor, saying that the clamps were breaking upon installation and that he shifted to an older batch to keep the line moving.

Worried now about the impact a lack of usable hose clamps could have on productivity and costs, the plant manager clicks on a hyperlink in the table and views a list of hose clamps used on the factory floor, including part numbers, a short description, dimensions, manufacturer, and date of last shipment. He puts in a rush order for new hose clamps from a different supplier and then sends an e-mail to the chief engineer to determine whether the hose clamps were breaking because of a defect or because the supplier shipped the wrong part. Later that day, the chief engineer confirms the manager's hunch that the supplier shipped the wrong part.

Thanks to the BI portal and his quick action, the plant manager averted a slow-down on the assembly line, which could have cost his company hundreds of thousands of dollars, and easily persuaded the supplier both to ship a new batch of hose clamps free of charge and to cover the cost of rush shipments to replace the incorrect parts.

BENEFITS OF TACTICAL DASHBOARDS

Finance Department Overhaul

In 2001, Mark Schwetschenau, senior vice president and controller at the International Truck and Engine Corporation, launched an internal program to transform the company's finance and accounting group from a financial record keeper to a proactive partner with the business. He believed that the finance group should play a more integral role in helping the $9.7 billion manufacturer of trucks, buses, and diesel engines in Warrenville, Illinois meet the growing demands of global competition, new regulations, and emerging markets as well as the company's own aggressive revenue and cost goals.

To meet these challenges and transform the finance group, Schwetschenau set forth a few principles to guide his group's efforts, each of which involved overhauling the way the company creates, delivers, and uses financial information:

- Provide access to financial information at any time
- Focus on analysis rather than data collection
- Deliver proactive rather than reactive analysis
- Use financial data as a predictive tool to guide decisions

Schwetschenau's mandate set in motion a flurry of initiatives, including projects to accelerate the closing of financial books, standardize the company's information infrastructure, and replace antiquated operational systems with new packaged applications. One of the most important projects, however, called for the creation of a Web-based reporting portal—in essence, a tactical dashboard—that puts accurate, actionable information in the hands of financial managers and analysts so they can contribute to the bottom line instead of just count it.

International Truck and Engine's KBI Portal

Today, International Truck and Engine's key business indicator (KBI) portal enables more than 500 financial executives, managers, and analysts to examine more than 130 key performance indicators that are updated daily. The KBI portal enables financial managers to improve operational performance and help avert hundreds of thousands of dollars in expenses and shipping delays.

"Our goal [with the KBI Portal] is to create a competitive advantage by providing access to timely, actionable information while at the same time increasing the quality and availability of that information," says Kathy Niesman, Director of Financial Systems at International Truck and Engine, who sponsored the information-centric initiatives in the financial transformation program.

Although the KBI portal was funded and developed by the finance department, it is not departmental in scope. Because finance and accounting touch every part of the company, the KBI portal extracts data from more than 32 operational systems spanning the company's five major divisions—trucks, engines, buses, parts, and financing—and stores the data in the company's enterprise data warehouse, which existed prior to the KBI portal initiative. As a result, usage of the KBI portal is rapidly growing and spreading beyond the bounds of the finance group.

"Now that the information is readily available, the KBI portal is bridging the gulf between departments, especially finance and operations," says Jim Rappé, group leader of enterprise data warehousing at International Truck and Engine. "Now, financial folks are interested in viewing operational metrics and operational managers want to see financial data."

In addition, the KBI portal has replaced a hodge-podge of paper-based reports and analytical systems that financial managers in the company's business groups once used to monitor and manage operational performance. Before the KBI portal, each business group would distribute three-ring binders containing operational reports at monthly or quarterly performance reviews. Now, they hook a laptop to a projector and review their group's performance via the KBI portal on the Web.

NEXT-GENERATION BUSINESS INTELLIGENCE

Tactical Dashboards Lead the Way

International Truck and Engine's KBI portal is an excellent example of a tactical dashboard. It represents the efforts of one department to consolidate reporting, join it with timely data for analysis, and deliver it via a Web-based portal.

In Chapter 6 we defined a tactical dashboard as a "reporting portal." However, do not be fooled by the term "tactical"—these dashboards, when designed properly and anchored by an enterprise data warehouse, deliver untold value to the company. Specifically, tactical dashboards deliver the following benefits:

- **Single Version of Truth.** Gives the department a consistent set of data, metrics, and reports that everyone uses and trusts.

- **Consolidated Reporting.** Replaces multiple, redundant reports and applications with a standard reporting system that meets the information needs of all users, from business analysts to front-line workers and executives.

- **Proactive Analysis and Action.** Delivers timely, detailed information that lets users explore a problem or opportunity and take action before it is too late.

In essence, tactical dashboards revolutionize the concept of a "report"— replacing it with a performance management system that parcels out data to users on an as-needed basis (see Spotlight 8.1).

SPOTLIGHT 8.1   WHAT IS A REPORT?

The term "report" has so many meanings today that it requires clarification.

Standard Reports. Traditionally, a report is a highly formatted, static set of data that are generated on a regular basis and distributed to users in paper or (more recently) electronic format. Today, however, standard reports offer little value to knowledge workers—executives, managers, analysts, and front-line staff. The data are too little, too late, and too static to do much good.

Over the years, there have been many variations of standard reports. For example, management reports compare organizational performance to budgets or plans each month; financial reports deliver balance sheets and income statements for both internal and external audiences; production reports create large volumes of pixel-perfect invoices or statements on a scheduled basis; operational reports publish results captured by a single operational system.

Interactive Reports. The next-generation of "reports" are dynamic, detailed, and interactive. They let users then drill down into detail, switch to an adjacent subject area to explore information from different perspectives, or link to other related reports. Interactive reports dynamically filter the data based on a user's profile so the person only sees the data they're authorized to view. Dynamic reports also let users take snapshots of the data at any level and publish these "live views" to colleagues via email or the Web.

Interactive reports can be generated using traditional report design tools, parameterized reporting techniques, OLAP tools, visualization techniques, or other types of technologies. They are a key component in many performance dashboards. In fact, if given a dashboard or portal interface, interactive reports may be indistinguishable from a tactical dashboard.

"A dashboard is the way most users want to view information," says Ryan Uda, program manager at Cisco Systems, Inc., a provider of networking equipment, software, and services. Uda says his team considered giving users the ability to create their own reports but decided against it. "People have so much going on in their work lives—e-mails, phone calls, meetings—the faster they can access and digest information, the better. A dashboard makes employees more productive because it drastically reduces the number of steps they need to take to get the information they need."

Because of their intuitive design, tactical dashboards spread quickly beyond their departmental confines to other business units and the organization as a whole. This is because managers and analysts find tactical dashboards a quick and intuitive way to measure the progress of their projects and processes on a daily or weekly basis. Tactical dashboards also make it easy for these users to drill down beyond the surface metrics in order to analyze critical issues and forecast trends.

CHARACTERISTICS OF TACTICAL DASHBOARDS

Layered Views

Chapter 1 described how performance dashboards have three layers of information: a graphical summary view, a multidimensional view, and a transactional view. This section shows how International Truck and Engine created these three layers within its KBI portal.

Top-Level View

Exhibit 8.1 shows the home page of International Truck and Engine's tactical dashboard, which was created in-house using Web software. Essentially, it is a Web

EXHIBIT 8.1   HOME PAGE OF A TACTICAL DASHBOARD

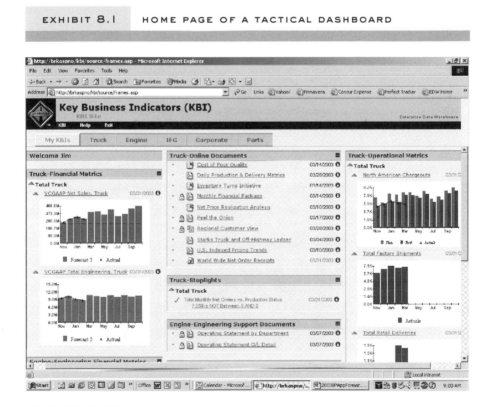

International Truck and Engine's tactical dashboard is a Web portal that groups critical metrics within six tabs. Each page shows a few key metrics, documents, and alerts and gives users the ability to drill down into metrics for more detail.

Source: Copyright © 2005 International Truck and Engine Corporation. Reprinted with Permission.

portal that gives the company's financial managers all the information they need to keep tabs on the company's operations, among other things. The KBI portal provides a separate tab for each division in the company, including a MyKBI tab that lets users select metrics and documents from a predefined list they are authorized to see. They can then place the objects in one of three columns on the screen and position them vertically based on their preferences.

The metrics on this home page use bar charts to display data and trends rather than symbols to convey state of the business or process (i.e., good, bad, or normal). This is one major difference between a tactical and a strategic dashboard: tactical dashboards focus more on performance data while strategic dashboards focus more on performance state. However, International Truck and Engine's bar charts do provide a barely visible trend line that compares actual data with plan, but this is not the dominant feature of the charts.

The middle column in the dashboard home page lists reports and documents in a variety of formats (Excel, PDF, Word, and HTML), which gives the tactical dashboard more of a portal feel compared with operational or strategic dashboards. Some of the documents are secured, requiring a password to view them. Below the documents is an alert, titled "Total Truck," showing that truck revenue is not meeting targets. Users can click on the alert and bring up a "report," which is actually a chart and table that helps them begin to figure out how to handle the situation. Whereas most operational dashboards provide alerts, few tactical dashboards do, making International Truck and Engine's site an exception to the rule.

Descriptive Properties

International Truck and Engine does a good job of providing descriptive information about the objects in the KBI portal. These descriptions help users better understand the origins and makeup of a metric or report. Each object on the screen, including documents and alerts, is time-stamped to show when it was last refreshed. By clicking on the blue circle to the right of the time stamp, which has an "i" in it that stands for "information," users can check an object's descriptive properties—what IT professionals call metadata—such as the name of the object or report, the name of the business owner of the object or report, when it was last refreshed, output format, location, text description, and other details (see Exhibit 8.2).

Second Level

To explore an individual metric in more depth, users click on the metric's hyperlinked title to open an online analytical processing (OLAP) tool that lets users "slice and dice" the data dimensionally. The tactical dashboard makes this transi-

EXHIBIT 8.2   DESCRIPTION PAGE

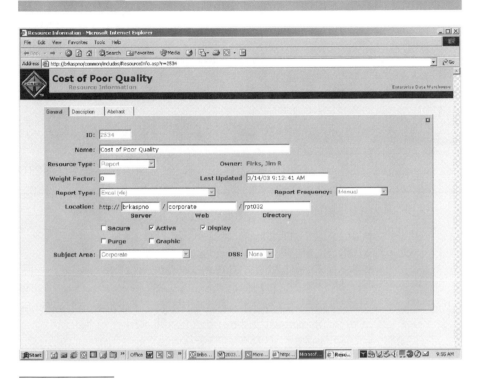

The International Truck and Engine Corporation provides information (or "metadata") about the metrics and objects in the tactical dashboards, as shown above.

Source: Copyright © 2005 International Truck and Engine Corporation. Reprinted with Permission.

tion from custom portal to commercial OLAP tool seamless to users. They do not need to do anything but click on a hyperlink to switch between the two.

Exhibit 8.3 shows a chart of the number of factory-invoiced vehicles for the past five months. To view factory-invoiced shipments for a specific plant, the user clicks on the "Production Plant" filter above the chart and selects a plant. Also, the manager can change the row and column filters to view the data by a different distribution channel, fiscal year, region, and so on. The manager can also change the metric calculation from count to revenue or margin.

When users find a chart or view they think is meaningful, they can hit the "print" button above the OLAP menu bar to print the view in PDF format. They can also hit the "refresh" button to update the data in the view or click on the "Excel" button to output data to an Excel worksheet for further analysis.

EXHIBIT 8.3   SAMPLE ANALYTICAL SCREEN

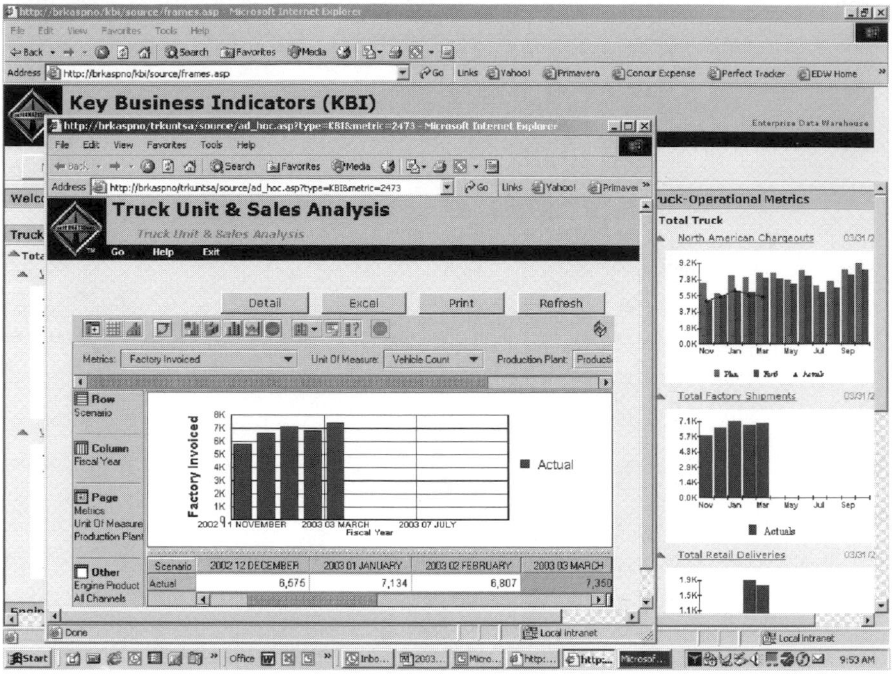

Users can drill down from the front page of the dashboard to an analytical screen that lets them change perspectives on the data, a technique known as "slicing and dicing."

Source: Copyright © 2005 International Truck and Engine Corporation. Reprinted with Permission.

Third Level

Most importantly, if users still have questions about the shipments in a specific plant, they can click the "Detail" button to display individual transactions at a plant for a given time period. Because transaction data are stored in International Truck and Engine's data warehouse, not the OLAP cube that powers the analytical screen, the system redirects the query to the data warehouse and displays the data in tabular format in a separate window (see Exhibit 8.4).

Again, this context shift from an OLAP tool to an SQL database happens transparently to end-users, and the SQL is generated automatically. Users do nothing but wait about five seconds or so for the query to return, which is very fast considering that International Truck and Engine's data warehouse is two ter-abytes in size. They can then drill further into the data warehouse information by

EXHIBIT 8.4 DRILL THROUGH TO TRANSACTION DATA

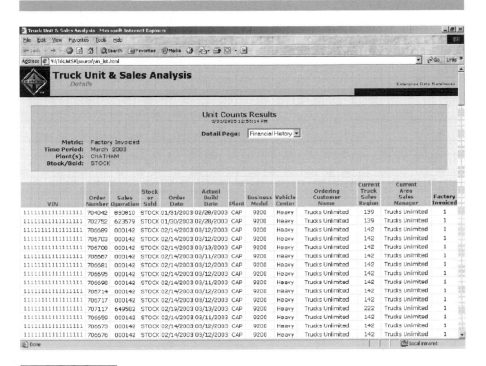

The International Truck and Engine Corporation lets users drill from the analytical screen in Exhibit 8.3 to a detailed view of data, shown above. (The data in this chart are scrambled.)

Source: Copyright © 2005 International Truck and Engine Corporation. Reprinted with Permission.

clicking on an individual truck's vehicle identification (VIN) number to bring up the order information and building specifications for that truck.

The challenge for International Truck and Engine is to homogenize the views in each of its three performance dashboard layers. Currently, each layer has a very different look and feel and different ways of manipulating information. If it blends these three layers into a coherent whole, it will make the system easier to use and reduce training requirements.

Guided Analysis

Natural Navigation

Because of their multitiered delivery of data, dashboards naturally guide users from higher level to more detailed views of data. This built-in navigation provides a basic form of guided analysis that is sufficient for many users. However, some organizations want to provide even more structured navigation to prevent users from getting lost in the data and submitting poorly designed queries that return incorrect results. These organizations want to accelerate "time to analysis" and effective decision making by minimizing the number of clicks users need to make to discover relevant data.

One financial services firm based in Boston uses hyperlinks embedded in the data to guide users. For instance, a profit/loss report might show columns of data for expenses, revenue, and headcount, each of which is hyperlinked. Clicking on expenses pivots the data and presents an expense-appropriate view. From there, users can click on a business unit to view expenses for that unit, and so on. In essence, the hyperlinks help define how users navigate from one screen or view to the next.

"Our dashboard is set up to present very business-specific views of information. The business thinks of expenses in a very specific way and they want to make sure that anyone who looks at that information is seeing it from their perspective so there is no confusion. That's what guided analysis does. It forces a path, yet gives them flexibility so they can change direction as they pass along the way," says the company's director of financial reporting and analysis.

The Limits of a Web Interface

In addition, the Boston financial services firm does not want managers or executives to drill down to infinite layers of detail because they don't want them to get lost in the data. "We don't want to overwhelm users with too many navigation options and dimensions to explore. So, we lead managers to an appropriate place and level of detail but then we expect them to call their business analyst to do additional analysis, if necessary," says the BI director. He added that the company's business analysts use a more sophisticated analytical tool that runs against the same data as the tactical dashboard used by the managers and executives.

Externalized Guidance

Other companies offer guided analysis that is more externalized, a kind of online help desk to assist users in selecting the next report to view. Direct Energy Essential Home Services, for example, takes this approach. Its guided analysis uses decision trees to step users through a series of "yes/no" questions to identify appropriate reports to view based on the content of the data they are viewing. For example, if the ratio of closed to pending sales is low in a sales revenue report, users can use a decision tree to find a "sales pending" report, read its description, and launch the report, if desired (see Exhibit 6.8 in Chapter 6).

Architecture of a Tactical Dashboard

The architecture that International Truck and Engine uses to support tactical dashboards is similar to Quicken Loans' architecture except that it does not support the "real-time" components, namely, the real-time data store and ODS. International Truck and Engine uses a data warehouse to standardize and integrate information from across the company as well as OLAP cubes and a reporting portal to deliver the information to users in a highly intuitive format that is easy to navigate and exceptionally fast (see Exhibit 8.5).

Back-End Systems

Specifically, International Truck and Engine's BI architecture collects source data and then loads the data in their original format into a relational database, which is the *staging area* for the data warehouse. It then uses a commercial extraction, transformation, and loading (ETL) tool to clean, validate, and integrate the source

EXHIBIT 8.5   INTERNATIONAL TRUCK AND ENGINE'S ARCHITECTURE

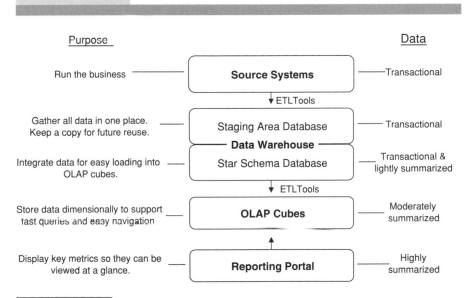

The diagram above shows a high-level view of International Truck and Engine's KBI portal architecture, along with the purpose of each layer in the architecture and the type of data that it maintains. This is typical of most BI architectures.

data and load them into another relational database, modeled as a star schema, which speeds query processing (see Chapter 3 for information on star schemas).

Front-End Systems

Once the data are in a star schema format, International Truck and Engine distributes subsets of the data to *OLAP cubes*, which are designed to support specific applications, such as the KBI portal among others. The OLAP cubes contain summary level data, not transaction-level detail, which is kept in the data warehouse. OLAP cubes are optimized to provide fast response times to a series of rapid-fire queries, such as "Let me see revenues by product for the northeast region" followed by "Let me see margins by product SKU in the Boston office." When users hit the bottom of the cube and seek more detailed data, the cube seamlessly queries the data warehouse and displays the data for the user.

The report portal contains the highest level metrics, which are static images of charts culled from the OLAP cubes. When users log in to the KBI portal, the charts and other objects in their views are automatically refreshed to reflect the most recent data and updates.

Levels of Summarization

International Truck and Engine uses a classic BI architecture to aggregate data at different levels of detail and support different types of analysis: the KBI portal home page provides highly summarized data and views of metrics; the OLAP cubes provide lightly summarized data and multidimensional views of the data; and the data warehouse provides transaction-level data for detailed examination.

CHALLENGES

The delivery of effective tactical dashboards presents many challenges; most of them revolve around creating a BI infrastructure that consolidates and integrates data from multiple data sources and standardizes definitions, rules, and metrics.

1. Perceptions

The first problem that companies encounter is convincing executives that they need to build a BI infrastructure to support the kind of analysis they desire. Some think that operational reports or Excel-equipped business analysts are sufficient to meet the organization's information needs. Others have tried data warehousing and been burned by a runaway project that cost too much, took too long, and never delivered value. "Data warehousing is a dirty word in our organization," says one

BI manager. "To get funding, we focus on business benefits that we will deliver and we avoid using that term."

2. Standardizing Terms

A more difficult challenge is standardizing the meaning and rules for shared metrics, such as "gross sale," "net margin," "profit," shared reference data, such as customer, product, or on-time delivery. Many business units are wedded to their view of the world and do not want to change. Sometimes the only way to get different business units to agree on standard definitions and terms is for the CEO to lock them in a room until they reach a consensus.

"Because we had so many sources of customer information, I finally had to stop the press, get some people in the room and ask, 'What is a customer?' It took me about a year to come up with a concise, comprehensive definition that everyone agreed with," says Wanda Black, director of information resource management at a privately held manufacturing firm.

Although it is important to have corporate standards for critical metrics and rules, this does not mean that local groups have to forfeit their way of looking at data. The company can give each business group its own data mart that preserves its view of the world as long as its data come from the enterprise data warehouse and its definitions can be mapped from local definitions to corporate standard.

3. Consolidating Analytical Systems

Part of the standardization process usually involves consolidating renegade and redundant analytical systems, which is often a never-ending task. Research shows that companies need to consolidate on average 2.1 data warehouses, 4.5 operational data stores, 6.1 data marts, and 28.5 spreadmarts (see Exhibit 8.6). On average, it takes organizations three years to break even on a project to replace these structures with an enterprise data warehouse. However, the cost savings thereafter range from $2 million to $3 million a year in hardware, software, and staffing charges.

International Truck and Engine has an ongoing project called "Release X" that identifies reporting applications that overlap with its KBI portal and tries to shut them down. So far, International Truck and Engine has shuttered 40 of 66 reporting systems on its "hit list," but it keeps discovering new ones each week. "You have to be eternally vigilant," says International Truck and Engine's Rappé.

Sometimes converting users from other applications is easy. "Often, users don't know the KBI portal exists and they get excited when they see the functionality and level of detail it provides," he says. In other cases, however, users are reluctant to use the KBI portal if it does not contain all the data in their existing application. In those cases, Rappé adds the requested information to a requirements list,

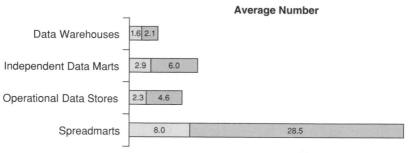

EXHIBIT 8.6   ANALYTICAL CONSOLIDATION PROJECTS

Completed vs. Planned Consolidations

Organizations have only consolidated about a third of all nonintegrated analytical structures. Data based on 521 respondents.

Source: Wayne Eckerson, "In Search of a Single Version of Truth" (*TDWI Report Series*, 2004).

which he includes in a future release. Once the release is issued, he notifies the group that the KBI portal is ready to meet its needs and then works with the group to convert to the new environment.

"Although we've saved money by turning off a number of systems, the benefits are more far reaching than the cost savings," says Rappé. "Once the KBI portal and data warehouse become better known throughout the organization, it causes groups to rethink the need to build an analytical application from scratch, which saves hundreds of thousands of dollars in development costs and licenses."

4. Rapid Development

To meet new and changing user requirements and stay ahead of analytical silos, the team responsible for delivering tactical dashboards must move quickly. They can no longer spend six to nine months developing new views or reports; they must deliver capabilities in days or weeks.

To accelerate development by an order of magnitude, companies must take an entirely new approach to developing analytical applications. This involves rethinking the way it gathers requirements, develops new functionality, and builds reports.

Instead of following a rigid set of steps to create a specification, developers need to work directly with end-users in a more iterative fashion. Developers need to sit side by side with users and flesh out requirements in prototyping sessions rather than using hand-written specifications. They need to establish technical teams that specialize in building different aspects of the tactical dashboard architecture—the data warehouses, OLAP data marts, dashboard reports, ad hoc reports—so they can work efficiently and effectively with minimal overlap and maximum coordination. They also need to train power users in every department to create reports from standard templates on behalf of their colleagues.

Accelerating development also requires that technical teams centralize business rules for cleaning, integrating, and calculating data on a server instead of in report files that cannot be reused. In the same way, the teams need to standardize report components—charting engines, query engines, layouts, list boxes, user prompts, and so on—so each can be reused in subsequent applications instead of being created from scratch or purchased anew each time. The team then needs to wrap these components in a Web service so that any application can access them and consume their XML output. The use of Web services creates a plug-and-play services-oriented architecture that makes it easy for developers to add, change, or enhance applications instead of trying to foresee every possible user need in advance.

SUMMARY

Departmental and Daily. Tactical dashboards are designed so that managers and analysts can quickly view the information they need to manage a process or measure their progress toward achieving a local objective. Although tactical dashboards may include metrics derived from a company's strategic plan, they are usually focused on optimizing the effectiveness of a department or group. They usually update data on a daily basis, although some tactical dashboards will query source systems to supplement historical data with up-to-the-minute information.

Next-Generation Reports. Tactical dashboards, in essence, represent a new way of delivering reports. Old-style reports are too static and out of date to help users work proactively to drive the business. In contrast, the new generation of reports is interactive and detailed. Such reports let users track a few key metrics at a high level and then drill down to detail or switch to an adjacent subject area. Interactive reports let users take snapshots of the data at any level and publish these "views" to colleagues via e-mail or the Web. When given a dashboard or portal interface, there is little difference between interactive reports and tactical dashboards.

OLAP-Enabled Data Warehousing Architecture. The architecture for a tactical dashboard is a classic data warehousing architecture that extracts and integrates data from multiple source systems and delivers it to a target relational database. More often than not, companies that deploy tactical dashboards use OLAP servers as data marts to deliver extremely fast performance so users can navigate information at the "speed of thought."

Robust Infrastructure Required. The main challenges in delivering successful tactical dashboards revolve mostly around creating a robust data warehousing infrastructure that supports a consistent view of key business terms and rules, such as "sales," "customer," or "net margin." Standardizing definitions can be political, but it is the first step toward consolidating information so that everyone in the company is working off the same data.

Rapid Development. It is also imperative that technical teams innovate new processes and techniques to accelerate the development of new features and data views to keep up with rapidly changing business questions and initiatives. Without rapid, iterative development techniques that can spit out new reports and views in days and weeks rather than months or years, a tactical dashboard will quickly become irrelevant, and users will search elsewhere to obtain the information they need.

CHAPTER 9

Strategic Dashboards in Action:
Hewlett Packard Co.

*O*n a sunny October day in 2004, about a dozen senior vice presidents from Hewlett Packard Co.'s Technology Solutions Group (TSG) discuss how to translate new strategic goals created by HP's Executive Council into tactical measures and initiatives for the group. The main thrust of the new corporate strategy is that increasing customer loyalty is the best way to drive future revenues. The Executive Council settled on this strategy after observing results in Hewlett Packard TSG's strategic dashboard and conducting further analysis that showed a direct correlation among customer satisfaction, customer loyalty, and revenue growth.

Proud of their contribution to the new corporate strategy, the Hewlett Packard TSG executive team discusses options to increase customer satisfaction and loyalty and measure the results better in their Balanced Scorecard, known as the Hewlett Packard Performance Measurement and Management System (PMMS). First, they come up with new initiatives to bolster customer satisfaction, such as overhauling automated telephone attendant programs, establishing a new account management model for top customers, and measuring customer satisfaction throughout the duration of a consulting engagement.

To measure customer loyalty better, as well as the impact of these new initiatives, the team decides to replace its current loyalty metric, which is based on blind surveys of customers conducted by a third-party market research firm, with an index that measures a variety of operational events known to affect customer satisfaction. To drive home the importance of the new strategy, initiatives, and measures, the team then decides to link the new loyalty metric and several operational metrics that drive it to Hewlett Packard TSG's incentive compensation plan.

Shortly after the meeting, all senior vice presidents communicate the new strategy, initiatives, and measures to their managers in each division and region of the group. Two weeks later, the new customer loyalty index appears on every Balanced Scorecard in Hewlett Packard TSG throughout the world. Just one quarter later, the Hewlett Packard TSG executive team sees a noticeable uptick in customer loyalty scores worldwide, and they soon expect to see a corresponding increase in revenues.

BENEFITS OF STRATEGIC DASHBOARDS

Hewlett Packard "Scores" Big

The above scenario is a far cry from the way Hewlett Packard TSG executives and managers ran the division before it implemented a strategic dashboard using a Balanced Scorecard methodology. Hewlett Packard TSG consists of Hewlett Packard's consulting, technology services, and software business units on a global basis.

The "Before" Scenario

Before 2001, the $12 billion division of Hewlett Packard had no means of consistently measuring regional and unit performance against company objectives and holding individuals accountable for the results. It also had dozens of reporting systems with overlapping or contradictory metrics that made it impossible for users to find performance data quickly and cost significant sums of money to maintain.

"The Balanced Scorecard is one of the most effective means of reinforcing Hewlett Packard TSG's vision and business strategy and translating it into information that people can act on," says Martin Summerhayes, a program director at Hewlett Packard TSG who spearheaded the project, which has generated a three-year $26.1 million return on investment and vastly improved individual and group performance and accountability. "It's true that what gets measured, gets done. And we reinforce this by basing compensation in part on Balanced Scorecard results."

Single Version of Truth

Hewlett Packard TSG's strategic dashboard (the PMMS) provides a single place where executives, managers, and supervisors at all levels within Hewlett Packard TSG can check the status of their group's performance against strategic objectives and examine detailed reports about exception conditions. The solution offers a single, easy-to-use Web interface that puts critical data one click away from all users, enabling them to make better and faster decisions. PMMS now displays 100 metrics that provide a single view of the business for 8,700 Hewlett Packard TSG employees throughout the world.

Cascading Scorecards

The strategic dashboard is more than just an "executive scorecard," although that is how it was first deployed in 2001 in the Europe, Middle East, and Africa (EMEA) region. Since then, Hewlett Packard TSG has rolled out the strategic dashboard to each of the division's four worldwide operating regions at multiple levels within the organization, sometimes down to individual field offices where a supervisor may manage a dozen engineers. Each scorecard in this hierarchy is linked to the one above it so performance metrics roll up from the bottom to the top of the organization. The performance information is widely publicized so users and groups can compare their performance with that of others at their level and below.

More Than a Pretty Face

PMMS is also more than just a scorecard of summarized performance results. It also provides analysis and reporting layers common to all performance dashboards, enabling users to explore performance results and examine detailed reports, if they desire. As a result, PMMS now meets the information needs of 80 to 90 percent of the division's employees and has significantly improved worker productivity and accountability.

"Managers and supervisors no longer waste time creating custom reports using ad hoc business intelligence (BI) tools, and they can't 'spin' the numbers to make their performance look better than it is. And because everyone across all business units and regions can see the results, people are more motivated to do well," Summerhayes says.

Tangible Benefits

In 2004, Hewlett Packard TSG's strategic dashboard generated $20.5 million in cost savings on $1 million total expenditures. Specifically, Hewlett Packard TSG saved $10.6 million by increasing worker productivity, primarily by reducing the time several thousand Hewlett Packard TSG employees spend looking for reports and information each month; it reduced training costs by $1.3 million because it no longer had to spend $5,000 per user to train a worker in the use of ad hoc BI tools; and it reduced reporting costs by $8.6 million by shutting down dozens of reporting systems that overlapped with PMMS.

Although these gains have made Hewlett Packard TSG more efficient internally, the strategic dashboard has also helped the company make strides toward achieving its strategic objectives. For example, since the introduction of PMMS, Hewlett Packard TSG has raised its customer satisfaction scores three to five percentage points in its four major divisions. It has also reduced the number of missed service-level commitments—a key metric at Hewlett Packard TSG—by an order of magnitude.

BALANCED SCORECARDS

Top-Down Deployment

Hewlett Packard TSG's strategic dashboard uses the Balanced Scorecard methodology. Although there are many methodologies that organizations can use to create strategic dashboards, the Balanced Scorecard is by far the most popular today.

As discussed in Chapter 6, the primary goal of a strategic dashboard is to align individual and group activities to a company's vision and strategy. Unlike operational or tactical dashboards, strategic dashboards are generally implemented in a top-down fashion, starting with top executives and working their way down to the lowest levels of the organization. However, strategic dashboards sometimes originate within divisions or regions and then expand to the enterprise, which is what occurred at Hewlett Packard TSG.

Monthly Updates

In addition, strategic dashboards are generally updated monthly, reflecting the strategic nature of the metrics and data they deliver. This was initially true for Hewlett Packard TSG's strategic dashboard, but as it cascaded scorecards throughout the regions and down multiple levels in the organization (i.e., region, subregion, country, district, and office), it added many operational metrics that are updated daily or weekly.

Methodology

The Balanced Scorecard methodology has gained great favor among corporate executives in the past 10 years. As originally conceived by Robert S. Kaplan, professor at Harvard Business School, and David P. Norton, president of the Balanced Scorecard Collaborative (BSC), Balanced Scorecards provide executives with a more "balanced" set of metrics beyond financial measures to evaluate intangible assets more accurately, predict future performance better, and balance short- and long-term business objectives.

In its most elemental form, the Balanced Scorecard is a performance measurement system that calls for balancing measures: financial and nonfinancial, external and internal, short–term and long-term, historical and future, and quantitative and qualitative across multiple facets of the business.[1] A classic Balanced Scorecard groups objectives and metrics into four major perspectives: financial, customer, learning and growth, and internal processes (see Spotlight 9.1).

SPOTLIGHT 9.1   BALANCED SCORECARD METRICS

A Balanced Scorecard, as defined by Robert S. Kaplan and David P. Norton, groups objectives, measures, targets, and initiatives into four perspectives: financial, customer, learning and growth, and internal processes. However, some organizations create their own perspectives that align more closely with the way they run their business.

Financial Perspective. The Financial perspective contains measures that indicate whether a strategy is achieving bottom-line results. Financial metrics are classic lagging indicators. The more common ones are:

- Profitability
- Revenue growth
- Economic value added

Customer Perspective. The Customer perspective defines the organization's target customers and the value proposition it offers them, whether it is efficiency (low price, high quality), innovation, or exquisite service. Most customer metrics are lagging indicators of performance, as follows:

- Customer satisfaction
- Customer loyalty
- Market share, "share of wallet"

Internal Process Perspective. Delivering value to customers involves mastering numerous internal processes, including product development, production, manufacturing, delivery, and service. Organizations may need to create brand new processes to meet goals outlined in the Customer perspective. Common metrics are:

- Patents pending, ratio of new products to total products
- Inventory turnover, stockouts
- Zero defects, on-time deliveries

Learning and Growth Perspective. This perspective measures the internal resources needed to drive the other three perspectives. These include employee skills and information technology. Typical metrics are:

- Employee satisfaction, turnover rate, absenteeism
- Training hours, leadership development programs
- Number of cross-trained employees, average years of service

Most executives quickly discover that the Balanced Scorecard methodology is more than a performance measurement system; it is also a strategic management system that they can use to execute strategy and manage organizational performance. Kaplan and Norton now describe the Balanced Scorecard as a tool to create a "strategy-focused organization"—in which strategy becomes the driving force of organizational activity and communication. The Balanced Scorecard focuses the energy of an organization into achieving strategic goals and objectives that are represented by key performance indicators (KPIs) customized to every group in the company.

According to the BSC, there are five principles that distinguish strategy-focused organizations. The BSC is a professional services firm that promotes and enhances the Balanced Scorecard and assists companies in becoming strategy-focused organizations. The five principles, which are described on the BSC web site (www.bscol.com), are as follows:[2]

1. **Translate the strategy into operational terms.** A Balanced Scorecard is not a list of measures, it is a description of an organization's strategy. One hallmark of a strategic dashboard—unlike most operational and tactical dashboards—is that you can discern the company's strategy by examining the objectives and metrics in it. Organizations define objectives and metrics using a strategy map, which has become an integral part of the Balanced Scorecard methodology (see Exhibit 9.1).

    A strategy map defines and depicts a series of cause-effect linkages among objectives in the four perspectives. These linkages define executive assumptions about resources and processes that drive customer value and financial results. The strategy map makes it easy for executives to see whether something is missing from their strategy and to test their assumptions once the scorecard is populated with data.

2. **Align the organization to the strategy.** The next step is to align the rest of the organization to the strategy defined in the corporate scorecard. This is usually done in a top-down manner, starting with the executive office of the company, a division, or a functional group (i.e., finance or sales). Once completed, the corporate scorecard becomes a template and reference point for managers at the next level to create their own scorecards. These lower level scorecards contain objectives and metrics that influence the objectives and measures in the scorecard one level above. This process continues down through successive levels of the organization until all groups and individuals are aligned through a cascading network of interlocking scorecards.

3. **Motivate the organization by making the strategy everyone's job.** In a knowledge economy, executives must educate everyone in the company about the strategy so they know what it is and how to execute it. This is done in three ways. First, organizations need to establish a formal mar-

EXHIBIT 9.1   A STRATEGY MAP

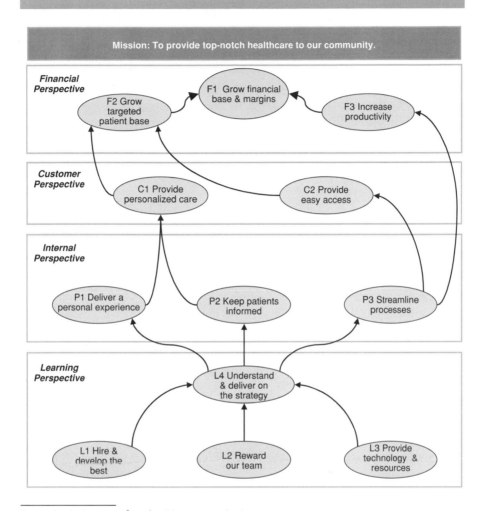

A sample strategy map for a healthcare organization.

Source: Reprinted with permission from "Align the IT Resource with Organization Strategy," keynote presentation by Robert S. Kaplan, TDWI BI Strategies Summit, May 2004.

keting and communications plan for the initiative, using every opportunity to communicate the purpose and benefits of a Balanced Scorecard to each constituency in the company.

Second, organizations must empower users to create their own scorecards and define the objectives and measures that they deem will have the greatest impact on overall strategy. Instead of telling workers what to do, executives and managers must seek their input because workers often know the best ways to get things done in the trenches. Last, companies should tie compensation incentives to scorecard metrics to get the attention of workers. However, executives should proceed cautiously on this score until there is general consensus around the validity and accuracy of metrics and objectives in the scorecards.

4. **Learn and adapt to make the strategy a continual process.** Organizations need to embed the Balanced Scorecard into the fabric of the organization. The first place to start is to use the strategy to drive the annual budgeting and planning process instead of the other way around. Executives should reference the Balanced Scorecard when prioritizing initiatives and allocating financial and staff resources for the coming year. There are now many techniques to accomplish this, including continuous budgeting and rolling quarterly plans.

Second, the executive team should use the Balanced Scorecard as the agenda for the monthly performance meetings and as a central place for business unit and department heads to record comments about performance results. Inevitably during these meetings, executives and managers will discuss the assumptions behind the Balanced Scorecard—whether the objectives and metrics accurately capture the company's strategy and correlate with financial results. These discussions help managers better understand the nature of their business, the strengths and weaknesses of their strategy, and what levers to pull under what conditions to influence performance.

5. **Mobilize change through executive leadership.** The Balanced Scorecard alone will not instigate the changes required to ensure that an organization achieves its strategy. Strategy by definition describes a destination that the organization strives to reach but has not yet. Besides a Balanced Scorecard, executives need to craft a compelling vision of the future state of the organization toward which everyone is heading. They also need to assemble a leadership team that knows how to execute knowledge-based strategies and that values the timely delivery of information. Finally, they need to make bold changes in the way the company is organized. Often, this means abolishing functional silos and restructuring the company around strategic themes or value-chain processes that align with its core value proposition to customers.

DEPLOYING STRATEGIC DASHBOARDS

Preparing the Organization

The BSC has published dozens of case studies of organizations that followed the five principles above to transform themselves into "Strategy-Focused Organizations." A common characteristic of these organizations is that they see major business value improvements within two years of deploying a strategic dashboard and additional benefits as the footprint of the system increases inside the organization. This is exactly what happened with Hewlett Packard TSG.

The project team that deployed the initial strategic dashboard in Hewlett Packard TSG's EMEA region has been turned into a program office that makes the system available to other groups in Hewlett Packard TSG at their request. To date, the team has rolled out new versions of the strategic dashboard in each of the division's four regions using the same application platform and BI infrastructure that it developed for EMEA. The team is now helping the regions drive the strategic dashboard to lower levels of their organization and expects to do the same for the rest of Hewlett Packard in the future.

Prior to rolling out the strategic dashboard worldwide, the program team gathered senior executives together to hash out guiding principles for the global initiative (see Spotlight 9.2). The aim was to ensure that each regional group implemented the strategic dashboard in a uniform fashion with predictable results. More importantly, the program team wanted each group to use identical metrics for key value drivers linked to the division's overall strategy so executives could compare performance across regions and groups. Standardizing these metrics proved to be a considerable challenge; it required executives to harmonize dozens of measures into a few standard ones that could be used worldwide.

SPOTLIGHT 9.2   GUIDING PRINCIPLES AT HEWLETT PACKARD TSG

Prior to rolling out its strategic dashboard, senior executives at Hewlett Packard TSG hashed out 12 principles to guide the global rollout of the strategic dashboard. They are:

- **Evangelize the initiative.** Senior executives should add to their list of roles and responsibilities the requirement to be a positive advocate for the initiative.

- **Make it pervasive.** Drive use of the strategic dashboard to all levels of the organization, not just senior leadership.

- **Manage it centrally.** Develop and maintain the strategic dashboard as a centralized system, using a worldwide program team to manage and maintain the system, supplemented by regional and business unit teams to assist in regional deployments.

- **Link metrics to factors needed for success.** Devise metrics that reflect the key strategies that each group needs to focus on during the next three years.

- **Define high-quality metrics.** All metrics should be measurable, significant, consistent, and agreed to by all.

- **Have a balanced approach to measurement.** Do not just measure financials, but also customer satisfaction and loyalty, employee satisfaction, and other business needs.

SPOTLIGHT 9.2   *(CONTINUED)*

- **Metrics should consist of past, present, and future indicators.** Leading indicators signal future performance whereas lagging indicators report past performance.

- **Less is more.** Aim to have less than 20 metrics per scorecard.

- **Review and revise regularly.** Conduct regular reviews to make sure that scorecards and metrics are being used and kept in sync with corporate standards and strategy.

- **Share metrics across the organization.** Scorecards should contain both "shared" measures that exist in every scorecard and "local" measures that are unique to each organization.

- **Use as a basis for recognition and reward.** Once firmly established, the strategic dashboard should be a factor in bonus payments and other incentive programs.

- **Kill two processes for every new one.** Reports developed for the strategic dashboard should replace two or more existing reports or reporting systems.

These guiding principles helped the project team work quickly and effectively with other groups that wanted to use the strategic dashboard. The principles showed that top management stood behind the initiative and gave it considerable momentum throughout the division. They also provided a lever to push executives and managers to adopt new approaches for measuring and managing performance with which they may not be entirely comfortable.

Designing the Dashboard

Like other performance dashboards, strategic dashboards deliver data at multiple levels of granularity, starting with graphical indicators at the top level and detailed reports at the bottom level. Hewlett Packard TSG's strategic dashboard consists of two distinct Web-based applications to create this multitiered effect: Libra, which displays the top-level scorecard views and second-level time-series tables and charts, and Muse, a reporting system that delivers both interactive and standard reports.

Libra Scorecards

Libra scorecards display performance state and trends using colored arrows. The scorecards can be either "balanced" or "unbalanced." Balanced scorecards contain metrics in the four perspectives defined by Kaplan and Norton. The "balanced" scorecards are used primarily by higher level executives who need a more comprehensive view of organizational performance. The "unbalanced scorecards" generally consist of metrics in two perspectives only and are used by managers and supervisors who oversee lower-level business processes. Hewlett Packard TSG's strategic dashboard currently contains hundreds of scorecards used by different groups and individuals throughout the division.

Muse Reports

Muse contains a list of standard reports in a hierarchy of folders available to users over the Web. Muse did not start as a full-fledged reporting system, although it is turning into one. Muse currently stores data in OLAP cubes, like Libra. Initially, Muse only extracted data for metrics in Libra when performance was below target for a given period. Today, Hewlett Packard TSG is expanding Muse to contain much lower levels of operational data and support daily operational reporting. Muse's reporting scope will undoubtedly continue to expand as more groups and users within Hewlett Packard start relying on PMMS as their primary reporting and analysis tool. It is moving towards becoming a full-fledged data warehousing environment.

Libra and Muse run independently of each other but are seamlessly integrated, allowing users to drill down seamlessly from the graphical summary view to operational details. Executives often can view Libra data without accessing Muse, whereas lower level managers often access Muse reports directly, bypassing Libra. Let us look at sample screenshots from Hewlett Packard TSG's strategic dashboard to get a better feel for how the performance management system works.

Top-Level Scorecard View

Exhibit 9.2 shows the top-level scorecard view of Hewlett Packard TSG's strategic dashboard. The scorecard divides the metrics into the four classic Balanced Scorecard perspectives: customer, finance, internal, and learning and innovation. Each perspective has between two and four metrics, allowing executives to view the status of all key areas in one glance (and staying within the company's 20-metric limit per scorecard). However, some metrics have sub-metrics, indicated by the "+" sign to the left of the metric title.

Arrows

Hewlett Packard TSG uses colored arrows to indicate monthly performance status for each metric. The color of the arrow indicates whether performance is above or below a predefined target. These targets are established by senior managers or executives on the basis of budgetary goals, external benchmarks, or fore-

EXHIBIT 9.2　TOP-LEVEL VIEW OF A BALANCED SCORECARD

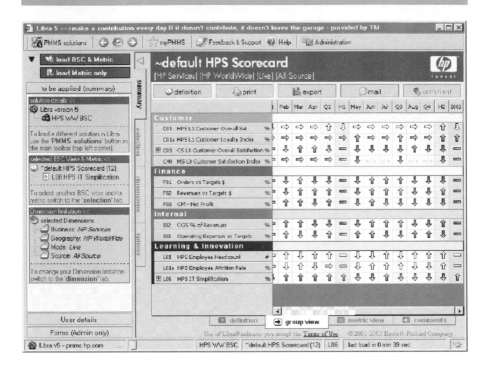

The front page of HP Services strategic dashboard conforms to a classic Balanced Scorecard approach with metrics grouped into four perspectives. (Data do not reflect actual performance.)

Source: Copyright © 2005 Hewlett-Packard Co. Reprinted with Permission.

casts based on past performance. Managers set baseline targets and aspirational (i.e., "stretch") targets. Most goals are defined within the administrative menu of the scorecard application. Some budgetary goals are loaded into the scorecard directly from the planning or budgeting application, which are primarily Excel spreadsheets.

A red-colored arrow indicates that performance is below the baseline target, a green-colored arrow indicates that performance is above target but below the aspirational goal, and a blue arrow means that performance exceeds the aspirational goals. (Dashes indicate that no comparison data are available, and white arrows indicate that executives have not yet defined a target for the metric.) "We have no yellow arrows because you are either performing as expected or not. But we encourage exceptional performance and high motivation, which is why we use blue arrows," says Summerhayes.

The direction of the arrows indicates performance trends. For instance, a sideways arrow pointing to the right indicates that performance has remained relatively unchanged for the past month or quarter depending on the measurement frequency. An arrow pointing up or down indicates that performance has increased or declined by a predefined percentage. Each metric uses a different percentage to calculate positive or negative trends. To see numbers instead of arrows, users can make their cursors hover over an arrow or change the scorecard's settings to display only numbers or numbers and arrows.

The combination of arrows and colors delivers a lot of information at a glance. For instance, a green arrow pointing down means performance is above target but trending in the wrong direction, which might prompt managers to explore this metric in more detail. Conversely, an upward trending red arrow may show that work done last month to correct a problem is already paying off although performance is still not up to snuff.

Other Features

The scorecard view lets users click on the "definition" tab above the main panel to view the properties of a metric, such as who owns it, where the data came from, when it was refreshed, how it was calculated, and so on. In the same way, users can also print the screen, export it (to Microsoft Excel, HTML, JPEG, or PowerPoint), e-mail it to a colleague, or add a comment to a metric. In addition, users can create a customized version of the scorecard (MyPMMS), provide feedback to developers, or get online help.

Second-Level, Multidimensional View

To analyze and explore data behind the arrows, users click on the name of the metric and the system loads data for it, usually as a chart or table that shows monthly performance data compared with both target and aspirational goals. In Exhibit 9.3, a manager has "drilled into" a metric called "IT Simplification" and pulled up the past 12 months of performance data. A quick glance at the chart shows that the group had a major setback in November, then improved gradually during the next two months, and achieved its goals thereafter.

To change views of the data, users click the "View" button on the menu bar or the "selection" and "dimensions" tabs on the left-hand side. Here, users can view the data by geography, time, or business unit. Unbalanced scorecards, which display metrics for only one or two of the business perspectives, support additional dimensions, such as customer, partners, products, and channel.

EXHIBIT 9.3   SECOND-LEVEL VIEW OF PERFORMANCE METRICS

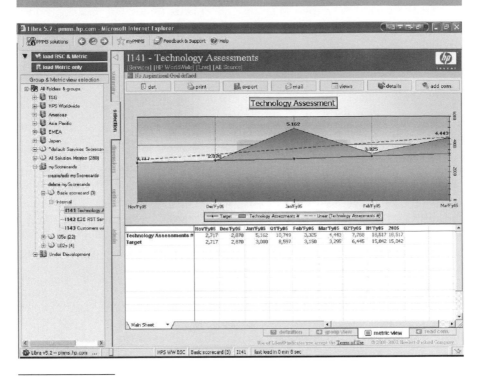

Hewlett Packard TSG's strategic dashboard lets users drill down from an iconic graphical view of key metrics to interactive charts and tables. (The data do not reflect actual performance.)

Source: Copyright © 2005 Hewlett-Packard Co. Reprinted with Permission.

Third-Level Detailed View

Spreadsheet View

To drill into more depth, users can click the "Detail" button on the top menu bar, which either displays the data in a spreadsheet or connects the user to the Muse reporting system. The spreadsheet view loads data into pivot tables or pivot graphs that let users swap rows and columns, change chart types, filter and sort the data, or insert new columns. In short, the spreadsheet view lets them "slice and dice" in a familiar spreadsheet context. Users can also export data to their desktops as Excel files or JPEG charts (see Exhibit 9.4).

EXHIBIT 9.4   PIVOT TABLE VIEW

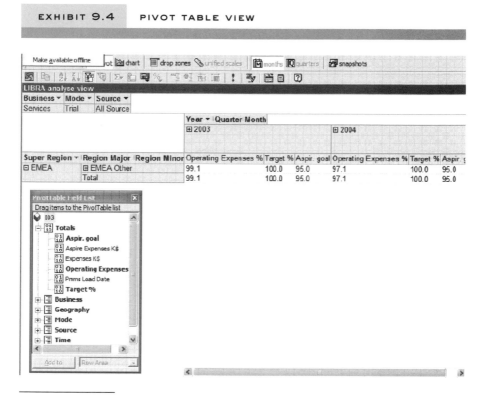

By clicking on the detail button, users interact with data in a pivot table or pivot chart (i.e. spreadsheet) within a Web browser. Users can export these data and view them on their desktop for offline analysis. Data do not reflect actual results.

Source: Copyright © 2005 Hewlett-Packard Co. Reprinted with Permission.

Muse Reports

The link to the Muse reporting system allows users to go the Muse home page or directly to a report related to the data they were viewing. Although this is a context shift for users—from Libra to Muse—the switch is made transparently to them. The system automatically passes query parameters to Muse, which brings up the appropriate report among the hundreds it maintains (see Exhibit 9.5).

Although Libra and Muse OLAP servers are located in different data centers, users never know they have switched between two different systems. Like International Truck and Engine, Hewlett Packard TSG's challenge is to blend the look and feel and functionality of all three layers into a more homogenous whole to make the system easier to use and reduce training.

EXHIBIT 9.5 A MUSE REPORT

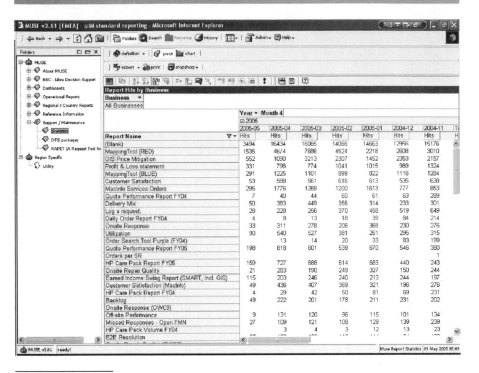

Hewlett Packard TSG's strategic dashboard provides users with transparent access to detailed reports, such as the one above, which also uses online, interactive pivot tables to display detailed data stored in OLAP cubes. (Data do not represent actual results.)

Source: Copyright © 2005 Hewlett-Packard Co. Reprinted with Permission.

Muse is a "one-stop shop" for reports and files, sparing users from having to spend hours looking for the right report. The data come from the same sources as Libra, thus ensuring that everyone is working from the same set of data, preserving a "single version of the truth."

Like Libra, Muse uses online analytical (OLAP) cubes, which enables users to "slice and dice" by multiple dimensions and drill down to detail. However, Muse stores more detailed data in the cubes and lets users drill through the "bottom" of a cube to more detailed data stored in a back-end relational database. In addition, Muse reports may display the data in many different formats—HTML, Excel, Brio, Business Objects, and so on. Developers publish reports (i.e. OLAP views) and other files to folders arranged in a hierarchical fashion, like Microsoft Explorer.

Architecture

Custom Coding

The PMMS team created the strategic dashboard by writing custom code using Microsoft .NET and leveraging Microsoft Office Web Components already installed on user desktops. Both Libra and Muse servers use Microsoft SQL Server for collecting and staging data, Microsoft Analysis Server to store data in OLAP cubes, and Hewlett Packard TSG's corporate portal to display graphical indicators.

The team decided to custom-build the strategic dashboard because at the time there were no commercially available tools that Hewlett Packard TSG felt were mature enough to deliver the functionality it needed. Also, by leveraging two in-house developers and existing equipment, the team spent just $370,000 to build and maintain the strategic dashboard during the first 12 months. In 2005, Hewlett Packard TSG expects to spend about $670,000 total, down from $1 million last year, reflecting greater economies of scale and fewer requests for new scorecards.

Data Infrastructure

The BI infrastructure is conceptually designed as a three-tier pyramid (see Exhibit 9.6). The top layer consists of highly aggregated data that delivers "knowledge." This layer populates balanced and unbalanced scorecards and views of individual metrics. The data in this layer are stored in a dozen or so Microsoft OLAP cubes, which are updated monthly. The Libra system holds a mere 100 megabytes of data and is maintained in a Hewlett Packard TSG data center in Atlanta, Georgia.

The middle layer consists of lightly aggregated data that deliver "information" in the form of Muse reports and files. Like Libra, the data are stored in OLAP cubes, which are updated at different intervals, from daily to monthly, depending on the nature of the reports they support. Muse consists of about 2,500 cubes that hold 200 gigabytes of data. Hewlett Packard TSG distributes the OLAP cubes across four regional data centers to keep the data closer to source systems and the primary users.

The bottom of the pyramid consists of the data from 40 different sources that feed the strategic dashboard, including data warehouses and operational systems. Most data are held for three years. What is unique about this approach is that it only captures data about exception conditions, not data for each metric at all times. For example, Muse only captures *missed* service-level commitments instead of all commitments. This substantially reduces the amount of data the strategic dashboard needs to load and store on a regular basis, improving performance, eliminating bottlenecks, and minimizing the team's dependence on IT teams for data.

EXHIBIT 9.6   BI INFRASTRUCTURE AT HEWLETT PACKARD TSG

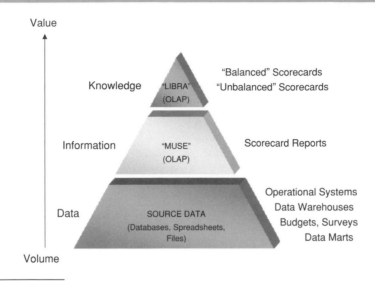

The BI infrastructure supporting Hewlett Packard TSG's strategic dashboard consists of two different systems, one that delivers a scorecard view of metrics (Libra) and one that delivers standard reports for scorecard metrics (Muse).

Source: Copyright © 2005 Hewlett-Packard Co. Reprinted with Permission.

As PMMS become Hewlett Packard TSG's primary means of distributing information to employees, its BI infrastructure will expand to house more data across more subject areas at more levels of detail. In essence, PMMS is an enterprise data warehouse in the making.

SUMMARY

Purpose. Strategic dashboards align actions with strategy. A strategic dashboard embodies an organization's strategy and presents it to users in a dashboard format so they can quickly view where they need to make adjustments to achieve the strategy and meet group or individual goals. Most organizations that deploy strategic dashboards use the Balanced Scorecard approach, which helps organizations develop and execute strategy by defining a balanced set of objectives and metrics across all facets of the business.

Principles. The Balanced Scorecard Collaborative, founded by Kaplan and Norton to promote and enrich the Balanced Scorecard methodology, defines five major principles for becoming a strategy-focused organization. These are: 1) translate the strategy into operational terms, 2) align the organization with the strategy, 3) motivate the organization by making the strategy everyone's job, 4) learn and adapt to make the strategy a continual process, and 5) mobilize change through executive leadership.

Hewlett Packard TSG represents a classic example of how an organization can implement a strategic dashboard quickly and reap tremendous benefits. Initially supporting a single region within Hewlett Packard TSG, the strategic dashboard now supports every region and unit in the group. The strategic dashboard consists of two distinct systems that are integrated transparently to users: Libra, which provides scorecard and top-level views of data, and Muse, which provides interactive reports containing detailed data about the performance metrics.

Hewlett Packard TSG built the performance management system in-house because at the time there were no commercially available tools that met their needs. Over time, PMMS will expand its BI infrastructure to support larger volumes of detailed data and become the single source of consistent information for the organization.

NOTES

1. Daniel Meade, "The Art and Science of Measurement: The Nature of Indicators on the Balanced Scorecard," BetterManagement.com.
2. Reprinted with permission by Robert S. Kaplan.

PART THREE

Critical Success Factors:
Tips from the Trenches

CHAPTER 10

How to Launch the Project

Launching a performance dashboard project is often the easy part—only if you are a senior executive with a vision for empowering the organization with information to achieve short- and long-term objectives. But, if you are lower in the organization and have little influence on strategic initiatives and budgets, what do you do? How can you translate your vision into tangible reality?

This chapter will discuss strategies that individuals have used to launch performance dashboard projects. The first set of strategies revolves around selling the project. Success here requires persistence, excellent communications skills, and political savvy. The key challenges are finding a visionary executive, building support among key senior executives, and securing funding.

The next set of strategies revolves around managing the project. This requires excellent organizational and team-building skills and an ability to keep a project on track. Key challenges are creating an energetic, competent team, managing expectations, and evangelizing the solution to front-line staff.

SELLING THE PROJECT

Find a Sponsor

Chapter 4 showed that there is a direct correlation between an active, committed sponsor and the success of a business intelligence (BI) project, such as a performance dashboard. Thus, the first task in implementing a performance dashboard is to find an energetic, committed business sponsor and sell him or her on the value of the project. The best sponsors exhibit numerous characteristics that can make or break a project (see Spotlight 10.1).

SPOTLIGHT 10.1   CHARACTERISTICS OF A GOOD SPONSOR

Is there a litmus test for good sponsors? Although sponsors come in all sizes and shapes, the best sponsors exhibit the following characteristics:

1. **Respected.** The sponsor should be well known in the company and have a solid track record for making positive contributions over the years. The sponsor's opinion should carry significant clout on the executive steering committee.

2. **Knowledgeable.** The sponsor should understand the company inside and out, having served in numerous capacities over many years. The person should also know how technology can be applied to improve the company's competitive position in the marketplace.

3. **Well Connected.** The sponsor should have many allies and few, if any, foes. The sponsor should know the key players whose support is required for the project to succeed. Avoid sponsors with an archenemy who will try to sabotage a project.

4. **Established.** The best sponsors are well established in their positions and will not abandon the project in midstream. Avoid recruiting young executives eager to climb the corporate ladder or veterans a year or two from retirement. "Losing a sponsor midstream was the worst thing that happened to us," laments one manager of business performance.

5. **Committed.** The sponsor needs to commit his or her most precious commodity to the project: time. Avoid sponsors who have a vision but are too busy to evangelize the project, attend meetings, make decisions, and allocate resources. They also must be willing and able to commit other people's time to the project, especially business analysts who can interpret data and business requirements for the technical team.

6. **A Good Communicator.** A good sponsor knows how to communicate the project's rationale effectively to every constituency in the company and how to galvanize enthusiasm for the project on a sustained basis.

7. **A Good Role Model.** A good sponsor backs up words with actions and uses the performance dashboard to manage the business, either directly or indirectly.

Although few executives possess all seven characteristics, strive to find executives who exhibit most of them, or who do not have any glaring weaknesses.

Wait for a Visionary Executive

There are several techniques for finding a business sponsor. The first is to scout the executive ranks for someone who has a vision of how information technology can improve the organization. Often, these executives are easy to spot: they are new to the company or business unit and have experience leveraging information technology in a previous position. These types of executives often find you before you find them.

This was the case at Hewlett Packard Technology Solutions Group (TSG) when a new vice president of customer service in the European division "drove some new thinking" into the program, according to Martin Summerhayes, program director at Hewlett Packard TSG. The executive asked Summerhayes to spearhead a new measurement framework, which quickly turned into a strategic dashboard using a Balanced Scorecard approach. (See Chapter 9 for a profile of Hewlett Packard TSG.)

Sometimes executives just need to hear the right presentation in the right context to turn formative ideas into a concrete vision and plan. For example, the CIO of a large wireless telecommunications firm attended a workshop delivered by Robert Kaplan, professor at Harvard Business School and co-creator of the Balanced Scorecard methodology. The CIO was so impressed that he recruited the company's CFO to attend the next workshop session, and both of them then sold the concept to the rest of the executive team.

Find a Sponsor with "Information Pain"

When a sponsor does not come looking for you, the next best option is to look for an executive of a business unit that is suffering from lack of timely or accurate information. Sometimes the executives running these groups are willing to sponsor a performance dashboard project if they are convinced it will alleviate their "information pain." Once you have identified the right executive, then you need to sell him or her on the idea.

Selling to Sponsors

Cost-Benefit Analysis

The first task in selling a project is to make a business case that shows the costs and benefits. Unfortunately, this is not always easy because the biggest benefits of a performance dashboard are intangible and difficult to quantify: quicker access to information, better decisions, and more effective plans. Nevertheless, it is imperative to quantify the benefits in dollars and cents. The project team at the International Truck and Engine Corporation, for example, estimated that a performance dashboard would save the company the equivalent of ten full-time staff positions.

"Since we couldn't realistically estimate revenue or costs from giving users access to more timely data, we justified it on the number of hours analysts would save each month collecting and formatting financial data. We knew the tangible and intangible returns would be substantially higher, which has proven to be true, but we couldn't estimate the full value upfront," says Jim Rappé, manager of enterprise data warehousing at International Truck and Engine.

Benchmarks

Besides presenting a cost-benefit analysis, another way to bolster the case is to present what the competition is doing. Executives are eager to know how their business compares with their direct competitors or with the industry as a whole. Showing how a direct competitor uses a performance dashboard to advantage can have a major influence on whether executives commit to the project. Secondarily, industry benchmarks might reveal that your company needs to increase its investment in BI to keep up with the competition. Many industry groups, associations, or major consultancies publish such benchmarking data. If no such data exist, commission a research firm to conduct a custom study.

Prototypes

A picture is worth a thousand words. Showing a prototype of the performance dashboard is a quick way to demonstrate the benefits. With a prototype in hand, be ready to show it to anyone at any time. For example, one ambitious project manager spent months wheeling a computer across a corporate campus before he found a sponsor willing to commit to the project. (This was before the advent of Web applications!) Prototypes also generate a great deal of immediate feedback, which can help refine the application and project to meet users' needs. One word of caution: make sure potential sponsors realize that the prototype is not a finished application and requires additional time, money, and staff before it can be transformed into a production application.

Build It and They Will Come?

Some individuals take matters into their own hands: they build a performance dashboard first and then look for a business sponsor to promulgate it throughout the enterprise. Although most experts discourage using this "build it and they will come" approach, some teams have used it with success, given the right circumstances.

For example, the information management team in the finance department of a large, decentralized company built a tactical dashboard that provides a single, consistent source of financial information across all business units. Historically, the team built separate analytical applications to meet the needs of each business unit. However, the team realized that it could meet everyone's needs more efficiently and effectively by creating a Web-based tactical dashboard. The team believed there was pent-up demand for a centralized solution because financial analysts were spending too much time collecting and formatting data and too little time analyzing it, undermining the overall productivity and effectiveness of the corporate finance group.

"Since our company is so decentralized, the CFO was initially skeptical that we could consolidate disparate reporting systems and get everyone using the same financial data. But given the pressure to reduce expenses and runaway spreadsheets, we figured that if we developed the system that it might take off," says the BI director at the company.

So far, the strategy has worked. The tactical dashboard now supports more than 600 users who submit two million queries a month on average, representing more than half the financial analysts in corporate finance and one-third of relevant business users in the rest of the company. To boost user adoption to 100 percent, the team is now "selling" the application to the CFO and a finance transformation team that is developing recommendations about how to increase the value that the finance group delivers to other business units. "We believe the CFO will eventually endorse the application as a corporate standard," says the manager.

Wait for a Catalyst

Sometimes the best cost-benefit analysis, prototype, or strategic rationale are not enough to gain executive commitment. In that case, you have to wait for an external catalyst to reshape the business landscape and change the way executives perceive the value of the project. The most common catalysts are mergers and acquisitions, deregulation, and economic downturns.

For example, TELUS, the second largest telecommunications company in Canada, with revenues in excess of $7 billion, struggled for several years to put together a Balanced Scorecard for its operations group. A team assigned to the project collected reams of paper and documentation and defined several measures but never succeeded in launching the project. That changed in 2001 after a new executive team kicked off an operational efficiency program to get the company back on a solid financial footing after it was buffeted by industry deregulation, several subsequent mergers, and the economic downturn that started in 2000. The new program became the catalyst the performance dashboard project needed.

"The company had always pursued efficiency improvement, but now there was no choice! Executives needed to reduce the operating costs significantly without lowering customer service levels. The only way to do that was to implement the performance management system," says Kevin Lam, manager of business performance at TELUS.

It also helped that TELUS brought in managers from non-regulated enterprises who were more receptive to using performance dashboards and BI systems. The scorecard team presented a business case to one of these executives, saying the system would deliver a balanced set of measures that would be consistent at all levels of the company. They estimated the new system would increase the productivity of the operational workforce by five percent and save the company millions of dollars. Within short order, the executive became a key sponsor, says Lam (see Spotlight 12.1 in Chapter 12).

Selling to Mid-Level Managers

Many technical projects garner top management support but never gain traction because the project team fails to gather the support of mid-level managers. As mentioned in Chapter 4, these managers control departmental budgets and funds, and their actions and words convey to their staff whether or not to take executive mandates seriously. Mid-level managers may also feel threatened by a performance dashboard that displays their group's performance to the entire company in an unvarnished fashion.

The best way to gain the support of mid-level managers is to leverage an executive sponsor to open doors to departmental managers and staff. It is critical to become a persistent, visible, and vocal advocate of the project at this level of the organization, according to Jim Rappé at International Truck and Engine. "I'll go to the vice president or director and get 50 minutes at their staff meetings to provide background on the KBI portal, explain what's in it for them, and demonstrate the application. I also spend a lot of time talking one-on-one with people to market and sell the project," he says.

Selling Staff

It is also critical to gain the support of the front-line staff whose performance the system will most likely monitor. In many organizations, the staff is understandably jaded and cynical. Many believe, rightly or wrongly, that management will not give them enough resources to meet the goals and objectives in the performance dashboard or enough freedom to optimize performance using strategies and tactics that aren't officially sanctioned.

"Our initial performance management system was built at a time when the prevailing thinking was that you use it to go and beat up the [workers]," says a senior vice president at a services company who asked not to be named. "Quickly, workers questioned the validity of this metric or that data and you begin debating the accuracy of the data, and it's a downward spiral from there."

Another senior director who wished to remain anonymous says, "We had strong support from the top, but I don't think we've done enough to get the folks at the level below them to become really invested in this. There is a lot of skepticism with front-line employees. Many don't believe the numbers that [departments] report and vigorously comment [on] why some directors get performance bonuses [based on those numbers]."

Both managers said it was important to include staff in the process of developing metrics and targets to get their buy-in. It is important to tell the staff in advance about the project and give them the opportunity to provide feedback both during the design and development stages as well as after the application is deployed through online feedback links or formalized review sessions.

SECURE FUNDING

Although every performance dashboard requires funding, there seems to be little correlation between money and success. In fact, it appears that new projects fare better if they operate on a shoestring budget, while projects that enjoy hefty initial budgets tend to run into problems.

Bootstrapping a New Dashboard

Many new projects get the buy-in of executives who do not necessarily control the purse strings at an operational level. This is what happened at Hewlett Packard TSG: the executive sponsor assumed that funding would come out of a regional budget. "Thus, I started with no dedicated budget, no full-time staff, and no hardware or software," says Summerhayes.

To get by until he could secure formal funding, Summerhayes "stole" two part-time developers from other projects and "found" some hardware they could use to build the system. In seven weeks, this makeshift team delivered the first version of the scorecard, which contained nine metrics and supported 800 users. Summerhayes was then able to divert money from other projects and hired 11 developers and two project leads. Within 18 months, the new system contained 120 metrics and supported 5,500 Hewlett Packard TSG users worldwide.

Direct Energy Essential Home Services also bootstrapped its performance dashboard. Even though the dashboard project was high priority, it was not given any money, largely because the company was preoccupied with reorganizing itself to thrive in a nonregulated environment. Executives expected the IT department to allocate the time of some staff to work on the project, which it did; in a few months, it delivered a bare-bones application that proved useful in the field. "Now that the business climate has stabilized, we plan to invest more, perhaps purchase a commercial dashboard solution," says John Lochrie, senior vice president at Direct Energy.

The advantage that bootstrapped projects have is that they are driven by small teams of business and technical people who are highly motivated and charged with a mission to move quickly to meet demand. They know the only way to sustain the project is to deliver quick wins to the business and create momentum. In contrast, larger teams with bigger budgets often take on bigger projects with bigger expectations that are challenging to meet. With more staff to coordinate, more users to satisfy, and more requirements to meet, they often experience problems.

In 2003 the District of Columbia decided to automate the way it handles agency performance data as part of a multimillion dollar campaign to modernize all administrative services. In early 2004, it purchased an integrated business performance management solution (i.e., budgeting, planning, and dashboarding) and began developing more than 1,200 scorecards for 56 agencies covering 19,000 employees that was scheduled to go "live" in November, 2004 (see Spotlight 10.2 and Exhibit 10.1).

SPOTLIGHT 10.2   STRATEGIC DASHBOARDS IN A GOVERNMENT AGENCY

Although many companies have introduced strategic dashboards, few have implemented them on the same scale as the District of Columbia. In 2004, the District began rolling out more than 1,200 scorecards to 56 agencies. The scorecards contain metrics and initiatives defined in each agency's performance-based budget that emanate from each agency's strategic plan objectives set by the Mayor of the District. The District of Columbia is working hard not to buckle under the scope of the project although it has had to postpone the delivery of the full system until 2006.

The scorecards largely automate an existing manual performance management process. Previously, each month agencies sent Microsoft Word-based reports with their comments to the city administrator's office, where analysts would review the reports, validate the data, and send questions or comments back. At the year's end, the city administrator's office would consolidate the data in a Microsoft Access database. The new system automatically collects and displays performance results and commentary in a Web-based dashboard available to directors and administrators in each agency and the Mayor's office.

The scorecard solution will help the city government to become more efficient in delivering high-quality services. It will expand the breadth of information collected about agency programs and activities while improving the quality and consistency of performance-related data. This will enable analysts in the Mayor's office to perform deeper analysis of agency performance and spend less time collecting, verifying, and massaging the data. It will also enable agency heads and program and activity managers to see exactly where they stand against their performance and budgetary targets at any time and better forecast demand for their services by viewing performance trends online over multiple years. The District publishes performance data from its scorecards in budget and performance reports that it sends to the U.S. Congress for review.

"Our discussion with the agencies will be much richer because more people will be entering the data and reflecting on our comments," says Doug Smith, director of Strategic Planning and Performance Management in the District's Office of the City Administrator, "and as we get more data into the system, we will press agencies harder in their budget submissions to more accurately forecast demand and the dollars they need to meet that demand and maintain service quality."

Despite its early success, the District still has work ahead. It needs to build grass roots support for the system among workers in the agencies and train users both to upload data using the new system and to meet data delivery deadlines. So far, the District has purchased licenses for 1,000 users, limiting usage of the scorecards to managers, analysts, and agency employees assigned to perform data entry for the system.

Because of the large scope of the project and other unexpected problems, the District has postponed the time when it plans to have all agencies on line with the system until 2006. "We bit off a little more than we can chew, but we are making progress," says Doug Smith, director of Strategic Planning and Performance Management in the Office of the City Administrator.

EXHIBIT 10.1   A STRATEGIC DASHBOARD IN THE DISTRICT OF COLUMBIA

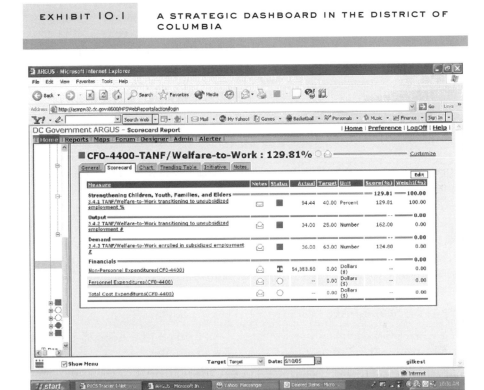

Like many organizations, the District of Columbia does not use the four perspectives of a classic balanced scorecard. Instead, it has customized its scorecards to reflect each agency's strategic goals and objectives contained in its performance-based budget. This screenshot shows a scorecard for a single strategic objective ("Improve welfare-to-work ratios") within the Department of Employment Services. The software lets users switch from stoplight views to tables or charts using the tabs below the scorecard title. Another tab shows the performance of initiatives associated with each objective and commentary about monthly performance results. (Numbers are based on test data.)

Source: Courtesy of the District of Columbia.

Funding Established Projects

Although new projects seem to thrive in a bootstrap environment, established projects require stable funding. BI managers often complain that funding for their projects is always at risk because executives and strategies shift quickly. This requires them to spend a great deal of time selling the project just to survive instead of delivering new functionality to meet user requirements.

Funding for established BI projects is usually split between the IT department and business units. The IT department pays for maintenance of the existing environment, and business units pay for extensions to it, usually new applications that require the extraction of new sets of data from operational systems. Sourcing and integrating new data into an existing environment usually takes at least three months to define user requirements, design the reports, and test the application. If the data are already in the BI environment, deploying new analytical applications can take anywhere from two hours to two days to two weeks.

WHERE TO START?

One of the most common questions that people ask about performance dashboard projects is where to start. The best place to start is where there is an energetic, committed sponsor. However, a sponsor is not enough to guarantee the success of a project. It is also important to evaluate the group the sponsor represents to determine how receptive it is as a whole to using a performance dashboard. The readiness assessment checklist in Chapter 4 is a good way to compare and contrast several groups in an organization to find the best place in an organization to launch a project (see Exhibit 4.11 for a sample worksheet to evaluate multiple groups).

Enterprise Scope Takes Years

Even when a CEO initiates a performance dashboard project, it does not become an enterprise application overnight. Top-down-driven projects need several years to percolate throughout an organization. For example, a wireless telecommunications company spent nine months creating a corporate scorecard for the executive team and another nine months developing custom scorecards for each member of the executive committee. Meanwhile, the company is also creating the technical and application infrastructure for the strategic dashboard so it can roll out scorecards to all groups in the organization.

Shared Services?

There is considerable disagreement about whether performance dashboards—Balanced Scorecards in particular—can be effectively initiated in a shared service function, such as finance, IT, or human resources, which provides support services to all the product and service groups in the company.

"The biggest mistake I've seen is to assign a [strategic dashboard] project to someone from finance, human resources, or information technology where the primary focus is on one of these areas," says Summerhayes. He says finance groups focus too much on financial measures, human resource groups focus too much on workforce issues, and IT departments spend too much time and money building the correct architecture and infrastructure. "A scorecard project should be business led to help balance all of these constituent parties, but you need to include all of these from the start," says Summerhayes.

Multiple Touchpoints

However, others believe that a shared service function is an ideal place to start a performance dashboard project. "A finance-led initiative touches almost every area of the business. We see order entry, the supply chain, and operations across all divisions in the company," says Rappé. Each time International Truck and Engine populates its data warehouse with a new subject area, almost every division in the company can leverage the data. Thus, the finance group's tactical dashboard has quickly become a substantial enterprise resource.

On the whole, it does not matter where you start a performance dashboard initiative as long as you have a committed sponsor, a receptive organization, and a proper understanding of how to deliver business value with the tools.

CREATE A STRONG TEAM

Once a performance dashboard project gets approved and funded, the next step is to create a capable team to define the metrics, create the dashboard, evangelize the solution, and train the users.

Project Champions

The team is led by a project champion or business driver who either pitched the idea to the business sponsor or was asked by the sponsor to spearhead the project. The project champion must possess a versatile mix of skills. According to John Monczewski, senior manager of reporting at Booz Allen Hamilton, project leads must have strong knowledge of the business and performance management concepts and excellent communications skills. They must be enthusiastic and relentless promoters, excellent team builders, consummate salespeople and politicians, and superb managers of time, resources, and projects. "They must truly be the champions of the project," he says.

Executive Steering Committee

The first thing the team should do is create an executive steering committee to oversee the project. The executive steering committee consists of the business sponsor, the project champion, and representatives from every group or business unit that ultimately will use or support the performance dashboard. The purpose of this group is to drive consensus on the definition and meaning of critical metrics, prioritize major enhancements, and sustain funding. Committee members should have clout in their own organizations so they can effectively evangelize the value and importance of the project back home.

Politically, it is wise to invite executives who might have reservations about the project to sit on the steering committee. This gives you more opportunity to sell them on the value of the project and helps you proactively develop workarounds to aspects the executives might find objectionable. You can also keep them better apprised of project developments that affect their area as well as intercept inaccurate rumors or hearsay that might adversely color their opinion of the project. Even if they decline to join the group, they will be flattered by the invitation. You can usually get them to agree to be on the committee mailing list to receive meeting summaries and updates.

Project Managers

Iterative Development

The team needs experienced project managers to establish a project plan, coordinate resources, manage scope and requirements, and keep the project on track and in budget. Much has been written about how to manage technical projects, and that information will not be repeated here. However, because performance dashboards are best developed in an iterative fashion, project managers should make sure they allow plenty of time for business users to provide feedback to the development team on designs and deliverables.

Marketing Plan

The project plan should also include a marketing plan that is critical to selling the project to lower levels of the organization and stimulating usage and adoption once the team rolls out the solution. The marketing plan should define target customer segments inside the company that need to use or support the performance dashboard. For each segment, the marketing plan defines what messages to communicate, how frequently, and through what media or channels, as well as who will deliver the message. It may be wise to consult a marketing manager in your own company to help you set up the plan, which can make or break your project.

Project Dashboard

The project team should also apply performance management principles to manage its own project. That is, the team should define a mission statement, goals, objectives, and values to guide the project and then create a performance dashboard to measure their project every step of the way! The team's experience in building its own performance dashboard is a quick and clever way to train the team on performance dashboard concepts, best practices, and pitfalls.

The "KPI Team"

To define metrics, some organizations prefer to form a key performance indicator (KPI) team, whereas others hire business analysts to interview managers and subject matter experts. Consensus-driven organizations generally prefer to use KPI teams, which are comprised of two to seven business experts from various parts of the company. KPI team members are subject matter experts who are authorized to make decisions on behalf of their group. Ideally, they work full time on the project until it is complete, which could be several months or more depending on scope. The best KPI teams use an external facilitator to ensure that the team creates a balanced set of metrics that accurately portray and predict performance.

Business Analysts

Other organizations use business analysts or other methods to gather requirements and define metrics. For example, Hewlett Packard's Summerhayes hired two seasoned business analysts to conduct metric interviews. Both analysts have more than 15 years of business experience inside Hewlett Packard and are experienced managers who can "talk the talk."

The analysts first interview the group's top executive who wants to introduce the strategic dashboard to their organization and then follow up with subject matter experts who can explain the nuances of the business processes the scorecard will measure. When two or more executives use conflicting metrics, Summerhayes gets them together to hammer out the differences. Once the metrics are defined, the TSG project team hammers out a contract in which the group promises to provide data to the program team on a scheduled basis and meet quarterly to assess the progress of the initiative, usage trends, and what metrics (if any) need to be revised to meet strategic objectives and user requirements.

Likewise, TELUS's Lam recruited business analysts from the operations group to help collect requirements, standardize metrics, and develop sample screens. "We used our analysts to build a close working relationship with our development team," he says.

Using Surveys to Gather Requirements

International Truck and Engine Corporation took a different approach. Prior to conducting one-on-one interviews, the dashboard team sent a survey of open-ended questions to 27 financial managers across all divisions in the company. About two-thirds of the managers responded, and their comments generated 133 KPIs, many of which were common across multiple divisions. Business analysts then followed up the survey with one-on-one meetings to get a firm grasp on the business context in which managers were using the metrics.

"Our survey was a great way to help financial managers brainstorm all the KPIs they might need. If we had done 30-minute one-on-one interviews, we may not have gotten all the KPIs that we did. The survey gave them time to think about the issues, reference their existing reports, and provide thoughtful replies. We think this approach generated higher quality information than individual interviews," says Rappé.

The Technical Team

Besides a project champion and business analysts, the performance dashboard team contains technical specialists who translate metrics into a working application. If the technical team uses a commercial tool, it is best to include one or more vendor consultants on the team on a long-term basis. The best technical team members interact continuously with business users and other members of the team. Often, they accompany business analysts on interviews and feel comfortable calling subject matter experts to get clarification.

Small Teams

Good technical teams have few members. This enables the team to work quickly and efficiently meet user requirements and deadlines. "We keep ETL developers, report developers, and Web developers in the same room so they work collaboratively, which is ultimately more efficient than an assembly line approach where one group hands off work to another," says Kevin Lam, former manager of business performance at TELUS.

Longevity

The longer a technical team stays together, the more efficient it becomes. Technical team members learn each other's strengths and weaknesses and develop pride in their collective accomplishments. "I find developers with lots of drive and enthusiasm and give them plenty of freedom to experiment, which makes them excited to come to work every day. Also they can be very creative in developing solutions, where the business can only outline the issue," says Summerhayes.

SUMMARY

Launching a performance dashboard project is exciting when there is a visionary executive who understands the value the solution can provide and is eager to devote time and resources to make it happen. However, finding such sponsors is not always easy. Sometimes it is impossible to get a sponsor until the business landscape shifts or a new executive comes on board with a vision for using a performance dashboard to drive the organization in the right direction.

Selling the Project. Once you find a potential sponsor, you need to make a business case that describes the intangible benefits and quantifies the tangible ones. It is also helpful to develop a prototype to show what the performance dashboard might look like or find benchmark data that compare your organization with industry norms or its top competitors. In a worst-case scenario, it may be necessary to develop the application, at least for a smaller group, and seek a corporate sponsor after the fact to deploy it over the whole enterprise.

It is also imperative to sell the project to middle management and staff. First, this requires the sponsor to evangelize the solution and open doors for further meetings at the departmental level. Follow up meetings with one-on-one discussions and make sure you seek the feedback of managers and staff at all phases of the project, from design to development to post-deployment.

Secure Funding. Many teams bootstrap performance dashboards without initial funding. However, this does not give executives and managers license to choke the flow of money to these projects. Fast-growing or established projects require regular infusions of cash or else they lose momentum and die. Established projects need sustained funding to continue expanding into other parts of the organization. Usually, the IT department covers maintenance costs, whereas business units pay for extensions to the platform.

Where to Start? There is no right or wrong place in the organization to start a performance management project, whether it is an operational, tactical, or strategic dashboard. Each can be deployed initially to a single group or department and expanded to the rest of the enterprise over time. However, the best performance dashboards grow incrementally and iteratively one department or subject area at a time.

Create a Strong Team. A performance dashboard team consists of individuals with both business and technical expertise. The team establishes a tight rapport with the business and moves quickly to meet their requirements. An executive steering committee guides and evangelizes the project and drives consensus on metric definitions. Project managers incorporate iterative development techniques, develop comprehensive marketing plans, and use performance dashboards to measure their own progress and success.

CHAPTER 11

How to Create Effective Metrics

TOOLS OF CHANGE

One of the most common questions people ask about performance dashboards is "How do we define effective metrics?"

The answer is important because the metrics govern how employees do their jobs. The adage "What gets measured, gets done" is true. Metrics focus employees' attention on the tasks and processes that executives deem most critical to the success of the business. Metrics are like levers that executives can pull to move the organization in new and different directions. In fact, among all the tools available to executives to change the organization and move it in a new direction, performance measures are perhaps the most powerful.

Subsequently, executives need to treat metrics with respect. As powerful agents of change, metrics can drive unparalleled improvements or plunge the organization into chaos and confusion. If the metrics do not accurately translate the company's strategy and goals into concrete actions on a daily basis, the organization will flounder. Employees will work at cross-purposes, impeding each other's progress and leaving everyone tired and frustrated with little to show for their efforts. In short, the company will be efficient but ineffective.

Suboptimized Processes

A trucking company, for example, that measures performance by the percentage of on-time shipments may drive hauling costs skyward because the metric does nothing to discourage dispatchers from sending out half-empty trucks to meet their schedules. To keep costs in line, the company needs to add a second metric that measures the percentage of unused cargo capacity in outgoing trucks, and it needs to revise the first metric so it emphasizes meeting customer expectations for fast, reliable shipments rather than just on-time deliveries. This combination of metrics gives dispatchers leeway to contact customers and renegotiate shipping schedules if they know the customer may be flexible.

Another classic example is a call center that pays bonuses to customer service representatives based on how many customers they talk to per hour versus how many customer problems they solve. Representatives paid by the number of clients they talk to per hour are not likely to take the time to understand a customer's problem or provide a satisfactory response, especially when complex problems are involved. To address this problem, some call centers create a special team to handle complex calls; such calls are then measured by how effective the representatives are at problem solving, not how many calls they handle per hour.

Many organizations take a close look at the performance metrics when designing strategic dashboards. This is because the Balanced Scorecard methodology encourages organizations to create metrics that are leading indicators of performance rather than lagging indicators (i.e., financial metrics). However, the two examples given above demonstrate the importance of creating effective metrics in operational and tactical environments as well. Creating effective metrics is critical to the success of any performance dashboard.

The Art of Creating Metrics

Crafting sound metrics is more an art than a science. Although a metrics or KPI team may spend months collecting requirements, standardizing definitions and rules, prioritizing metrics, and soliciting feedback—in short, following all the rules for solid metric development—it still may not succeed. In fact, there is a danger that metrics teams will shoot for perfection and fall prey to "analysis paralysis." In reality, KPI teams can only get 80 percent of the way to an effective set of metrics; the last 20 percent comes from deploying the metrics, seeing how they impact behavior and performance, and then adjusting them accordingly.

"Only when you put the metrics out there, do you really understand what behaviors you are driving," says John Lochrie, senior vice president of Direct Energy Essential Home Services.

UNDERSTANDING METRICS

Types of Metrics

Key Performance Indicators

Metrics used in performance dashboards are typically called key performance indicators (KPIs) because they measure how well the organization or individual performs an operational, tactical, or strategic activity that is critical for the current and future success of the organization. There are two major types of KPIs: leading and lagging indicators. Leading indicators measure activities that have a significant effect on future performance, whereas lagging indicators, such as most financial metrics, measure the output of past activity.

Leading Indicators

Leading indicators are powerful measures to include in a performance dashboard, but are sometimes difficult to define. They measure key drivers of business value and are harbingers of future outcomes. To do this, leading indicators either measure activity either in its current state (i.e., number of sales meetings today) or in a future state (i.e., number of sales meetings scheduled for the next two weeks), the latter being more powerful because it gives individuals and their managers more time to influence the outcome (see Spotlight 11.1).

SPOTLIGHT 11.1 SAMPLE LEADING INDICATORS

It is easy to define lagging indicators, but it takes imagination and persistence to identify leading indicators. One must follow the trail backward from results measured by a lagging indicator to a first-mover driver. Because each lagging indicator or outcome has numerous drivers, the key to defining effective leading indicators is to find the one or two drivers that have the greatest effect on the results desired by executives. Here are a few examples of leading indicators and the outcomes (or lagging metrics) they influence.

Leading Indicators or Value Drivers		Lagging Indicators or Outcomes
Number of clients that sales people meet face to face each week	→	Sales revenue
Complex repairs completed successfully during the first call or visit	→	Customer satisfaction
Number of signed, positive employee suggestions each week; ratio of positive to negative comments	→	Employee satisfaction
Number of parts for which orders exceed forecasts within 30 days of scheduled delivery	→	Per unit manufacturing costs
Number of days with lowest prices for comparable products	→	Market share
Number of customers who are delinquent paying their first bill	→	Customer churn
Number of loyalty rewards cashed in each month	→	Customer loyalty

For example, Quicken Loans identified two KPIs that correlate with the ability of mortgage consultants to meet daily sales quotas: the amount of time they spend on the phone with customers and the number of clients they speak with each day. Quicken Loans now displays these two "current-state" KPIs prominently on its operational dashboards. More importantly, however, it created a third KPI based on the previous two that projects every 15 minutes whether mortgage consultants are on track to meet their daily quotas. This "future-state" metric, which is based on a simple statistical regression algorithm using data from the current state metrics, enables sales managers to identify which mortgage consultants they should assist during the next hour or so.

Brainstorming Leading Indicators

Most people are so well trained at measuring outcomes instead of drivers that it takes them a while to shift their mental focus and become adept at creating effective KPIs. Consultant Paul Niven suggests using facilitated brainstorming sessions to break mental logjams. Whenever a user suggests a metric, the meeting facilitator should say, "Good, what drives the performance of that measure?" The individual or group then brainstorms new metrics, and the facilitator repeats the question. Before long the group has performed a root-cause analysis of the initial metric and generated one or more effective leading indicators.[1]

Diagnostic Measures

Some measures do not necessarily fit neatly into a leading or lagging indicator category, but they are still important to capture. In most cases, these metrics signal the health of various operational initiatives or processes and are good candidates for a departmental or workgroup dashboard. Niven calls these types of KPIs "diagnostic" metrics. Some examples might be net margins on key product lines, profitability of the top 10 percent of channels, or days of sales outstanding.

KPI CHARACTERISTICS

Actionable KPIs

Besides predicting future performance, KPIs have numerous other characteristics (see Spotlight 11.2). Perhaps the most important attribute of a KPI is that it is actionable. That is, if a metric trends downward, users should know what corrective actions to take to improve performance. There is no purpose in measuring activity if users cannot change the outcome.

SPOTLIGHT 11.2   TWELVE CHARACTERISTICS OF EFFECTIVE KPIs

1. **Aligned.** KPIs are always aligned with corporate strategy and objectives.

2. **Owned.** Every KPI is "owned" by an individual or group on the business side who is accountable for its outcome.

3. **Predictive.** KPIs measure drivers of business value. Thus, they are "leading" indicators of performance desired by the organization.

4. **Actionable.** KPIs are populated with timely, actionable data so users can intervene to improve performance before it is too late.

5. **Few in number.** KPIs should focus users on a few high-value tasks, not scatter their attention and energy on too many things.

6. **Easy to understand.** KPIs should be straightforward and easy to understand, not based on complex indexes that users do not know how to influence directly.

7. **Balanced and linked.** KPIs should balance and reinforce each other, not undermine each other and suboptimize processes.

8. **Trigger changes.** The act of measuring a KPI should trigger a chain reaction of positive changes in the organization, especially when it is monitored by the CEO.

9. **Standardized.** KPIs are based on standard definitions, rules, and calculations so they can be integrated across dashboards throughout the organization.

10. **Context driven.** KPIs put performance in context by applying targets and thresholds to performance so users can gauge their progress over time.

11. **Reinforced with incentives.** Organizations can magnify the impact of KPIs by attaching compensation or incentives to them. However, they should do this cautiously, applying incentives only to well-understood and stable KPIs.

12. **Relevant.** KPIs gradually lose their impact over time, so they must be periodically reviewed and refreshed.

Accountability

An actionable KPI implies that an individual or group exists that "owns" the KPI, is held accountable for its results, and knows what to do when performance declines. Without accountability, measures are meaningless. Thus, it is critical to assign a single business owner to each KPI and make it part of his or her job description and performance review. It is also important to train users to interpret the KPIs and how to respond. Often, this training is best done "on the job" by having veterans transfer their knowledge to newcomers.

Some companies attach incentives to metrics, which always underscores the importance of the metric in the minds of individuals. However, just publishing performance scores among peer groups is enough to get most people's competitive juices flowing. It is best to assign accountability to an individual or small group rather than a large group, in which the sense of ownership and accountability for the metric become diffused.

Empowered

Companies also need to empower individuals to act on the information in a performance dashboard. This seems obvious, but many organizations that deploy performance dashboards hamstring workers by circumscribing the actions they can take to meet goals. Companies with hierarchical cultures often have difficulty here, especially when dealing with front-line workers whose actions they have historically scripted. Performance dashboards require companies to replace scripts with guidelines that give users more leeway to make the right decisions.

Timely

Actionable KPIs require right-time data. The KPI must be updated frequently enough so the responsible individual or group can intervene to improve performance before it is too late. Operational dashboards usually do this by default, but many tactical and strategic dashboards do not. Many of these latter systems contain only lagging indicators of performance and are only updated weekly or monthly. These types of performance management systems are merely electronic versions of monthly operational review meetings, not powerful tools of organizational change.

Some people argue that executives do not need actionable information because they primarily make strategic decisions for which monthly updates are good enough. However, the most powerful change agent in an organization is a top executive armed with an actionable KPI.

David Parmenter, the CEO of Waymark Solutions, a performance management consultancy in New Zealand, recounts the story of Lord King, chairman of British Airways, who reportedly turned around the ailing airline in the 1980s using a single KPI: the timely arrival and departure of airplanes.[2]

"[Lord King] was notified, wherever he was in the world, when a British Airways plane was delayed over a certain time, say two hours. The British Airways airport manager at the relevant airport knew that if a plane was delayed beyond this threshold, he or she would receive a personal call from the Chairman. It was not long before British Airways planes had a reputation for leaving on time," says Parmenter.

Trigger Points

The British Airways story illustrates another characteristic of KPIs. They trigger a chain reaction of process improvements throughout the organization. Effective KPIs sit at the nexus of multiple interrelated processes that drive the organization. When activated, these KPIs create a ripple effect throughout the organization and produce stunning gains in performance.

For instance, late planes affect many core metrics and processes at airlines. Costs increase because airlines have to accommodate passengers who miss connecting flights; customer satisfaction declines because customers dislike missing flights; worker morale slips because they have to deal with unruly customers; and supplier relationships are strained because missed flights disrupt service schedules and lowers quality.

When an executive focuses on a single, powerful KPI, it creates a ripple effect throughout the organization and substantially changes the way an organization carries out its core operations. Managers and staff figure out ways to change business processes and behaviors so they do not receive a career-limiting memo from the CEO.

Easy to Understand

In addition, KPIs must be understandable. Employees must know what is being measured, how it is being calculated, and, more importantly, what they should do (and should not do) to affect the KPI positively. Complex KPIs that consist of indexes, ratios, or multiple calculations are difficult to understand and, more importantly, not clearly actionable.

However, even with straightforward KPIs, many users struggle to understand what the KPIs really mean and how to respond appropriately. It is critical to train individuals whose performance is being tracked and follow up with regular reviews to ensure they understand what the KPIs mean and know the appropriate actions to take. This level of supervision also helps spot individuals who may be cheating the system by exploiting unforeseen loopholes.

"We hold forums where we show field technicians how our repeat call metric works and how it might impact them. We then have the best technicians meet with others to discuss strategy and techniques that they use to positively influence the metric," says Ripley Maddock, director of customer management at Direct Energy Essential Home Services.

It is also important to train people on the targets applied to metrics. For instance, is a high score good or bad? If the metric is customer loyalty, a high score is good, but if the metric is customer churn, a high score is bad. Sometimes a metric can have dual polarity, that is, a high score is good until a certain point and then it turns bad. For instance, a telemarketer who makes 20 calls per hour may be doing exceptionally well, but one who makes 30 calls per hour is cycling through clients too rapidly and possibly failing to establish good rapport with callers.

Accurate

It is difficult to create KPIs that accurately measure an activity. Sometimes, unforeseen variables influence measures. For example, a company may see a jump in worker productivity, but the increase is due more to an uptick in inflation than internal performance improvements. This is because the company calculates worker productivity by dividing revenues by the total number of workers it employs. Thus, a rise in the inflation rate artificially boosts revenues—the numerator in the metric—and increases the worker productivity score even though workers did not become more efficient during this period.

Also, it is easy to create metrics that do not accurately measure the intended objective. For example, many organizations struggle to find a metric to measure employee satisfaction or dissatisfaction. Some use surveys, but some employees do not answer the questions honestly. Others use absenteeism as a sign of dissatisfaction but these numbers are skewed significantly by employees who miss work to attend a funeral, care for a sick family member, or stay home when daycare is unavailable. Some experts suggest that a better metric, although not a perfect one, might be the number of sick days since unhappy employees often take more sick days than satisfied employees.

Relevant

A KPI has a natural life cycle. When first introduced, the KPI energizes the workforce and performance improves. Over time, the KPI loses its impact and must be refreshed, revised, or discarded. Thus, it is imperative that organizations continually review KPI usage.

"We usually see a tremendous upswing in performance when we first implement a scorecard application," says Martin Summerhayes, a program manager at Hewlett Packard Technology Solutions Group (TSG), "but after a while, we often see performance trail off again. In the end you can't control people, so you have to continually reeducate them on the importance of the processes that the metrics are measuring or you have to change the processes."

Performance dashboard teams should track KPI usage automatically, using system logs that capture the number of users and queries for each metric in the system. The team should then present this information to the performance dashboard steering committee, which needs to decide what to do about underused metrics. For example, Hewlett Packard TSG holds quarterly meetings to review KPI usage, which it tracks at a detailed level. "If a metric isn't being accessed, we go back to the owners and see whether they still want it. If not, we remove the metric," Summerhayes says.

EXHIBIT 11.1   HOW OFTEN DO YOU MODIFY KPIS?

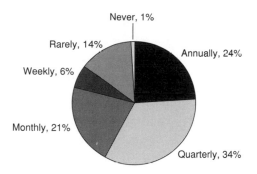

Never, 1%

Rarely, 14%

Annually, 24%

Weekly, 6%

Monthly, 21%

Quarterly, 34%

Most companies modify KPIs annually or quarterly. Based on 360 respondents.

Source: Wayne Eckerson, "Best Practices in Business Performance Management: Business and Technical Strategies" (*TDWI Report Series*, 2003).

Research from The Data Warehousing Institute (TDWI) shows that most organizations modify KPIs on a quarterly or annual basis. Only 15 percent of organizations "rarely" or "never" modify KPIs. The most common reason for modifying KPIs is to adapt to changes in business strategy (77 percent) followed by the need to make KPIs "more relevant" (see Exhibits 11.1 and 11.2).

EXHIBIT 11.2   WHY DO YOU MODIFY KPIS?

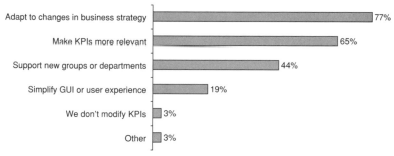

Adapt to changes in business strategy — 77%

Make KPIs more relevant — 65%

Support new groups or departments — 44%

Simplify GUI or user experience — 19%

We don't modify KPIs — 3%

Other — 3%

Most companies modify KPIs to adapt to changes in business strategy or make KPIs more relevant. Based on 360 respondents who could select more than one choice.

Source: Wayne Eckerson, "Best Practices in Business Performance Management: Business and Technical Strategies" (*TDWI Report Series*, 2003).

CREATING METRICS

Gathering Requirements

Most performance dashboard teams use interviews and surveys to gather requirements as a way to determine the right KPIs to create. Interviews are usually done by business analysts who ask open-ended questions to top executives about the business strategy, objectives, goals, and expectations for the project, among other things. The analysts then gather additional detail by interviewing mid-level managers and subject matter experts who can fill in the details of specific processes, identify data sources, and discuss the metrics used in current reports, what those metrics mean, and how they are calculated.

Requirements Forms

To guide business analysts during interviews, most project teams create a template or requirements form to capture requirements in a standardized way. This ensures that analysts ask a consistent set of questions and gather a comprehensive set of information that is easily synthesized and standardized.

Hewlett Packard TSG, for example, uses two forms to define new metrics for its strategic dashboard, one to gather business requirements and one to define technical specifications. The business requirements form or template asks for a general description of the metric, how it aligns with corporate strategy, the name of the metric, its owner, its target and stretch goals, and how the metric is calculated, among other things (see Exhibit 11.3).

The technical specification document provides technical details for each proposed metric. For example, it asks for data sources and formats, extraction logic, scorecard layouts, target specifications, analytical layouts (including columns, rows, data types, formats, and formulas), chart views, and security requirements. Most importantly, the form asks for the business and technical owners of the metrics so project team members can follow up with additional questions, if needed.

Understand Metric Usage

Although the above data about proposed metrics is important, most project teams find it is critical to understand the context within which the business plans to use the metrics. This usually involves follow-up interviews or creating use-case scenarios that document the processes and ways in which people use the metrics.

For example, International Truck and Engine Corporation conducted follow-up interviews with several managers, who shared that they usually ask a business

EXHIBIT 11.3   BUSINESS REQUIREMENTS FORM

P M M S	PMMS LIBRA Metric Request Form **Submitted By:** _____ **Date:** _____
Business or Function	*What business or function do you request a metric for:*
Region/Country Scope	*What is the geographical scope of the metric:*
Metric Perspective	*What balance scorecard perspective does the metric fit in? Customer, Financial, Internal, Learning:*
Metric Title	*Give a brief name to the metric (less than 20 characters)*
Metric Description	*Describe the metric in business terms*
Business Justification & Strategic Importance	*Define if the metric is a strategic metric or an operational excellence measure and justify it. How does the metric measure progress towards strategy execution?*
Metric Business Owner, Subject Matter Expert, Business IM Owner	*Define the owners of the metric either from the business or the function that will be measured on the results (can be name or job title). Also, who collects, reviews, approves and reports the data?*
Metric Goals	*Specify both the target and stretch goals for the metric (indicate over what time period) Also, how is the goal selected and who approves the goal?* **Target :** **Stretch:** **Goals setting process and approval from:**
Definition, Calculation, and Criteria	*How is the metric calculated? What criteria is used? Identify any differences between WW or Sub-Region definitions.*
Data Source and Availability	*What is the data source for the actual results and how is it collected? When is the data available? (i.e., which workday, every six months, annually, etc.)*
Supporting Reports	*What detailed reports are available to support the metric results?*
Related Metrics	*List of upstream metrics (influenced by this metric)?. List of downstream metrics (have influence on this metric)?*
Additional Information	*Input additional information related to the metric.*
Status	*Status of the metric request from the PMMS WW Program Office team (approved, pending additional info), targeted implementation date, etc.*

Sample form used by Hewlett Packard TSG to capture requirements for a strategic dashboard.

analyst to create a detailed report for them when they notice a downward trend in a metric. The team quickly realized it could provide significant value to the managers and free up analysts' time if it provided detailed data and reports alongside the metrics.

Validating Metrics

Elusive Nuances

The problem with many metrics is that they are difficult to understand or implement. Sometimes the metric does not accurately capture the nuances of a business process, making it difficult for the project team to figure out what data to capture and how to calculate it.

For example, executives at Direct Energy requested a "repeat call" metric to track the efficiency of field service technicians, but it took the project team considerable time to clarify the meaning of the metric. For example, field service technicians primarily repair home energy equipment, but they can also sell it. So, is a repeat call a bad thing if the technician also brings literature about replacement systems or makes a sale? Or, what if a homeowner only lets a technician make minor repairs to an aging system to save money, but then calls shortly afterwards because the home's furnace broke down again?

Most business processes contain innumerable nuances that must be understood and built into the metric if it is to have any validity, especially if the metric is used as a basis for compensation. The worst-case scenario is when employees discover these nuances after the metrics have been deployed, which stirs up a hornet's nest of trouble and wreaks havoc on both the performance management system and compensation policies.

Missing or Corrupted Data

Sometimes, the data to support a metric simply do not exist, or they are in poor condition and difficult to integrate. The most well-defined KPIs are irrelevant if there are no data to support them. Executives who want to create a strategic dashboard frequently assume the data warehouse or some other system contains all the data necessary to support their metrics. To get a handle on data issues early in the process, executives need to appoint a systems analyst to scout data sources for potential KPIs so executives can decide whether to revise a proposed KPI or create a new system or process to capture the data they want.

Data that are in poor condition and chock full of missing or invalid values, duplicate records, or inconsistent data types might take weeks or months to clean up, if at all. Here, executives need to decide whether the metric is important enough to warrant a major data reconditioning project or should be dropped or replaced by another. Another common problem is that the data required to populate a metric are spread across multiple systems that capture and format data differently. Even if the distributed data are in good condition, which they usually are not, the project team must expend significant effort to integrate the data in a consistent fashion.

"Data integration is critically important but it is often overlooked, especially by the business side of the house," says Patrick Morrissey, manager of performance management at Business Objects. "Business people often don't know there is a problem until the technical team reports back that it can't deliver all the relevant KPIs. The larger the organization, the bigger the data integration challenge."

Establish a New Process

In some cases, it is fairly simple to create a new process to capture high-quality data for a KPI. For example, executives who want to track the number of clients that each salesperson meets face to face each week can have the sales department fill out a time sheet of appointments and submit it to the performance dashboard team each week. Similarly, executives who want to track customer satisfaction can commission market research firms to conduct blind surveys and submit the results for inclusion in the strategic dashboard.

However, not all KPIs can be populated with manual data. Sometimes executives may need to commission the creation of a new operational system. For example, executives who want to track daily grocery sales at the SKU level might need to build a multimillion dollar transaction system to obtain the data. Executives need to weigh the value of the KPI and the processes it measures against the cost of building the new system.

Project Delays

Experts say that most strategic dashboards are missing 20 to 30 percent of the data they need when starting out but that this should not delay or postpone the project. The organization can still benefit from the other metrics while it builds systems to capture the remaining data. However, these problems underscore the importance of having technical people on the project team to ascertain the true costs of delivering the required data to populate KPIs.

Standardizing Metrics

Standardizing Terms Is Key to Integration

A big challenge in creating KPIs is getting people to agree on the definitions of terms, such as sales, profits, or customer. As mentioned earlier in this book, standardizing terms is critical if organizations are going to distribute performance dashboards to different groups at multiple levels of the organization and roll up the results. Without standards, the organization risks spinning off multiple, inconsistent performance dashboards whose information cannot be easily reconciled.

Scope Increases the Challenge

The challenge in standardizing terms increases with the scope of the project and the number of distinct groups the performance dashboard supports. The more groups and people, the more divergence there will be in the definitions of terms, rules, and calculation that compose a metric. Sometimes the only way to resolve these differences is for top executives to get together and hash out a standard with which they all can live.

"We have two distinct businesses, commercial and government, and the measurements each uses are very different, which makes it very challenging to develop corporate-wide standards," says John Monczewski, senior manager of reporting at Booz Allen Hamilton. "We've had strong backing from our CEO to make this work and we've made a lot of progress. But even with that, it takes a lot of time. Our partners have decided to postpone trying to resolve some issues until a later time."

Hewlett Packard TSG faced a similar situation. "We wanted a worldwide metric for cost reduction and we discovered that the operation and finance people had 32 ways to measure cost reduction. Some of these were duplicates, others measured different facets of costs. The project team arranged a meeting between two top financial executives and they agreed to standardize on six metrics for cost reduction," says Summerhayes.

Prioritizing Metrics

Less Is More

One thing many people ask about KPIs is: "How many should we have?" The short answer is: "As few as reasonably possible." There is a natural tendency among organizations to keep adding metrics and never delete any. As a result, they lose their power to grab the attention of employees and focus their behavior on key value-added activities. "There is always a temptation to add more metrics as time goes on," says Direct Energy Essential Home Services' Maddock. "When people have too many metrics to track, the message gets blurred."

Guidelines for Metrics per User

Some experts say that organizations should limit the number of KPIs to between three and seven metrics per user, because most people have difficulty concentrating on more than seven things at a time. However, the optimal number of metrics depends more on a person's role and level in the company than on an arbitrary number.

As a rule of thumb, workers managing operational processes should track fewer metrics, probably less than a handful because they have less time to respond to issues, whereas executives responsible for setting strategic direction should view many more metrics, perhaps a dozen or more. To reduce the visual confusion of displaying a lot of metrics on the screen at once, designers should group metrics in folders or tabs or nest related metrics under a lead metric.

Guidelines for Metrics per Dashboard

From an organizational perspective, a performance dashboard may have dozens of metrics or more. The total number of metrics depends on the size of the organization, the scope of the project, and the complexity of the organization's business model. Large organizations with complex processes may require hundreds of metrics to measure performance accurately.

Hewlett Packard TSG's Summerhayes, for example, says that it often takes multiple metrics to measure key processes from end to end. For example, a repair call resolution metric might require five sub-metrics to capture performance accurately at each stage in the repair process, from taking an order and scheduling the repair to validating the repair and receiving customer payment. One metric may not shed enough insight to help managers know what part of an end-to-end process is experiencing problems.

If in doubt about how many KPIs to create, err on the high side. What does not get measured, does not get done, and what does not get done can hurt the organization. The key to selecting metrics judiciously is to validate that they are aligned with strategic objectives and distribute them to performance dashboards at the appropriate level in the organization. Not all metrics need to appear on the top-level scorecard; most, in fact, should be delegated to lower-level ones.

According to research from TDWI, most organizations adhere to the "less is more" rule regarding KPIs. Organizations deploy a median of 20 KPIs in the entire Performance Dashboard and a median of seven KPIs per user (see Exhibit 11.4).

Another common question that people ask is how often they should refresh metrics with new data. The primary factor is the role of the user of the metric and the frequency with which they need to make decisions. If the person is an executive with primarily strategic decision-making responsibilities, then monthly or quarterly updates are probably fine. Of course, if the executive wants to monitor critical operational processes, as many do, then the updates should happen in right time.

Balancing Metrics

The most important characteristic of a KPI is that it leads to positive outcomes. This is easier said than done. A KPI alone will not change behavior or improve

EXHIBIT 11.4   AVERAGE AND MEDIAN KPIS

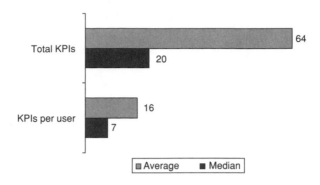

Organizations that have deployed Performance Dashboards average 64 total KPIs (16 median) and 20 per user (7 median). The median numbers reflect the larger number of organizations. Based on 360 respondents.

Source: Wayne Eckerson, "Best Practices in Business Performance Management: Business and Technical Strategies" (*TDWI Report Series*, 2003).

performance. It is merely a tool to communicate what workers need to do to help the company achieve its strategic objectives and, in the process, improve their position in the company.

"Measures without meetings are useless," says Maddock. "Unless managers hold regular sit-down meetings with their staff to review performance, nothing will change. Managers need to ask, 'What are you doing about this number? How will we avoid this happening next time?'"

Organizations as a whole appear to be struggling to find KPIs that impact employee performance, according to research from TDWI. Only 13 percent said their KPIs are "very effective" at changing employee performance; 34 percent said they were "fairly effective." Meanwhile, 23 percent said their KPIs were only "somewhat effective," and 19 percent were not sure (see Exhibit 11.5).

Finding Loopholes

One problem is that users often try to circumvent established KPIs out of laziness or personal gain. "Users always look for loopholes in your metrics," says Direct Energy's Maddock. At Hewlett Packard's TSG, to prevent users from "fudging" customer satisfaction numbers, the company hires a market research firm to audit customer surveys.

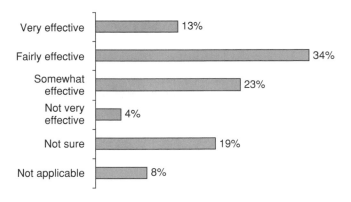

| EXHIBIT 11.5 | HOW EFFECTIVELY DO KPIS CHANGE EMPLOYEE PERFORMANCE? |

Very effective — 13%
Fairly effective — 34%
Somewhat effective — 23%
Not very effective — 4%
Not sure — 19%
Not applicable — 8%

A third of respondents say that KPIs are "fairly effective" at changing employee performance. Based on 360 respondents.

Source: Wayne Eckerson, "Best Practices in Business Performance Management: Business and Technical Strategies" (*TDWI Report Series,* 2003).

Sub-Optimization

In other cases, KPIs may unintentionally undermine each other. For instance, a logistics group that is trying to streamline inventory costs may decide to reduce inventory, which makes it difficult for a retail store to prevent stockouts of fast-moving items—a key performance measure for them. "We've seen our staff take unexpected action to boost a metric that turned out to undermine other measures," Maddock says.

Strategy Maps

One way to avoid having metrics undermine each other and sub-optimize processes is to create strategy maps that show cause-and-effect linkages among objectives and the metrics that represent them. Strategy maps can help executives clarify their assumptions about what drives the business and debug the objectives and metrics that comprise the strategy. If a positive improvement in one metric doesn't lead to an expected bump in a related one, then this is a sign that executives need to examine their assumptions behind the linkages. It may cause the team to revise the metrics or create a new one that sits between the previous two and links to both.

Putting Performance in Context

By definition, KPIs provide context. They show users or groups what is an acceptable level of performance. KPIs embed organizational expectations in the form of targets and thresholds.

Targets and Thresholds

Targets define a desired state at a particular point in time. For example, a target might be a 10 percent growth in net profits by year end. Ideally, targets are set by executives and managers with input from subordinates. Targets can come from many sources: annual budgets, strategic plans, forecasts, industry benchmarks, competitors, or comparisons with a previous point in time, such as last year, last month, or last week. Thresholds, on the other hand, provide an upper and lower range of acceptable performance for each target in a given time period. Thresholds generally operate on a graduated rolling basis; that is, the thresholds gradually increase each period, usually monthly, until the desired end-state or target is reached.

Target Scope

Organizations may want to establish several types of targets for various KPIs. Most KPIs will have an *annual target* that is decomposed into weekly or monthly targets and thresholds. In addition, some KPIs may have a three- to five-year goal that serves as a *stretch target*. This type of target may be applied to operational processes that are critical to the strategy or that need substantial improvement. Executives set stretch targets either by getting input from workers and managers in the trenches, hiring consultants to assess the efficiency and potential of existing processes, or referring to industry benchmarks that define "best in class" performance.

The final type of target is a *visionary target*. This target reinforces a company's vision statement of where it wants to be in five to ten years. The visionary target should galvanize employees and create a sense of unity and purpose that causes the organization to perform at a much higher level. Executives usually set visionary targets in response to competitive threats. For example, President John F. Kennedy's 1961 call to "land a man on the moon and return him safely to Earth" before the end of the 1960s was a response to the Soviet Union's success in putting the first man into orbit.

Creating Realistic Targets

Setting realistic targets is not easy. Targets should not be so challenging that they discourage workers, nor should they be too easy, which creates complacency.

Also, managers should be aware of ways that workers may try to circumvent targets or "game the system." Often setting targets is a matter of trial and error. However, it is best to get as close to realistic targets as possible at the outset to avoid problems.

The best way to create targets is to interview executives and managers in an attempt to understand their goals and objectives for the areas they manage. They may often use last year's targets or goals as a basis for creating targets for the upcoming year. Other sources of targets may be industry benchmarks or customers and suppliers, which may already have standards by which they measure your organization. For instance, a manufacturing company may expect a supplier to deliver 95 percent of shipments on time and in full with proper bar codes or RFID labels.

It is important not to set targets in a vacuum. Although it is tempting for executives and managers to set targets based on their own knowledge of the business, such unilateral goal setting does not engender goodwill among the people who are responsible for achieving the goals. It is critical that executives gather input from employees to understand what targets are reasonable and gain their buy-in to the project. Ultimately, employees are doing the work and should feel that the goals are reasonable.

Technical Considerations

Technically, it is not easy to apply targets and thresholds to metrics. Developers need to create a rules engine that lets users define targets and thresholds for each KPI using a simple Boolean engine (i.e., "if, then, else" rules). The rules need to be applied on a periodic basis to data stored by a repository managed directly by the performance dashboard or a related data mart or data warehouse. This can happen on an event-driven basis (e.g., when the database is updated) or at regular intervals (e.g., every ten seconds, ten minutes, or ten days).

Alerts

The system should also let developers and end-users define rules about when and how users should be notified if parameters are exceeded for a given metric (i.e., alerts) as well as when and how to initiate automated actions based on those alerts (i.e., agents). Visual alerts should be accompanied by text that explains the problem, a report that users can click to see actual data, and a URL to initiate additional action, such as to refresh a report or display contact information for someone to call. The rules engine should accept events from third-party systems as well.

SUMMARY

Agents of Change. KPIs are powerful agents of organizational change. Creating effective KPIs is challenging; it is more of an art than a science. It is easy to create poor metrics that cause performance to decline, business processes to be suboptimal, and users and executives to be frustrated. To avoid these problems, organizations should understand the characteristics exhibited by effective metrics.

Leading versus Lagging. The two primary types of KPIs are leading and lagging indicators. Lagging indicators measure past activity, whereas leading indicators measure drivers of future performance. Performance dashboards should contain a healthy dose of leading indicators to optimize future outcomes.

KPI Characteristics. Effective KPIs exhibit many other characteristics. They are actionable, empowering users to intervene in a process. Actionable KPIs, by definition, must be updated frequently enough so that empowered users can take action in a timely manner. Also, KPIs must be few in number, easy to understand, and have an owner who is accountable for the outcomes. KPIs also put performance in context by applying targets and thresholds to performance. The targets may be based on the annual budget or plan, three- to five-year strategic plans, or a top executive's long-term vision for the company. Targets are typically applied using thresholds that define low and high levels of acceptable performance.

Far-Reaching Impact. Effective KPIs trigger positive change. They sit at the nexis of many core processes. When the organization focuses on a KPI, it creates a ripple effect of positive changes throughout the organization, especially when the CEO actively monitors and manages that KPI. Effective KPIs are also based on corporate standards so they can be integrated across performance dashboards, if needed. Standard definitions and rules for calculating metrics enable companies to aggregate data from lower to higher level views in the performance dashboard.

Reality Check. It is important to select KPIs that can be populated with data that do not undermine each other or create a loophole that lets users cheat the system. One way to vet KPIs is to create a strategy map that defines cause-and-effect linkages among objectives in the performance dashboard. Because KPIs lose their impact over time, organizations must continually reevaluate and refresh them. This involves monitoring system usage and getting feedback from members of the performance dashboard steering committee.

NOTES

1. Paul Niven, *Balanced Scorecard Step by Step: Maximizing Performance and Maintaining Results* (John Wiley & Sons, 2002), p. 116.
2. David Parmenter, "The New Thinking on KPIs: Why You May Be Working with the Wrong Measures," BetterManagement.com.

CHAPTER 12

How to Design Effective Dashboard Screens

This chapter focuses on how to design the "look and feel" of a performance dashboard so that it is easy to use and visually appealing. The visual interface—what users can see and do on the screens—can make or break a performance dashboard.

Workers do not have to use a performance dashboard; it is not a requirement for doing their jobs. They will use it if it makes them more productive and effective, but they will shun it if it is not intuitive and consumes too much time and effort for the value it delivers. They will go elsewhere to obtain the information they need or get by on intuition and gut feel.

Creating dashboard screens is challenging, and few people have the background in visual design techniques required to do a good job. Most rely on their own visual instincts, get feedback from users, and go from there. Unfortunately, this usually produces a visual interface that is cluttered and complex, forcing users to work too hard to discern the pertinent facts they need to know. Surprisingly, few organizations hire visual design experts to lend advice, and few have usability labs that observe workers using a piece of software and recommend enhancements to the visual design.

Nevertheless, designing dashboard screens and functionality is rewarding. It is the fun part of building performance dashboards, the grand finale when users finally see the fruits of the initiative and get excited about using the new system.

GENERAL GUIDELINES FOR MANAGING THE DESIGN PROCESS

Focus on Data and Process First

It is a fact that the quickest way for a magazine to boost sales is to put a picture of a pretty woman on the cover. In the same way, it's no exaggeration to say that a pretty "face" sells a performance dashboard. A surefire way to get executives excited about a dashboard project is to show them a mockup of a dashboard screen with their metrics wrapped in fancy graphics. However, selling a dashboard screen and delivering a performance management system are two different things. A project team should be wary of raising users' expectations too early in the process.

"It's often too easy to create a fancy-looking dashboard and get executive support. But if you don't have real data to put into it, it's really just smoke and mirrors. It's important that you do the necessary work to get to the point where the glitz is functioning properly. That includes defining metrics and targets as well as getting systems data. If we had gone in with glitz and glamour before building the infrastructure, we would have set unrealistic expectations and wouldn't be as far along as we are now," says Kevin Lam, performance manager at TELUS (see Spotlight 12.1 and Exhibit 12.1).

SPOTLIGHT 12.1   USING STRATEGIC DASHBOARDS AT THE DEPARTMENTAL LEVEL

In 2001, TELUS, a leading Canadian telecommunications company, implemented a strategic dashboard in its operations group that has enabled the company to increase the productivity of workers significantly, including field technicians, engineers, customer service representatives, dispatchers, and their supervisors and managers. Specifically, the Web-based scorecard helped increase workers' productive hours by 9 percent and reduce the time to complete a job by 16 percent, saving approximately $1 million to $2 million a month.

"The scorecard was one of the primary catalysts driving these productivity gains," says Kevin Lam, manager of business performance at TELUS. "It's given us line-of-sight visibility into our daily performance from our vice presidents all the way to individual technicians. Without the measurements and structure in place, we would have limited visibility on where we stand or how or what to improve."

TELUS kicked off the dashboard project in 2001 in response to a company-wide initiative to cut costs and improve operational efficiencies. The initiative was designed to reduce overhead and make the firm more competitive after a series of mergers, followed by the economic downturn in 2000 that hit the telecommunications industry particularly hard.

TELUS's goal was to reduce operating costs without long-term negative impact to government-regulated customer service levels. "We had tinkered with Balanced Scorecards as a way to measure and manage worker productivity, but now we had no choice. We had to be more efficient or lose market share," says Lam.

SPOTLIGHT 12.1   *(CONTINUED)*

Today, the firm provides "actionable scorecards" to 300 managers with visibility to over 2,000 front-line team members. Every scorecard displays the same metrics and targets, but the values differ based on a user's position in the firm. The information rolls up several levels from technician all the way to the executive vice president. This way users can see how their performance contributes to the overall productivity of the business unit, says Lam.

The system also lets users drill into and slice the information any way they want. They can view the information by level, metric, time period, or interval (i.e., daily, weekly, monthly). If required, they can even drill into transaction data, such as a trouble ticket, to find specific information about an incident. The information values are color coded so users can see how their performance compares with predefined targets.

The system replaced a hodgepodge of manually crafted Excel reports that never delivered consistent information in a timely or detailed fashion. "We could never have achieved significant productivity gains without changing the way we deliver and use information," says Lam.

EXHIBIT I2.I   A STRATEGIC DASHBOARD FOR THE OPERATIONS
                 GROUP AT TELUS

CSD Performance Metrics
Employee Level Metrics Report, Summary by VP
Timeframe is Weekly - From February 15, 2004 to February 21, 2004
Updated on 2004/04/13

Drilldown: (Next Level in Employee Hierarchy)

VP	Weeks	Productivity Factor	Availability OBJ<	Availability PCT	Managed Absence OBJ<	Managed Absence PCT	Utilization OBJ<	Utilization PCT	Training OBJ<	Training PCT	ADMIN OBJ<	Administrative Meetings PCT	OT OBJ<	Overtime PCT	OOT PCT
VP Name	08	71.33	80%	85.14%	3%	6.04%	92%	92.70%	5%	1.35%	3%	5.95%	8%	5.94%	1.87%
VP Name	08	72.82	80%	87.23%	3%	3.58%	92%	90.22%	5%	3.99%	3%	5.79%	8%	8.24%	.72%

Drilldown: (Next Level in Employee Hierarchy)

VP	Director	Weeks	Productivity Factor	Availability OBJ<	Availability PCT	Managed Absence OBJ<	Managed Absence PCT	Utilization OBJ<	Utilization PCT	Training OBJ<	Training PCT	ADMIN OBJ<	Adminis Meeti PC
VP Name	Dir Name	08	88.26	80%	84.20%	3%	8.67%	92%	83.92%	5%	1.14%	3%	
	Dir Name	08	80.42	80%	89.70%	3%	5.95%	92%	93.53%	5%	1.01%	3%	
	Dir Name	08	64.86	80%	82.03%	3%	3.06%	92%	87.94%	5%	1.19%	3%	
	Dir Name	08	65.22	80%	83.61%	3%	6.75%	92%	83.97%	5%	3.78%	3%	
	Dir Name	08	89.23	80%	83.58%	3%	7.24%	92%	94.90%	5%	.54%	3%	
	Dir Name	08	67.98	80%	73.20%	3%	2.30%	92%	89.76%	5%	1.36%	3%	
	Dir Name	08	66.91	80%	86.04%	3%	4.55%	92%	93.73%	5%	1.39%	3%	
	Dir Name	08	68.86	80%	88.90%	3%	4.37%	92%	95.94%	5%	.76%	3%	

The Performance Dashboard at TELUS Corp. is geared to an operations department. Everyone in the department, from vice presidents down to field technicians, receives the same display with the same metrics, but each view contains different values based on the person's role and level in the company. The system aggregates data from the lowest levels of the organization to the top levels. The view above is designed for vice presidents. By clicking on their name, vice presidents can drill down to see results for the directors that report to them, and so on down the line. (Data do not reflect actual results.)

Source: Courtesy of TELUS Corp.

When gathering requirements for a performance dashboard project, it is critical to focus on what information users need and how they plan to use it rather than how they want to view it. Focusing on screen layouts too early in the process restricts your ability to design an optimal visual interface; it is best to show a screen mockup at the end of the process once developers have a solid understanding of the information that users need to manage the business processes and projects for which they are responsible.

Know Your Users

It is one thing to build a robust performance dashboard with all the bells and whistles, and it is another to expect your workers to use it. As we discussed in Chapter 3, it is important to segment users by their technical and analytical capabilities and preferences. Just because one segment of users finds the screens easy to use does not mean that all segments will.

Executive Requirements

For example, to ensure that senior executives at Hewlett Packard Technology Solutions Group (TSG) would adopt its strategic dashboard, the project team trained executive administrators to use the tool and investigated how executives prefer to receive quantitative information. They discovered that some executives prefer to receive reports via e-mail, while others like to print out the views, and others prefer offline electronic versions that they can examine while traveling. "We tell executives, don't worry about accessing the tool, we'll train your assistants to get you the information," says Martin Summerhayes of Hewlett Packard TSG.

Power User Requirements

Although executives may need extra hand holding, power users need additional leeway. Power users are usually not satisfied with functionality geared to average users, who primarily want to monitor data, not analyze it. Although well-designed dashboards let users drill from high-level views to detailed transactions, the pathways are fairly structured and circumscribed. To satisfy power users who want unlimited freedom to explore, it is often necessary to let them access data and information directly using whatever tools they want. For example, power users at Quicken Loans use desktop OLAP tools to access the data warehouse and multidimensional cubes, whereas power users at Hewlett Packard TSG prefer query and reporting tools.

Make It Simple

Ironically, although fancy graphics and charts help sell performance dashboards, the "glitz" gets in the way once workers begin using the system. Designers eventually strip out items from screens to reduce their "busyness" and complexity. What is left may not look overly appealing, but it is quick and easy to use.

"Simple is best. We did a project we thought was spectacular, but users thought it was too complex. We created stoplights, up and down arrows, but it was too fancy. Some guys are new to this stuff so we had to make it foolproof," says TELUS's Lam.

Because TELUS's dashboard was designed for the company's operations department, Lam's team took out all graphics and charts and displayed only numbers, which were color coded, to make the performance dashboard look more like an operational report. Also, to prevent workers from getting lost in drill-down paths, every screen has the same layout and column names, and information never disappears, it is only added. Lam calls this "line of sight drill through." For example, when executives drill from a VP level to a Director level, they see rows of director-level performance data nested underneath the rows of VP-level data. This way, they always know where they are in the organizational hierarchy.

Lam's team also simplified the way users request ad hoc reports. They created an uncluttered screen that steps users through four prompts: 1) users select the metric and organization using drop-down list boxes or a keyword search, 2) users type in a date range or use a calendar function, 3) users select the output format (i.e., Excel, HTML, or PDF), and 4) users click on the "submit" button (see Exhibit 12.2).

Optimize Each Application

As described in Chapter 1, a performance dashboard is three applications in one: a monitoring application that conveys critical information quickly, an analytical

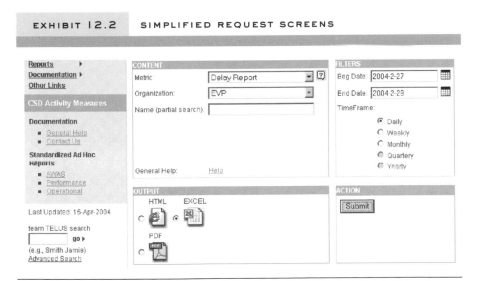

EXHIBIT 12.2   SIMPLIFIED REQUEST SCREENS

Source: Courtesy of TELUS Corp.

application that allows users to navigate and analyze large volumes of information, and a management tool that improves communication among executives, managers, and staff. When designing dashboard screens, it is important to know which of these three applications you are working on. Each application uses a different visual paradigm and requires different functionality.

Here are some guidelines for designing the "look" (i.e., screens) and "feel" (i.e., functionality) for each application in a performance dashboard. This book has addressed many of these items already, but here is a condensed and consolidated version.

Monitoring Application

- **Keep it selective.** Display only critical metrics that users need to achieve their objectives. Do not overwhelm users with too many things to monitor at one time.

- **Keep score.** The metrics should visually express *performance state* (e.g., superior, good, or bad), *performance direction* (e.g., trending up, down, or steady), and/or *performance progress* (e.g., gap between performance and targets). Operational dashboards will also display actual data or text.

- **Keep it sparse.** Do not clutter the screen with unnecessary or overly fancy graphics. Graphics should convey only the relevant information with a minimum amount of ink.

- **Highlight exceptions.** Use colors or symbols only to express out-of-bounds conditions or performance states.

- **Alert users.** Proactively notify users of out-of-bounds conditions via the Web, e-mail, or other high-impact channels.

- **Customize it.** Dynamically generate screens that are generically geared to every individual's role and responsibilities.

- **Personalize it.** Allow users to personalize the customized screens by selecting the objects they want to view from a predefined list.

- **View properties with one click.** Let users click on a metric to view its properties, such as how it was derived, who owns it, when it was last updated, and so on.

- **View information with one click.** Let users click on a metric name or symbol to view the information underneath in table or chart format.

- **Provide "right-time" information.** Although this is more of an infrastructure issue, it is critical to a monitoring application. Design elements must be populated with "right-time" information so users can proactively manage and optimize processes.

Analysis Application

- **Make it interactive.** Make sure users can switch views and contexts, access reports, and drill from high to low levels of detail using simple point-and-click techniques.

- **Make it structured.** Do not allow users to get lost in the information or have to drill up and back down when switching dimensions or formats (i.e., table to chart). Create easy-to-use prompts and predefined drill paths that structure how users navigate the information.

- **Make it guided.** Guide novice users through the process of analyzing and acting on performance information or finding relevant reports using wizards, context-sensitive recommendations, or online help.

- **Make it detailed.** Provide seamless and dynamic access to transaction data stored in a data warehouse or operational system.

- **Support multiple channels of delivery.** Allow users to access the dashboard system via alternative interfaces, including e-mail, wireless devices, or desktop applications.

- **Support disconnected usage.** Allow users to disconnect from the network and take the dashboard system and data with them for further analysis.

- **Support advanced analytics.** Let users perform "what-if" analyses, create and test scenarios, build forecasts, or create simple statistical models in the system or via third-party applications (e.g., Excel, data mining tools, or advanced visualization techniques).

Management Application

- **Publish it broadly.** Provide open access to the results throughout the company, especially among peers so they can compare their performances.

- **Exchange it widely.** Exchange performance information with other groups that have other dashboard systems to improve coordination and cross-pollination of ideas.

- **Compare to plan.** Use targets and goals from the budget, strategic plan, forecasts, or benchmarks so workers can gauge their progress and improve the accuracy of their forecasts.

- **Attach commentary.** Allow users to attach comments to dashboard views and respond to those comments. These threaded discussions provide an audit trail of ideas, decisions, and actions, which is useful for regulatory purposes as well as for new managers who want to learn how to manage specific processes.

- **Make it collaborative.** Let users set up a workflow that sends published dashboard views to a list of users for review and approval.

- **Make it timely.** Update the information frequently enough so users can take action to fix problems or capitalize on opportunities before it is too late.
- **Build in recommendations.** Build in recommendations for actions users should take based on the context of the information in the dashboard system.

Hire or Train Visual Designers

To optimize the design of the performance dashboard, it is important to get somebody on the team who has visual design expertise. Although few teams can afford to hire someone full or part time, they may be able to hire a consultant to provide assistance. Ideally, the consultant can educate the team about basic design principles and provide feedback on initial designs. It is also helpful for someone on the team to read articles and books on the topic or take a course on visual design before starting the process.

Usability Labs

In the best of all worlds, your company has a usability lab that can observe workers using the dashboard system in a laboratory setting. These labs use cameras to record hand and eye movements and interviews to determine the intuitiveness of an application and where users most get hung up in the visual interface. Usability labs usually provide good suggestions to improve even the most sound designs.

"We used [our company's] usability lab twice. We went initially to get advice about how to design the interface and get the dashboard up and running. Then, we went a few months ago after our dashboard went live to have it tested with real users. Some of the advice we got involved making small cosmetic changes, for instance that we should move some icons around and clean up the layout. But other advice gave us a better understanding of how the system behaves from the perspective of business users and where they find it confusing. We learned that people had difficulty drilling down into our data using parameterized drop-down lists. So now we're trying to address these issues in subsequent upgrades," says an IT director at a financial services company.

Use Prototypes

Once you have gathered all the information requirements and defined the metrics and targets, you are ready to design the look and feel of the dashboard system. The best way to get the process going is to deliver users a strawman proposal based on solid design principles. Then, let users tweak the layout and design as required but do not let them overhaul your design completely (unless it is really poor!). Also, do not start with a blank screen or let users create the strawman on their own. They have fixed ways of viewing information, usually limited by what they've grown accustomed to seeing and doing over the years.

However, sometimes, there is no way around user biases. In one company, executives insisted that the opening scorecard screen look exactly like the paper scorecard they had created during the strategy mapping process. Although this made sense in many ways—the company had published posters of the initial scorecard and hung them in the hallways throughout the organization—it forced the team to create a custom solution, which both the business users and technical team did not want to do.

SPECIFIC GUIDELINES FOR CREATING THE VISUAL INTERFACE

The first section of this chapter provided general guidelines for approaching the design process. The following section provides specific recommendations on how to create an effective visual interface for the performance dashboard.

First Impressions

First impressions make a big difference, today more than ever. In our busy, fast-paced lives, if something does not catch our eye immediately and draw us inward, we ignore it and move to something else. For this reason, it is imperative to spend considerable time and effort designing the initial screen of a performance dashboard. This initial view conveys the breadth, depth, and usability of the entire performance dashboard. If it does not resonate with users or portray the right information, they may not use it, or only use it begrudgingly.

Painterly Touches

A good dashboard designer is like an expert painter who conveys an image or evokes an emotion with a single stroke of the brush. The art of visual design is working sparsely, making sure that every element and figure on the screen is there for a purpose. Visual designers are ruthless in stripping out colors, shapes, images, or decorations that distract users or do not convey vital information.

Although few of us have training as artists or visual designers, there are a number of things we can do to enhance the visual appeal and usability of the dashboard and scorecard screens we create. The following are guidelines and techniques for creating screens that jump out and grab users, not require them to squint at and study the screen to discern relevant facts.

Much of the advice in this section comes from Stephen Few, principal of Perceptual Edge, a consulting firm that specializes in information analysis and presentation, and a faculty member of The Data Warehousing Institute. Few has written an excellent book entitled *Show Me the Numbers* (Analytics Press, 2004) and several articles in *Intelligent Enterprise, DM Review,* and the *Business Intelligence Journal* that are worth reading. He is also currently working on a book titled *Information Dashboard Design: Beyond Gauges, Meters, and Traffic Lights* scheduled for publication by the end of 2005. Few says he is a dedicated follower of Edward Tufte, whose 1983 book, *The Visual Display of Quantitative Information*, laid the conceptual foundation for how to display information clearly and cogently.

1. Display Information on a Single Screen

The first and toughest goal of a dashboard designer is to squeeze the information onto a single screen. Users should not have to scroll down or open another screen to view critical information. All relevant information should be instantaneously viewable.

> The fundamental challenge of dashboard design is to display all the required information on a single screen, clearly and without distraction, in a manner that can be assimilated quickly. If this objective is hard to meet in practice, it is because dashboards often require a dense display of information. You must pack a lot of information into a very limited space, and the entire display must fit on a single screen, without clutter. This is a tall order that requires a specific set of design principles.[1]

2. Minimize the Number of Metrics and Objects on the Screen

To put all vital performance information on a single screen, the designer must have a clear understanding of the information users need to monitor, its importance to them, and the order in which they want to see it. This helps designers determine the priority of information and its placement on the screen.

How Many Is Too Many?

Some experts say that dashboard screens should only have between three and seven metrics to have the greatest visual impact. However, few people want to restrict the number of metrics arbitrarily and risk excluding those that meet bona fide business requirements. To accommodate both principles, many designers nest lower priority metrics under higher priority ones.

Portal-Based Dashboards

Another way to prioritize metrics is to let users do it themselves using a dashboard's personalization capabilities. This lets users pick metrics that they want to see from a pre-approved list.

Some organizations also let users add other objects, such as documents, alerts, and Web links, turning the dashboard screen into a makeshift portal. Conversely, many organizations let users create personalized views of the corporate portal. One of the most popular elements to customize a corporate portal with is a KPI chart. So, here the difference between dashboard and a portal begins to blur. In any case, a personalized dashboard motivates workers to visit the application more frequently because it contains information and objects they deem important. The downside is that users always add too many objects to the screen, creating clutter and minimizing its visual impact.

3. Keep Graphical Icons Sparse

Graphical Elements

The only way to pack a lot of information onto a single screen is to abbreviate or summarize it. This is usually done by representing metrics as graphical elements. This keeps designers from having to put actual data onto the dashboard screen, which takes up valuable real estate and crowds the view.

However, most organizations get carried away when using graphical elements, spurred on by vendors who populate their dashboard solutions with eye-popping graphics that do a good job of catching attention but a poor job of communicating pertinent information quickly. Part of the problem is that most vendors try to simulate an automobile dashboard on a computer screen instead of focusing on the fundamental principles governing the visual display of information.

"Caught up in the race to out-gizmo one another, few vendors have taken the time to gain more than a superficial understanding of effective dashboard design. Without this knowledge as a foundation, these dashboards are destined for the trash heap," says Few.

Few has very specific recommendations for using graphical elements, or graphs, for short. As a general rule of thumb, every designer should ask: "Do the graphs provide the clearest, most meaningful presentation of the data in the least amount of space?" He adds that graphs should:

- Fit any size space
- Be appropriate for the task
- Display measurement, context, and state

Gauges, Thermometers, and Stoplights

Few dislikes radial gauges because they waste a lot of space due to their circular shape. "You can't put a lot of radial gauges side by side," he says. In this regard, Few prefers thermometers, which are linear and fit in a compact space. However, he says that most thermometers are overly decorative. "They are generally designed to look so much like the real thing that space is wasted on meaningless realism."

Less is More

He objects to stoplights for much the same reason, saying there is no reason to display three lights when one will suffice. "Don't waste visual content with an entire stoplight, just show a single icon (for example, a circle) next to a metric," he says. Going one step further, Few recommends not showing a symbol or icon at all unless it is important to do so, such as when performance falls below target. Users subconsciously recognize that the absence of an object carries meaning, like "no news is good news." In this example, users understand that a metric without a circle next to it reflects acceptable performance and there is no need to examine the data or take further action.

4. Display Context in Abbreviated Form

The main purpose of dashboard graphics is to display performance in context so users can quickly ascertain what is going on.

There are three aspects to context: 1) the *performance state*, which indicates whether performance is good or bad according to predefined thresholds; 2) the *performance trend*, which indicates whether performance has improved, declined, or held steady during the prior period; and 3) the *performance variance*, which shows how performance compares with the target for that period (see Exhibit 12.3 for a dashboard screen that displays all three contexts).

Performance State

The depiction of performance state is usually done by applying colors to a graph, symbol, or the metric itself (i.e., the text label). Performance states correspond to thresholds set by managers to identify ranges of performance. For example, a sales organization might have four performance states based on four ranges or thresholds of performance against a single target and associate colors or symbols with each state:

1. "Urgent" indicates that sales fell 10 percent or more below target (red)
2. "Caution indicates that sales were 10 percent or less below target (yellow)
3. "Normal" indicates that sales were up to 10 percent above target (green)
4. "Superior" indicates that sales were 10 percent or higher above target (blue)

An initial dashboard screen for an executive might display performance state by putting a color-coded circle next to the name of each metric, and that is it. A second-level screen might display performance state using color-coded numbers in a table or by showing a trend line in a chart whose background is painted according to threshold ranges.

EXHIBIT 12.3   DISPLAYING PERFORMANCE STATES

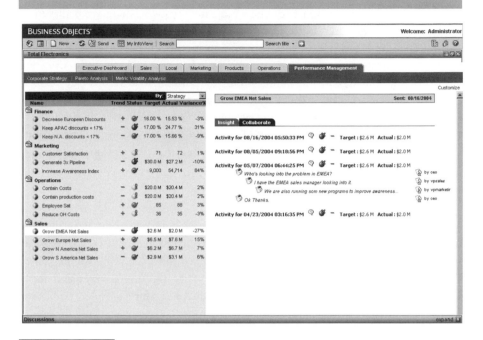

This Balanced Scorecard screen displays metric name, performance trends, status, target, actual, and variance from target from left to right in the left-hand column. The dashboard uses a colored symbol to indicate trend and both a colored circle and an icon to represent status to accommodate color-blind people. The right-hand panel embeds a threaded discussion on metrics where performance is below target.

Source: Courtesy of Business Objects S.A.

When using more than three performance states, it's wise to embed a key in the dashboard screen that translates the encoding. However, a key also forces users to work harder than they want. They have to study the screen to decipher its contents instead of being able to glance at it quickly and ascertain performance.

Performance Trend

A performance trend indicates the direction of performance data for a prior period. The trend indicates whether performance is moving up, down, or holding steady. Each "trend state" also needs to be calibrated with a threshold or rule that defines what is "up," "down," or "steady." The best way to show performance trends visually is with a symbol, such as an arrow or plus (+) and minus (−) signs.

An arrow supports a wide range of trends because it can be pointed in any direction. Plus and minus signs support only two trends, up and down. However, the absence of a plus/minus sign could also indicate "steady."

Hewlett Packard TSG displays both performance state and trend on its scorecard. It encodes block arrows with four different colors (i.e., red, green, blue, and white) to indicate performance status and points them in three different directions (i.e., up, down, and sideways) to convey performance trends (see Exhibit 9.2 in Chapter 9). This use of color-coded arrows is effective because it shows both state and trend using one symbol. However, since this does not work for color-blind people, users can configure the system to display data values instead of arrows or display data values only when they hover their cursor over the arrows.

Performance Variance

Performance variance compares actual performance with a target and calculates a variance. The target and variance can be displayed textually as numbers in columns or graphically on a line chart using two lines (i.e., one for targets or thresholds and one for data values) or a bar chart by plotting a target line across the bars. Performance variance can also be displayed using a simple graph, such as a thermometer or bullet graph (see below.)

Many companies like to apply multiple targets to a single metric. For instance, an organization may want to compare this month's net sales against the annual budget and results from the same period last year. Few recommends applying no more than two targets per metric to avoid creating overly complex graphical elements.

5. Use Color Intensities not Hues

Color has four characteristics that are helpful to know when one is designing dashboards:

- **Hue.** The color, such as red, white, or blue.
- **Lightness.** The shade of the hue, ranging from light to dark.
- **Saturation.** The amount of hue applied to a given area, ranging from little (pale) to total saturation.
- **Intensity.** Refers to both lightness and saturation, because each can be manipulated to increase or decrease the perceived intensity of a hue.

Few believes it is more effective to use a single hue with multiple intensities rather than multiple hues to depict performance states. It does not matter which hue is used—red, black, or blue—as long as it does not change. One reason to use different intensities instead of different hues or colors is to give the dashboard screen a consistent look and feel. Another reason is to increase the contrast between things that really need highlighting, such as an urgent, out-of-bounds condition, and those that do not. For example, an alert encoded as a red circle immediately catches a viewer's attention when the rest of the screen and graphs are cast in shades of gray.

A third reason to use intensities instead of hues is to accommodate color-blind workers, most of whom cannot differentiate between red and green. Ten percent of men and one percent of women are color blind to some degree, which makes using hues alone to depict performance states problematic. However, color-blind people can distinguish between intensities of the same hue. So one way to communicate state without adding an extra symbol is to use different intensities of the same hue. For instance, deep red can signify an urgent problem and dimmer red a less urgent one. Some dashboard designers add symbols or simple graphs to accommodate color-blind workers, but this is overkill and leads to cluttered screens.

6. Pay Attention to Position and Placement

The way designers position or sequence information on the screen reinforces its meaning. Position and placement become another way to communicate meaning and enhance the value of the dashboard.

Top Left to Bottom Right

According to Few, elements in the top left quadrant and the center get the most attention when set apart visually from what surrounds them. Next is the upper right and lower left quadrants, followed by the bottom right. Therefore, designers place elements that deserve more prominence in the upper left or in the center of a screen and leave plenty of white space around the objects. Designers also use arrows to step people from one section of the screen to another if there is a logical sequence or flow to the data. They also sometimes number elements to indicate a visual flow.

Groupings and Flows

It also helps to group like elements together on the screen to show that they are related. The same goes for items that need to be compared. Placing them too far apart makes the user's eyes work too hard to see and compare the items. When designers cannot place items together, they use hues, shapes, or fonts to show which elements are related to each other.

SAMPLE TECHNIQUES

Two Effective Graphical Elements

Few advocates two techniques that circumvent many of the problems with graphical elements today: sparklines and bullet graphs.

Sparklines

Sparklines are the brainchild of Edward Tufte and are ideally suited for performance dashboards because they give a basic sense of trends over time, skipping superfluous detail. Sparklines are designed for time-series data (i.e., measurements that occur in regular intervals over time), but they do not contain a quantitative scale. Sparklines are good when users require a quick, high-level perspective of historical performance in a highly condensed display.

Bullet Graph

A bullet graph is a linear widget, invented by Few, that uses the following: a single bar or data point to show actual performance, color intensities to show performance levels or thresholds, and one or more short lines to show comparative measures, such as a target. Bullet graphs let users quickly evaluate performance in context (i.e., comparisons and thresholds). They also take up less space than most simple graphs (e.g., gauges, meters, and dials) and can shrink to fit into a compact space without losing their legibility. However, because they are new, users may need some training to interpret them and become comfortable using them.

Sample Dashboard

Exhibit 12.4 shows a portion of a dashboard created by Few that applies the visual design principles and display techniques described above. Few's compact dashboard contains seven metrics for maximum impact. Each metric has an associated sparkline, a bullet graph, and actual data. (The only thing missing is the actual date or time interval being measured, although monthly is implied.) The sparklines show performance trends for the past 12 months. The bullet graphs show actual performance compared with year-to-date targets and thresholds. A red circle (which is the darkest circle in the exhibit) appears next to the names of metrics in which performance is below the target for the period, but circles do not appear next to metrics that meet or exceed monthly goals. The intensity of a circle's hue indicates the degree to which the metric is below target. For example, the "profit" metric has a circle with the most intense hue because it is below the bottom threshold, as indicated on the bullet graph. The other circles

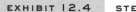

EXHIBIT 12.4   STEPHEN FEW'S SAMPLE DASHBOARD

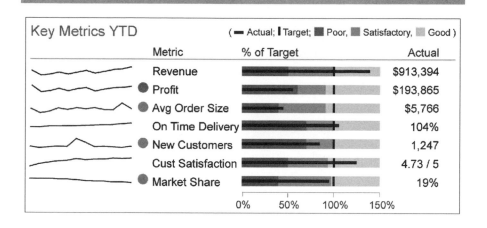

are colored with a less intense hue because their metrics are only slightly below target.

Few also sequences these elements from left to right in a way that tells a story. Users can view 12-month trends, followed by an alert, which prompts them to read the bullet graph to compare performance with targets and actual data. I would have preferred to see the metric names on the far left side, kind of as a row header, but Few placed the metric names between the sparkline and performance bar to simplify the screen. Because the metric names sit in the middle of these two graphical elements, there is no need to add a separate label for each element, which reduces clutter. It also removes the temptation to add row or column lines between the graphical elements as a visual divider, another design faux pas.

Although it may take a few minutes to become oriented to Few's dashboard, the value is obvious. It conveys much more information in a compact space than most dashboards. In a glance, users can view 12-month performance trends for each metric, month-end data values, and comparisons with targets and thresholds. Few's alerts jump out at users because they are colored with a different hue (red) than the rest of the elements, which are shades of gray. (Note: since the book is printed in black and white, these different hues are not distinguishable in Exhibit 12.4.) Also, the alerts (i.e., an abbreviated stoplight) only appear when an out-of-bounds condition exists. Less is more.

Although you may not be inclined to use the widgets or style in Few's dashboard, it clearly demonstrates basic principles of visual design and offers alternative ways of displaying information that most people have not considered.

NAVIGATION TECHNIQUES

Drill Paths

From the scorecard screen, which represents information graphically, users should be able to drill down effortlessly to see actual data. Unfortunately, software vendors have yet to devise a standard way to perform drill-downs, and many techniques employed today are not intuitive.

One-Click Drills

The ideal way for users to drill down is by left clicking on the metric name, indicator, or alert or whatever on the screen demands their attention. They click once and the information appears in the form of a table or chart that plots performance over time.

Unfortunately, few performance dashboards make it this easy. Some require users to right click, which is an awkward movement for many users. This causes a dialogue box to pop up that usually contains too many options and drill paths for users to absorb or remember. Other performance dashboards require users to click on one or more drop-down list boxes to specify the parameters of their drill and then click a "go" button. Although power users like having multiple drill paths and parameters, casual users do not.

Customizing Drill Paths

Rather than provide users with unlimited navigation, it is wise to discover all the possible drill paths users need in advance and bake them into the system. The technical team can then select the drill paths that each department or role requires and associate them with individual users' security profiles. This way users only see the drill paths that they need and aren't overwhelmed with too many options. Administrators can always expand the number of drill paths it makes available to departments or individuals, even providing unlimited navigation. This approach eases users into the system, delivering new functionality and navigational paths only when they are ready to use them.

Getting Lost

Another problem with dashboard navigation is that users often drill to a certain point and forget where they are. For instance, I watched one user drill down on a series of charts, but when he wanted to switch to a table view he had to drill back up the hierarchy and drill back down in the table view mode. (Actually, he could have switched formats in one click but did not know how; it was not intuitive.) This also happens when users switch subject areas or departments, say from viewing customer profitability by region to viewing product sales by channel. It also occurs when users drill through to data stored in another system, such as a data warehouse or transaction system and land in a separate window with different navigational techniques (if any at all) without a clear way to get back to their starting point.

To avoid having users get lost in the system, designers should dynamically map a user's navigational path through the information so they always know where they are, where they have been, and how to get back. These maps can be similar to computer pathnames or spider webs, for instance. Users should be able to click on any part of the map to return to a previous view.

Think Like a 12-Year-Old

To deliver high-quality performance dashboard interface, designers should think like a 12-year-old (or younger perhaps). Designers who spend every working hour building an application forget how alien the system is to someone using it for the first time. Designers need to build the system not for someone like themselves, but for a 12-year-old son or daughter who uses computers but not regularly or intensely (except perhaps to play computer games!). Ultimately, the key is to prevent users from getting "lost" in the data and overwhelmed by system functionality.

SUMMARY

Dashboard design is like putting icing on a cake. It is the fun part of building a performance dashboard. It is how you really connect to users. However, the design—no matter how well executed and visually attractive—is worthless if the team has not first done the hard work of creating effective metrics and targets and populating them with clean, valid data. The most important principle to remember when designing dashboard screens is "Get the data right first!"

With a solid foundation, dashboard designers can then begin the process of creating layouts and screens. The most common mistake is to make things too complex. K.I.S.S., or "Keep It Simple, Stupid!," should be the motto of every dashboard designer. Although many vendors sell glitzy dashboard displays that tantalize users with fancy graphics, most users prefer less glitz and more content once they begin using the system. Operational dashboard users take this a step further: they usually prefer text or numbers rather than graphics, which they find get in the way.

A good dashboard design conveys a lot of information with as few elements as possible. Users should be able to glance at the dashboard to view the information they need to achieve their objectives. If they have to scroll down or switch screens to assess their progress, they get frustrated. The screen should display a minimal number of elements in a compact way. This means representing metrics and context using simple graphs, hues, intensities, symbols, and charts. These graphical elements should be streamlined, not decorative, so they convey vital information quickly. They should also be placed on the screen or grouped together in a way that conveys meaning.

Colors or hues should be used sparingly, only to highlight out-of-bounds conditions. Graphical elements should use different intensities to display performance states, different symbols (e.g., arrows, icons) to convey performance trends, and different graphs to display performance variances.

Finally, the dashboard screen should provide intuitive navigation that lets users click once to drill down on graphical elements to view actual data. Drill paths should be structured so users cannot easily get lost in the information. The dashboard should dynamically map the user's path through the data so they always know where they are, where they have been, and how to get back.

NOTE

1. Stephen Few, "Dashboard Design: Beyond Meters, Gauges, and Traffic Lights" (*Business Intelligence Journal, 2005*).

CHAPTER 13

How to Link and Integrate Performance Dashboards

APPROACHES TO INTEGRATION

A common question that people ask about performance dashboards is how to integrate and link them. The question usually has one of two sources. Either they have read about the Balanced Scorecard methodology and want to know how to "cascade" scorecards throughout the organization, or they want to integrate two or more existing performance dashboards that were designed and developed independently.

In either case, the task is the same: align multiple performance management systems so everyone is working off a consistent set of information. When this happens, an organization starts to use information strategically. It can roll up or aggregate performance results from lower levels of the organization to higher levels and give executives an accurate and comprehensive understanding of overall organizational performance at any given moment. It also lets managers and staff compare their performance to internal peer groups, increasing motivation and performance.

Centralized versus Federated

Organizations can align and link performance dashboards using either a centralized or a federated approach. The centralized approach creates a single performance management system that spawns multiple, dependent dashboards and scorecards. The federated approach, on the other hand, dynamically integrates existing performance dashboards that run on different BI platforms and are administered by different technical teams.

The centralized approach works best in companies with centralized or hierarchical cultures in which a CEO or business unit head can get everyone to standardize on a common set of metrics and BI platform. In contrast, the federated approach works best in companies with more decentralized cultures where business units, departments, and workgroups enjoy considerable autonomy and frequently build their own IT systems. In reality, most companies neither have an entirely centralized or decentralized organizational structure, but something in between. As a result, the majority of organizations use a blend of both centralized and federated approaches to deliver a consistent set of performance management metrics.

CENTRALIZED APPROACH

The centralized approach builds integration into the design and project plan so all performance applications, whenever and wherever deployed, run on a common business and technical foundation, sharing common metrics, data, and functionality, and work together harmoniously.

In a centralized approach, performance dashboards are not physically distinct systems or applications; they are simply customized views of performance information generated by a single performance management system. The system dynamically generates custom views of metrics and information based on each user's role or security profile. The centralized approach makes it easy for technical teams to rapidly create multiple, customized performance dashboards for every individual and group in the organization.

Top-Down Deployment

The best way to deploy performance dashboards using a centralized approach is to work from the top down, starting at the executive level and then working down the organizational hierarchy in a systematic fashion.

Cascade Development

The first performance dashboard—or executive dashboard or scorecard—translates the organization's strategy into key performance indicators (KPIs) that measure performance at an enterprise level. The corporate view then serves as a template for all subsequent performance dashboards. Each business unit or group reuses KPIs from the corporate scorecard or creates new ones that directly influence executive-level objectives and metrics or that measure unique processes at the business unit or group level. Once the business unit scorecards are completed, the process repeats itself at the regional or district level, and so on down to the lowest level in the organization, which could be an office, a workgroup, or an individual.

Asking each business unit to figure out how to influence metrics in higher level performance dashboards unleashes considerable creativity. Paul Niven, in *Balanced Scorecard Step by Step*, writes: "One of the benefits of the cascading process is watching creativity bloom...as groups begin to contemplate how they might contribute to an organizational goal once considered well outside their sphere of influence."

Program Offices

The key to the top-down approach is to make sure each group adheres to the standard definitions and rules for metrics contained in the executive dashboard or scorecard and faithfully aligns their versions to the ones directly above them in the organizational hierarchy. This usually requires the organization to create a program office that oversees and coordinates development activities. The program office, which serves as an intermediary between the business and project teams, ensures that all development efforts adhere to standards for defining and linking metrics as well as predefined technical specifications.

Serial versus Parallel Development

Ideally, every performance dashboard is built on the same infrastructure and guided by the same project team, which ensures that every group adheres to corporate standards and processes for defining objectives and metrics. This ensures consistency, saves money, and reduces risk. The project team creates each performance dashboard in a serial fashion, one after the other and one level at a time.

However, the downside of a serial approach is that it can take considerable time to roll out performance dashboards to every group in the organization. Executives can accelerate the process by funding parallel development teams or allowing each business unit or group to create its own version of the performance dashboard on the same infrastructure. However, the organization needs to ensure that the program office has significant clout and resources to enforce standards among various development groups and ensure the consistent usage of metrics and information among all performance dashboards.

Bottom-Up Deployment

The opposite of top-down deployment is bottom-up deployment, whereby an initiative does not start in the executive office but in a business unit, region, or other group and spreads upward and outward from there. For example, a regional group at Hewlett Packard TSG initiated a strategic dashboard project to serve its own needs, but it was so successful that it quickly spread to every region and unit in the group (see Chapter 9). The problem with the bottom-up approach is that other business units and groups are usually developing similar systems. Invariably, these groups use different metrics, sources, staffs, and methods, making their systems incompatible.

A large number of operational and tactical dashboards start in a business unit or department and use a bottom-up approach to expand outward to the enterprise. In contrast, many strategic dashboards—because they align and focus the organization on strategic objectives—use a top-down approach.

Technical Requirements of a Centralized Approach

The centralized approach—whether working top down or bottom up—requires the technical team to create and manage all dashboards and scorecards on a standard BI platform. This approach offers greater flexibility at lower cost than developing individual performance dashboards from scratch. Technical teams quickly create new "views" (i.e., dashboards or scorecards) for individuals or groups without having to build a system or application or buy new servers and software. When users log on, the system checks their credentials and dynamically displays a unique dashboard or scorecard view. In this way, a single performance dashboard can support dozens or hundreds of distinct applications, which most users refer to as their "dashboard" or "scorecard."

The centralized approach also makes it easier for companies to maintain the consistency and uniformity of metric definitions and rules because they are stored and maintained in one place by one team. (Companies call a repository of metric definitions a "data dictionary," a "data library," or a "data glossary." Technical teams call it a "metadata repository.") Another benefit of the centralized approach is that organizations can support other analytical applications on the BI infrastructure other than performance dashboards. For instance, Quicken Loans built its BI architecture primarily to drive its operational dashboards but now uses it to support other analytical applications as well.

Systems Standards

A development team needs to define architectural standards for the performance management system. For instance, it needs to specify what technologies and products it will use for its Web servers, application servers, storage systems, databases, online analytical processing tools, programming languages, and reporting tools.

Although business managers often object to adhering to architectural standards because they can slow down or sidetrack a thriving project, standards ensure the long-term sustainability of a project. Standards ultimately reduce development, maintenance, and training costs for both business and technical staff and speed delivery of applications and solutions. The business and technical teams need to work together to optimize the business value of information technology, which often means making tradeoffs between adhering to technical standards and delivering immediate business value (see Chapter 14 for how to align business and technical requirements).

Application Standards

The team also needs to establish development standards to ensure reliable delivery, accurate data, and consistent application performance. Development teams that establish conventions for displaying, manipulating, and navigating data can work more efficiently and rapidly. They can reuse components, such as layouts, grids, graphs, and charts, instead of creating them from scratch each time. They can also optimize these components to deliver fast response times when users navigate the performance dashboard, submit queries, or download reports.

Unfortunately, many development teams are whipsawed by user demands and are unable to establish technical standards that would enable them to serve customer needs better in the long run. Instead, they spend significant time recreating the same components over and over again to meet the preferences of different groups whose needs are actually more similar than different.

For instance, a technical team in a telecommunications company that is developing a corporate scorecard complains that each department wants the same information displayed in different ways: the marketing department wants charts with a green background and special graphics; the engineering department wants the chart to display a map of the United States; and the finance group wants charts with two "y" axes that displays multiple metrics simultaneously. Each request requires the technical team to build or buy a new charting component. Even off-the-shelf components still take them considerable time to configure and test.

The senior IT manager of the technical team says, "The program office needs to go to the business and say, 'You must use these formats,' but they are reluctant to do so because they fear that business users will create their own charts and reports and not use the corporate scorecard."

The example above illustrates the pitfalls of developing performance dashboards that span multiple business units and departments. Project teams that build performance dashboards for a single business unit or department tend to avoid many of these issues. They can adhere to standards because there is greater homogeneity in the way people want to view and manipulate applications and data in the group.

Data Standards

Besides standardizing application components, the technical team needs to standardize data. This is accomplished in three ways: 1) by creating a data model that drives the performance dashboard; 2) by sourcing the appropriate data operational systems, file systems, and other places, both inside and outside the organization; and 3) by cleaning and validating data to ensure it meets user expectations for quality and accuracy.

Data Models. Every application, including a performance dashboard, needs a data model. A data model represents a business process within the structure of a database. It is the brains of the application. Without it, the application cannot work.

Logically, the data model defines "things" (e.g., employee, position, manager, and so on), attributes of those things (e.g., employee can be full-time, part-time, current, former, and so on), and relationships among things (e.g., an employee is hired by a manager). Physically, the model stores all this information in tables and columns within a relational database (or in other types of structures in specialized databases). Once deployed, the database captures events and adds rows to various tables (e.g., John Doe was hired as a part-time receptionist on January 17 by manager Jane Ray). Metrics apply calculations to the rows and columns and generate scores or values, also usually stored in tables.

Technical teams spend considerable time interviewing business users before creating data models. Their goal is to create models that accurately reflect the way the business works and deliver fast application performance when mapped into a database. The bigger the scope of the project and the more complex the processes, the longer it takes to create effective data models.

One advantage of commercial performance dashboard solutions is that they contain a generic data model that is tailored to managing performance in a large organization. Most vendors cull the experiences of numerous customers when creating generic data models and analytic applications. While the models usually need to be tweaked for individual companies, they can accelerate project development compared to starting from scratch.

"We purchased a [vendor product] for its data model, which jumpstarted the project for us. It helped us understand how to roll this stuff out. The vendor product now represents only 20 percent of our entire solution but it was worth having something to start from," says a senior manager of IT at a wireless telecommunications firm.

Data Sourcing. IT managers responsible for populating metrics with data must identify the most reliable sources for that data. This is not always straightforward. There may be 20 places to get customer data. Which is the right source given what the metric is designed to measure? Which sources contain valid, reliable data?

The technical team may decide to pull several fields from one source and a few from another source to populate the dashboard data model. This analysis and triage "takes weeks and months to work out with the business units," says one IT manager, "but now we have high-quality detailed data that people trust." The key is to recruit business analysts who combine a strong knowledge of the business with an acute understanding of the underlying data and systems. These individuals can make or break the data sourcing process.

Data Quality

Data Defects

The third aspect of standardizing data is the hardest: delivering high-quality data to a performance dashboard. Operational systems are often riddled with data errors—missing data, invalid values, incorrect data types and formats, invalid dependencies—that do not show up until a performance dashboard team tries to integrate data among multiple systems.

"Our [performance] dashboard constantly highlights issues with the quality of data coming from source systems," says one IT manager who asked not to be named. "We're at the end of the line and often have to deal with the garbage that others send down the pipe. We point out problems to source system administrators and ask the business owners to pressure the administrators to fix the problems, but that's all we can do. There is an institutionalized lack of rigor around maintaining high-quality information in source systems. They keep band-aiding the system, but we need to get it right at the source the first time."

Fixing at the Source

The cost of fixing data errors increases the further down the line they are identified. The worst-case scenario is when a data error slips into an application and can be detected by end-users. When this happens, end-users stop trusting and using the system, leading to the application's demise.

Obviously, the best way to achieve high-quality data is to prevent errors from occurring in the first place. This usually requires source system owners to apply validation routines to check the accuracy of data entered into applications and to inform downstream application owners whenever they add or change a field in the source system. It may also require developers to rewrite outdated applications and managers to reengineer business processes so workers are rewarded for delivering high-quality data.

Most technical teams let "bad" data pass through into the performance dashboards and do not try to clean it up. The theory, which is sometimes debated, says that the business will not be motivated to fix bad data at the source unless they know that problems exist. Since bad quality data can cause users to reject a new performance management system, many project teams schedule a "beta" or trial period where users can experiment with the system and identify bugs before they officially declare it a production system. After that point, many teams rigorously analyze incoming data and don't allow users onto the system until a business owner declares that the data is valid and ok to use.

Business Ownership

To obtain high-quality data, the business must view data as a critical asset, as valuable as equipment, people, or cash. To preserve this asset, companies need to create data stewardship teams that identify critical data elements and assign individuals responsibility for ensuring the integrity of each data element. These data "owners" are usually business analysts—individuals who understand the business and the data and can assess whether data values are in or out of range. Their expertise makes them uniquely qualified to identify data quality issues and develop data validation and cleansing programs.

Sometimes these analysts also have responsibility for checking the data in a performance dashboard after new data is added and officially validating its quality before users are allowed to access the system. For example, every day, a business analyst at a Boston-based financial services firm "certifies" that data in the company's financial dashboard is clean and accurate. The analyst runs tests on the data, and when everything looks okay, the analyst pushes a button that changes the dashboard's status from "preliminary" to "final" and adds to the bottom of each screen the time and date that it was officially certified.

FEDERATED APPROACH

The centralized approach works well when an organization builds a performance dashboard from scratch and rolls it out across the enterprise. Unfortunately, most organizations do not start with a clean slate. They may already have multiple performance dashboards, some of which overlap and compete for resources and endorsements from top executives. Given such an environment, project teams need to consider whether it makes sense to add another performance dashboard to the mix or leverage and extend what already exists.

The federated approach attempts to link existing performance dashboards into a seamless whole. This can be accomplished in a variety of ways. It can be as easy as transferring data from one performance dashboard to another or as challenging as standardizing metric definitions in multiple dashboards so they report performance consistently. A federated approach might also involve merging two performance dashboards or consolidating multiple dashboards into a single system. Sometimes organizations pursue multiple tactics at the same time.

Inventory

To bring order to the chaos, project teams should first create an inventory of performance dashboards that already exist in the organization. The inventory should document a number of characteristics, such as performance dashboard type (i.e., operational, tactical, or strategic), business domain, sample metrics, active users, platform used, and business owner, among other things (see Exhibit 13.1).

Project leaders can use this information to determine whether it makes sense to create a new performance dashboard from scratch or piggyback on top of an

EXHIBIT 13.1   SAMPLE INVENTORY

	Dashboard A	Dashboard B
Business Domain	Finance	Sales
Business Owner	John Doe	Jane Ray
Dashboard Type	Tactical	Operational
Usage Metrics	120 active users; 140 queries a day	200 active users; 400 queries a day
Platform/Tools	Excel, Essbase	Custom .NET
Data Sources	Mainframe, Excel	Sales tracking, pipeline
Updates	Monthly	Daily
Primary Metrics	AP/AR, DSOs	Orders, forecasts
Comments	Most data exist in the data warehouse	Heavily used custom application with active sponsor
Evaluation	Good candidate for consolidation	Keep as is

The first place to start in a federated environment is to identify existing performance management systems and collect information about their key characteristics, such as business owner, metrics, platforms, and so on. This side-by-side inventory helps executives triage existing systems, deciding which should stay, which should be merged or consolidated, and which should be eliminated.

existing one. The project leader can also use the inventory as evidence to convince a top executive that the organization has a burgeoning information management problem. The inventory can then serve as a guide to help an executive determine which performance dashboards should remain and which should be eliminated or merged and consolidated into others.

Horizontal Integration

There are two ways to integrate existing performance dashboards: horizontally and vertically. Horizontal integration is when two or more performance dashboards exchange information, creating a peer relationship among them.

Data Exchange

Horizontal integration works best when there are no inconsistencies or overlap among the metrics and data in the performance dashboards. Here, business groups simply agree to exchange performance data. For instance, the finance group might want its scorecard to display charts from a human resources (HR) scorecard and an operations dashboard maintained by those departments. This is a relatively straightforward process; the only question is whether the exchange is done dynamically or in batch. For instance, the finance group could have the HR department send it data via e-mail or file transfer protocol (FTP). If it wants a more automated exchange, the two groups could connect their performance dashboards via a custom interface or a middleware backbone and send updates in real time.

If the HR department does not want to export its data, then the finance group might create a link from its dashboard to the HR dashboard, allowing finance users to log in and view the appropriate information in the HR dashboard (see Spotlight 13.1).

SPOTLIGHT 13.1   HUMAN RESOURCES DASHBOARD

High-flying Cisco Systems, Inc., a maker of networking equipment and software that fueled the Internet boom, was the darling of high-tech investors. In 2000, Cisco Systems was affected by the downturn in the economy along with other high-tech companies. The surprise was not that the economy was slowing but the rate at which it fell. Reporting systems at the time were built around "stovepipe" applications and were incapable of providing visibility into rapid changes in the business.

Cisco Systems has taken a number of steps to improve the visibility of its sales pipeline and supply chain, including consolidating data into a corporate data warehouse and delivering tactical dashboards that make it easier and quicker for users to spot critical trends and issues that need to be addressed immediately. Users access data from an operational data store (ODS) that is updated every 15 minutes to deliver the most up-to-date bookings and inventory data. "Dashboards are the way people want to view reports and information. They provide an easy, intuitive way for workers to access relevant information for decision-making purposes," says Ryan Uda, program manager at Cisco Systems. "But dashboards are the icing on the cake compared to the task of getting accurate, timely data. At one point, Cisco had 30 plus systems managing bookings and backlog information; significant time and resources were committed to developing a single source of truth."

Since the downturn, Cisco Systems has delivered tactical dashboards to more than 2,000 users in sales, marketing, and HR departments (see Exhibit 13.2). The dashboards provide both historical data from the data warehouse or a data mart and "real-time" data culled directly from source systems or an operational data store. Collectively, the dashboards enabled the company to close down hundreds of operational reports and systems and increase worker productivity significantly.

"The data were always there, but locked away in databases most users couldn't access quickly or efficiently," says Uda.

EXHIBIT 13.2	CISCO SYSTEMS' HUMAN RESOURCE DASHBOARD

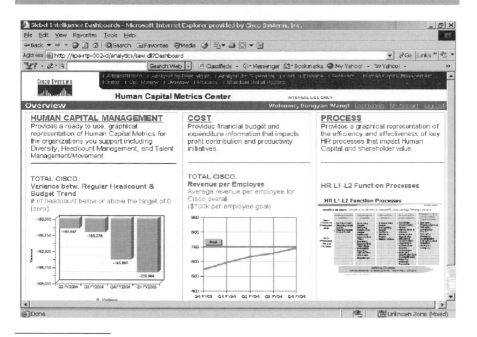

Cisco Systems uses a Web portal home page for its tactical dashboard that shows major categories of exploration and key high-level metrics divided into three columns. Users click on the text-based hyperlinks to see additional metrics for each area. (All numbers have been scrambled.)

Source: Courtesy of Cisco Systems, Inc.

Data Melding

Horizontal integration becomes challenging when performance dashboards track the same activity but calculate the metrics differently. For instance, an organization might have a metric called "total customer sales," but the marketing department calculates sales by tallying order commitments; the sales department by signed orders; and the finance department by payments received.

Most groups do not want to change the way they calculate metrics because the calculations represent the fundamental way they perceive the business. Unfortunately, this creates a problem when the CEO or CFO wants to know "total customer sales" for the entire company and can't get a valid answer. Just like the dueling spreadsheet phenomenon, the owners of each dashboard argue about whose data and metrics are right, leaving the CEO or CFO bewildered and frustrated.

Vertical Integration

Vertical alignment involves the integration of different types of performance dashboards into a virtual dashboard. Here, an organization with disparate operational, tactical, and strategic dashboards weaves them together so that users can navigate seamlessly from one to the other. This type of integration is tricky but not impossible.

For example, an operations group may have a strategic dashboard that tracks overall performance, a tactical dashboard for reporting and analysis, and an operational dashboard that monitors manufacturing processes. By integrating these dashboards, a user could view their performance in the scorecard view (i.e., strategic dashboard), then drill down into a report (i.e., tactical dashboard) and then view transaction details (i.e., operational dashboard) without knowing they are switching applications or systems.

To make this work, it is important that the three applications work off a common set of metrics. Then, developers need to create dynamic interfaces between each application so users can drill from one application to another without having to log in or reestablish their context. Typically, users can tell that they've moved from one application to the next because the data pops up in a new window and the screen and controls are different.

Another option is to use distributed query technology, or enterprise information integration (EII) tools to integrate data from different performance dashboards (see Chapter 3 for a description of EII). This approach creates a virtual view of data in other dashboards, queries them in response to user requests, and integrates the results on the fly and presents them to users. To improve performance in a distributed environment, administrators configure the systems to cache the results of commonly used queries and reports. Distributed queries work well when data volumes are small, data are relatively clean, and views do not require complex data joins or calculations.

CONSOLIDATION APPROACHES

Rather than trying to integrate disparate performance dashboards, sometimes it is best to consolidate them into a single system with consistent metrics and a common BI platform. Organizations have done this for years with independent data marts and data warehouses. Here are a few of the more common consolidation strategies.

1. Rehost

Organizations focused exclusively on reducing costs may simply opt to rehost existing performance dashboards onto a single operating platform. This "forklift" option enables firms to eliminate multiple servers and the staffs required to maintain them. However, rehosting does not change the dashboards in any way and does nothing to integrate data or deliver a single version of the truth. Its data model, metrics, and reports stay the same.

Sometimes, organizations rehost to replace proprietary technology or when a vendor withdraws support for a product, such as a database management system. Others rehost as a first step in a broader consolidation strategy.

2. Create from Scratch

Any homebuilder will tell you it is easier to build a new home than renovate an existing one. The same concept holds true for performance dashboards. Organizations that have multiple, redundant performance dashboards often decide that the easiest and most cost-effective option is to start anew.

In most cases, the architects of the new environment borrow heavily from the existing performance dashboards, but they also re-interview users and gather new requirements to build the most comprehensive and up-to-date dashboard possible.

One problem when starting from scratch is trying to figure out what to do with the existing performance dashboards. In some cases, the decision is easy. If end-users are not actively using the dashboards because they are unhappy with the performance, functionality, timeliness, or relevance, then it is a no-brainer to pull the plug. If it would cost too much to swap out tools, then it is best to leave the performance dashboard. For instance, one company determined that it would cost $16 million to convert its existing BI tool licenses to those of another vendor and decided not to make a change.

However, if a performance dashboard has a powerful business sponsor who wants to keep the application or if it has an active user base, then sometimes the best option is to "grandfather" the application and wait until the group is ready to migrate to the new environment. Sometimes, a CIO can accelerate that decision by withdrawing IT support for the grandfathered application. This makes it more costly for the group to continue using a nonstandard system.

3. Designate and Evolve

The "designate and evolve" approach involves designating one of the existing performance dashboards as the "corporate standard." The company then consolidates all other dashboards into the designated environment.

This frequently occurs when a larger company acquires a smaller one. The performance dashboard of the larger company becomes the corporate standard and the newly acquired performance dashboard is folded into it. This approach also makes sense when a company makes a strategic commitment to implement products from a specific vendor, whose performance dashboard product then is designated as the corporate "standard."

4. Backfill

When local groups hold considerable power, a politically acceptable approach is to backfill a data warehouse behind the existing performance dashboards. Here, the data warehouse serves as a staging area for the data contained in downstream performance dashboards. It consolidates all extracts and data feeds from source systems and logically integrates these data via keys and shared dimensions. Although this approach does not reduce the number of performance dashboards, it does reduce the number of source system extract programs that feed the dashboards.

5. "Conformed" Dashboards

One way to consolidate performance dashboards without physically integrating them is to restructure the dimensions and metrics in each mart so they "conform" with each other. Rather than start from scratch, an organization redesigns the data models and metrics used in existing dashboards so that they conform. They also standardize source system extracts so all dashboards are populated with the same data. This has the added benefit of reducing costs and complexity by consolidating multiple, redundant data feeds.

This approach is not without its challenges. Redesigning data models and changing extract feeds can wreak havoc on dashboard screens and reports. The redesign process can get unwieldy if there are a half-dozen or more performance dashboards that need to be conformed.

6. Dashboard of Dashboards

If your organization is highly decentralized and only the corporate group requires consolidated information, one option is to create a performance dashboard that pulls from all the existing dashboards, creating, in effect, a dashboard of dashboards. One benefit of this approach is that it does not change the existing dashboards at all, which is attractive politically. It also does not take much effort or money, but it does require the groups managing the existing dashboards to coordinate closely with the managers of the new downstream dashboard since any changes they make in the fields or metrics will affect the new dashboard.

SUMMARY

Centralized Approach. The best way to link performance dashboards is to use a centralized approach that enables a single project team to automatically generate custom dashboards designed to meet the information requirements of each group or individual in the organization. The centralized approach, however, requires a standardized architecture that specifies hardware and software components, programming conventions, a common data model, and a rigorous approach to ensuring high-quality data, among other things.

Top-Down Roll-Out. The best way to integrate performance dashboards using a centralized approach is to work from the top down. Here, the organization builds the corporate scorecard and uses it as a template to build lower-level scorecards. Each successive scorecard either reuses metrics from the previous scorecard or devises new ones to influence the higher-level metrics. This process enables organizations to "cascade" scorecards throughout the organization. To ensure consistency among cascaded scorecards, it is best if a single project team works with the business groups to build each scorecard on a common platform with consistent definitions of metrics.

Bottom-Up Roll-Out. In a bottom-up deployment, a business unit or department initiates a performance dashboard project. Through word of mouth, the project spreads throughout to the rest of the organization as various groups seek to reap the same benefits. Working bottom-up, however, can jeopardize data consistency if business units or departments create their own performance dashboards instead of building off an existing system.

Federated Approach. A federated approach tries to link existing, incompatible performance dashboards using a variety of techniques, including exchanging data via email or FTP or dynamically transferring files via middleware. Integrating non-overlapping performance dashboards is relatively straightforward, but integrating dashboards that define metrics differently and use different data models is challenging and sometimes more effort than it is worth.

Consolidation Techniques. Often, the simplest approach to integrating performance dashboards is simply to consolidate them into a single system. There is a range of consolidation techniques that mirror the way companies consolidate independent data marts and data warehouses. The most commonly used approach is "start from scratch," in which organizations build a new performance dashboard and either shut down or "grandfather" the legacy dashboards.

CHAPTER 14

How to Align Business and IT

PITCHED BATTLES

Tension Abounds

There has always been distrust between the business and the technical sides of an organization, but performance dashboard projects seem to heighten the tension to extreme levels. I have been in the technology industry for 17 years, and frankly, I've been shocked by the intensity of the distrust that I have witnessed between these two groups while researching this book.

Although there is much talk about the need to align business and information technology (IT) departments, little progress has been made. Part of the problem is systemic to IT departments and technical people, but another part involves the willingness of business executives and managers to engage with IT constructively on a long-term basis.

A performance dashboard project exacerbates the tension between business and IT because the two groups need to work closely together to deliver an effective solution. Unlike operational systems that are designed once and run for long periods of time without major modification, performance dashboards must continually adapt to the changing needs of the business. Consider this comment from a business manager who spearheads a performance dashboard project.

"We're supposed to submit a project plan that spells out what we are going to do every month and quarter and budget it out accordingly. But we can't operate that way. We know there will be a reorganization at least once a year, new processes, and potentially a major acquisition that forces the company to change strategy and move in a different direction. We have a project roadmap and cross check with the IT department, but we have to remain flexible to adapt to the business."

Battle over Control

In many cases, the pitched battle between the business and IT occurs because a business group has developed a performance dashboard outside of IT's purview but, due to its own success, can no longer keep up with demand. It needs IT's support and expertise to scale up the application and expand it to the rest of the company.

IT Ineptitude

The business is terrified about ceding control over the design, architecture, and budget of its pet project to a central IT group, which it views as slow, incompetent, and uncompromising. The business cites numerous examples of IT ineptitude to reinforce their notions that the IT department will suck the life blood out of the project and cause it to die a slow, inexorable death.

Here are a few comments from a business manager who used a small team of developers and rapid development techniques to build a performance dashboard in three months for an operations department.

"We need things today, not tomorrow, or else we go out of business. That's not how the IT world sees things; their business acumen is not the same and a sense of urgency is lacking. For instance, we asked IT for a data extract and they said it would take four months. We couldn't wait that long so we leveraged GUI-based technology ourselves and in one weekend created a temporary fix that worked well. But when IT finally delivered the extract, it had errors and required rework. After we launched the dashboard, it was so successful that it began consuming more disk space than they anticipated. Rather than working with us to come up with a satisfactory solution, they threatened to randomly delete our data unless we offloaded the data ourselves."

Spoiled Rotten

Of course, the IT group sees the business as a spoiled child who is too impatient and short-sighted to wait for IT to lay the necessary foundation to ensure the long-term success of their own system. IT is also bitter that the business expects them to deliver an ever-increasing number of "high priority" projects in shorter and shorter time frames while dealing with reduced costs, shrinking staff, and the constant threat of outsourcing and offshoring. One IT director recently lamented, "We work hard to meet the needs of our business customers but they are constantly adding and changing requirements, and they do not have the discipline to adhere to their own priorities. This makes it difficult for us to plan and impossible to succeed. It's a no-win situation."

The result is a tense standoff in which each group fulfills the other's worst predictions of each other. If the business has the upper hand, it will maintain control of the technical aspects of the project, creating another non-integrated system that will be costly to maintain in the long run. If IT gains control, it will halt development of new end-user functionality until it brings the infrastructure into conformance with its architectural standards and nothing of value will get accomplished.

So what can be done to slice through this Gordian knot? What will it take for both sides to enter into a relationship of mutual respect? Like a marriage on the rocks, business and IT need some serious counseling before they can work together effectively. Part of the counseling involves taking a number of baby steps that improve communication and overcome mutual distrust by helping each side better understand the other's challenges and dilemmas.

GENERAL COUNSELING

Counseling for IT

During the past ten years, IT has come to recognize that its job is not to deliver technology for technology's sake but to provide exquisite service to its customer—the business. Like an alcoholic who publicly admits the problem, this is a step in the right direction. However, this is only the first step. Verbal acknowledgment alone does not translate into remedial action.

To take the next step, IT must translate goodwill into action. The following questions can help an IT team determine whether it is paying lip service to meeting business needs or actually doing it. If the IT department can respond positively to most of the questions below, they are on the right path.

Does the IT team:

- Sit side by side with the business people it serves?
- Read the same trade magazines as its business counterparts?
- Attend the same conferences?
- Go to lunch regularly with business clients?
- Read the company's annual report?
- Read and understand the short- and long-term strategic plans for the company?
- Know the entire business process that drives the application it is developing or maintaining?
- Have an average ten years of experience in the company's industry?
- Have degrees in database administration and business administration?

What better way to align with the business than to eat, sleep, and breathe like a business person? Unfortunately, the IT department—by virtue of its being a separate organization within the company—often functions as a subculture that operates by its own rules. IT groups have their own jargon, incentives, reporting structure, and career paths, which are different from those of the business that it serves.

In contrast, technical teams embedded in departments or lines of business often enjoy a much healthier relationship with their business counterparts than corporate IT. Why? Rather than existing in a technical subculture, these "embedded" IT staff members sit side by side with the business people and function as a single team, with the same goals, bosses, and incentives.

Counseling for Business

Although IT groups generally get the lion's share of the blame for misalignment between business and IT, it takes two to tango, as they say. The business shares equal blame for the frustration that it feels towards IT—perhaps more so, because it does not always recognize how its actions and behavior contribute to the problem.

The business needs to understand that it changes too fast for IT to keep up. It harbors a short-term bias toward action and rarely takes a long-term view toward building sustainable value. This is especially true in U.S. companies, whose Wild West heritage makes them notorious for acting first and asking questions later. The business needs to slow down sometimes and ask whether change is really needed or if they are reacting in knee-jerk fashion to the latest event or issue of the day.

Decentralized organizations magnify this behavior, parceling out authority to divisions and departments to make decisions faster and in the context of local markets. Although there are advantages to decentralization, there are considerable downsides that contribute to the perpetual misalignment of the business and IT on an enterprise basis. The scores of analytical and operational silos, including the hundreds and thousands of pernicious spreadmarts that hamstring corporate productivity, testify to the business' fixation with speed and decentralized decision making.

Finally, the business has the upper hand in its relationship with IT and it often rules in a high-handed and capricious manner. In many organizations, executives threaten to outsource or offshore IT when it does not deliver sufficient value, rejecting the possibility that their own actions and decisions may have crippled IT's ability to function effectively. The business often lacks a reasonable degree of restraint and self-discipline when it comes to IT projects. One IT manager I talked with recently said his company's annual technology planning process is a sham because the business cannot discipline itself to live within its limits.

"Prior to the beginning of every calendar year, the business prioritizes IT projects for the next 12 months. Out of 90 projects, they identify 60 of them as 'high priority' and we create a schedule to deliver them," says the beleaguered IT manager. "But even before January 1st arrives, the business adds 20 more 'high-priority' projects to our list and adds another 20 projects before April. And then they tell us in March that we are already two months behind schedule!"

The IT manager said that he had negotiated a new project prioritization process with the business that required the business to operate in a "zero sum" environment. If they added projects after the budget was finalized, they needed to cut others. Although the IT manager was hopeful the new policy would succeed, he also half-jokingly commented that if he has to tell the business to abide by its new guidelines, he may stir up ill-will that might cost him his job.

ALIGNMENT TACTICS

Although it is not the sole source of the stalemate, the IT department needs to take the first step toward reconciliation. It needs to show that it wants to be an equal partner in the business, not an auxiliary that is more interested in technology than the bottom line. It can do this by becoming more responsive to business needs by improving the way it gathers business requirements, by adopting rapid development techniques, and by creating and selling a portfolio of analytical applications. To do these things, some organizations are creating an information management group that sits between the IT department and the business and is responsible for the timely delivery of information, reports, and analytics to users.

Business Requirements

According to Jill Dyche, partner at Baseline Consulting in Sherman Oaks, California, business requirements are the most "elegant bridge between IT and the business because each organization shares accountability for communicating and representing an understanding of what the business needs." However, many requirements-gathering sessions lead to less than stellar results. Part of the problem is that business users do not know what they want in a report or dashboard screen until they see it. Just asking what data users want to see invariably leads to the answer, "All of it," which helps neither side bridge the gulf.

Some organizations recruit business requirements analysts to interview users and translate their requirements into technical specifications for developers. Other organizations start with open-ended survey questions and then follow up with one-on-one interviews. Other techniques to gather requirements include joint-application design sessions, use case modeling, process modeling, and application storyboarding, among others.

Incremental Delivery

Once requirements are gathered, the technical team needs to step up and deliver value to the business much faster than it does today. Most IT managers understand that the days of five-year multi-million dollar projects are over; they know they need to deliver projects much faster with fewer dollars and guaranteed return on investment. The business no longer trusts IT to deliver the goods.

Speed without Compromise

However, most IT managers have not yet figured out how to deliver value fast without compromising architectural standards that are in the best interests of the company in the long run. Fortunately, there are solutions, and many come from the business intelligence (BI) arena. Because of the adaptive nature of BI systems, project managers have learned how to develop the architecture and infrastructure incrementally as they go along (see Exhibit 14.1).

Any IT manager will tell you that the hard part of building applications is not what you see on the screen but what lies underneath. Behind each application is an architecture that guides developers as they build a system that meets business requirements. At the heart of the architecture is an enterprise data model that

EXHIBIT 14.1   INCREMENTAL DEVELOPMENT TECHNIQUES

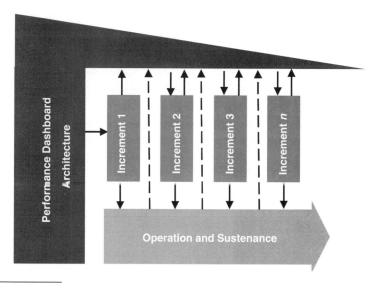

An incremental development methodology enables companies to create an enterprise architecture and infrastructure incrementally instead of all at once at the beginning of a project. The team delivers new infrastructure components and applications in three-month increments. Each increment extends and modifies the architecture in an iterative fashion.

represents how the organization works and how data elements relate to each other. Instead of spending months or even years creating this architecture, BI project managers now create it as they go along, one subject area at a time, usually in three-month increments.

During this three-month period, the technical team does the following: 1) gathers requirements for the new subject area (i.e., customer profitability); 2) extends the data model to support the subject area; 3) identifies what data to use among operational systems and elsewhere; 4) analyzes and maps the data to the target model; 5) documents these mappings or transformations; 6) develops reports and application screens; 7) tests and debugs the application; 8) pilot tests the application with users; 9) launches the application; 10) trains users.

"We roll out our KBI portal in incremental releases, and we treat each release as a production application. It doesn't launch until users sign off on it and we've gone through all the design and testing. This makes sure you have the numbers right," says Jim Rappé, an IT manager at International Truck and Engine Corporation.

Not Good Enough?

However, three months is still too long for most business managers to wait for applications or enhancements. Many business users want instant turnaround. The good news is that technical teams can meet these requirements if the data exist in a usable form. "If users ask for a new metric and the data are already in the data warehouse or an OLAP cube, we can do it in a few days," says Rappé.

Virtual Dashboards

If the data isn't already in a data warehousing repository and users don't want to wait, then a technical team in certain situations can populate dashboard metrics by querying source systems directly using enterprise information integration (EII) tools. Many commercial dashboard products use this technique to deliver dashboards quickly. The set-up is fairly straightforward and primarily involves mapping data in source systems to dashboard metrics. While this approach works well in a pinch, it inherits the liabilities of EII tools and distributed query techniques. The connections can be brittle and slow and often don't scale well to support large volumes of data or users, although this is improving. In general, this approach is appropriate as a way to prototype a performance dashboard or supplement it with limited amounts of external or real-time data stored outside of a BI repository.

Analytic Development Environments

On the front-end, newer BI tools, including many performance dashboard products, enable developers and power users to deliver minor enhancements in a few hours. Called analytical development environments (ADEs), these tools promise to accelerate development because they largely eliminate the need to write code. They are especially effective when deployed to a network of power users who can write reports on behalf of colleagues in their department. ADEs finally get the IT department out of the business of creating custom reports and applications for users (see Spotlight 14.1).

SPOTLIGHT 14.1   ANALYTICAL DEVELOPMENT ENVIRONMENTS: THE WAVE OF THE FUTURE

An analytical development environment (ADE) is a new generation of BI development tool that lets technically savvy business users create analytical applications rapidly, including performance dashboards. With an ADE, power users drag and drop visual components onto a graphical workbench where they can be connected and configured to create an analytical application without writing code.

ADEs, which are the technical complement to IDEs (integrated development environments), used to create transaction applications, promise to accelerate the development of performance dashboards and other analytical applications. Today, organizations spend way too much time customizing and extending BI tools and application packages to meet user requirements. On average, organizations customize about 33 percent of every packaged application and spend 7.5 months to deliver a final product—way too much time to meet fast-changing user needs.

The drag-and-drop nature of ADEs will shift development responsibilities away from IT staff and application developers. With an ADE, a power user can easily modify a packaged analytical application, flesh out a report definition, or create a new application or report from scratch once IT has established data connections and query objects. Thus, ADEs will once and for all get the IT staff out of the business of creating reports so they can focus on what they are best at: building robust data architectures and abstraction layers for end users.

Rapid Prototyping. ADE tools will also accelerate the trend toward rapid prototyping. Developers and power users can use an ADE tool in a joint application design session to get immediate feedback from users on data, application screens, metrics, and report designs. This iterative process results in better designed applications that are delivered more rapidly. Many vendors are shipping ADEs for specific applications to facilitate rapid prototyping. For example, many dashboard and scorecard solutions are ADEs.

Service-Oriented Architecture. The power behind ADEs comes from the fact that vendors have componentized the functionality of their BI tools. In the past, vendors hard-wired presentation, logic, and data functionality together. However, the advent of object-oriented programming and service-oriented architectures has enabled vendors to open up their products, componentizing functionality within a service-oriented architecture. The upshot is that ADEs enable developers to create multiple instances of components, store them centrally, and reuse them in other applications.

For more information on ADEs, you can download a 40-page report entitled "Development Techniques for Creating Analytic Applications" at www.tdwi.org.

A potential problem with ADEs is that whereas most accelerate development of the front end of the application, few address the back end. That is, most ADEs assume that the data are already loaded into a data warehouse or data mart or that the data are in good condition and can be accessed dynamically and integrated on the fly. Vendors that promise to build a dashboard in a day or week fall into this camp. Although they may have a slick-looking Web-based ADE, they assume that you have already done the hard work of cleaning up and integrating your data.

If the data do not exist for an analytical application, it usually takes technical teams three months at a minimum to source, clean, integrate, design, and test the data set and application before it can be rolled out. However, if the data exist, a developer or power user armed with an ADE should be able to create new views in several hours or days, depending on the complexity of the screens.

Portfolio Planning

One problem with the incremental development approach is that business users do not want their application delivered "piecemeal." They want it all at once or not at all. They do not see the usefulness of having a portion of the functionality they want or need and then waiting months or years for the rest. To curb the restless appetite of the business, it is helpful to unveil the bigger picture of where the project is going and how it will get there. You can do this by developing a BI portfolio that shows how IT can deliver a series of related applications built on a common infrastructure over a period of time, such as 18 to 24 months.

Jill Dyche, partner at Baseline Consulting in Sherman Oaks, California, created the chart shown in Exhibit 14.2 to help business executives understand the iterative process of building analytical applications and how they can accelerate the process if they want to pay the cost of creating parallel development teams.

The chart shows executives that they can get everything they want by building on a common infrastructure instead of adopting the "go-it-alone" approach. If they want their applications faster, they can pay for parallel development teams. This shields IT from accusations that it works too slowly, leaving decisions about speed and cost to the business.

Exhibit 14.3 shows the infrastructure that supports the portfolio of applications in Exhibit 14.2. The data model, which consists of multiple subject areas populated with data from multiple operational systems, is developed one subject area at a time. Each subject area, once added, multiplies the number of new applications that the environment supports.

In other words, there is not a one-to-one correlation between applications and subject areas. In fact, the value of the infrastructure expands exponentially as more subject areas are added. Each new subject area enables the organization to build many new applications on top of the integrated data. A data warehouse

EXHIBIT 14.2   BI DELIVERY PORTFOLIO

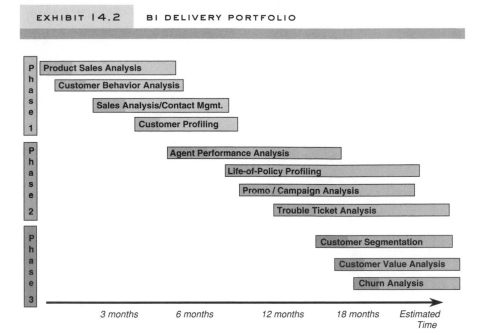

A BI portfolio makes it easier for executives to see that their needs will be met over the long term by building on a standard infrastructure. They can accelerate development using parallel teams but they will have to pay extra in the short run.

Source: Copyright © 2005, Baseline Consulting. Reprinted with permission.

with dozens of integrated subject areas can support an almost limitless number of applications, providing substantial business value. Once the data are stored in the data warehouse, applications can be delivered rapidly, in days or weeks (see Exhibit 14.4).

Debate over Standardization

One of the biggest stumbling blocks between the business and IT is the IT group's insistence on adhering to technical standards, which then become more important than delivering value to the business. As we discussed in Chapter 12, standardization enables the IT group to respond more quickly to user needs because the group can reuse skills, code, and products rather than start from scratch each time. However, IT's nearly zealous adherence to standards drives business people crazy.

"The head of information systems and architecture wants to restructure existing applications to run on a single set of ETL [extraction, transformation, and

EXHIBIT 14.3   INFRASTRUCTURE FOR A BI PORTFOLIO

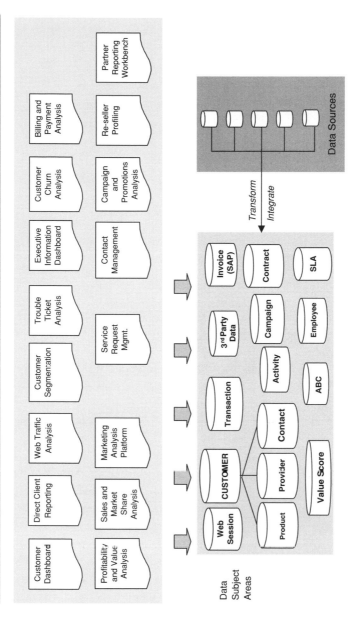

With a BI infrastructure, there is no longer a 1:1 ratio between applications and data structures. Each new subject area, which is populated with data from various data sources, multiplies the number of new applications that BI infrastructure can support.

Source: Copyright © 2005, Baseline Consulting. Reprinted with permission.

EXHIBIT 14.4   A BI INFRASTRUCTURE DELIVERS EXPONENTIAL VALUE

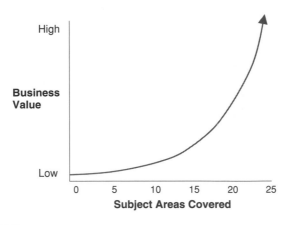

The value of a BI infrastructure increases exponentially as more subject areas are added. Each new subject area enables the organization to build many new applications on top of the integrated data.

loading] and BI tools. But one size doesn't fit all and what's it going to cost to harmonize everything into the new architecture? We spent a half million dollars on our scorecard—it's served hundreds of people for two years and it's stable—but it will cost $2 to $3 million to rebuild the application using the new standards. Meanwhile new work is backed up in the queue so where's the business value?" says one performance manager.

I recently attended a presentation by an IT manager at a health insurance company who had developed a strategic plan to foster a more collaborative partnership between corporate IT and the business. One of the more innovative elements in the plan was a way to create a standard application architecture that had buy-in from both the business and IT. The process of creating the standard architecture required both business and IT to evaluate current and proposed business applications, including performance dashboards. The plan calls for the business to evaluate the "business fit" of the applications and the IT department to evaluate the "architectural fit." The results of the evaluations are depicted on a quadrant chart that plots business fit on the y-axis and architectural fit on the x-axis (see Exhibit 14.5).

Applications in the lower left quadrant are candidates for elimination or consolidation—they are the low-hanging fruit that can help drive momentum behind the new architecture and standards. Applications in the upper right-hand quadrant represent an optimal fit from both a business and technical perspective and should be preserved.

| EXHIBIT 14.5 | APPLICATION SCORECARD FRAMEWORK |

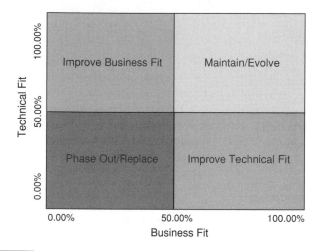

The quadrant chart above can be used to evaluate existing or potential applications in a company's portfolio. It is an excellent tool to help business and IT begin to communicate their needs and requirements in a more proactive, positive manner.

Applications in the remaining two quadrants—lower right and upper left—need modification before they meet both business and IT requirements. Business and IT leaders need to sit down and develop a strategy to bring each into compliance. The process of evaluating applications in this manner is one way for the business and IT to communicate their requirements to each other and overcome the mutual distrust that has darkened relations for years.

Structural Reorganization

Business Requirements Analysts

Another way to minimize the inherent conflict between business and IT is to use an intermediary to communicate between them. For example, many companies hire business requirements analysts to interview users and translate their requirements into technical specifications for developers.

However, these types of intermediaries have had mixed success. A business sponsor at a large insurance company said his firm hired specialists to "bridge the chasm" between the worlds of business and IT. "The results have been poor," he said. An IT manager was even more vocal: "Business requirements analysts are a big mistake because users never really know what they want when you ask them.

You need to show them something, and work iteratively, because your interpretation is never exactly what they had in mind. Plus, they'll come up with new things as they see the application."

Departmental IT

Other companies have experimented with embedding IT into departments and business units. We have seen that this can generate some extraordinarily successful applications, including some profiled in this book. However, this approach creates integration problems down the road. The business sponsor at the insurance company quoted above also tried this approach but said, "That method worked OK when we were constructing technology 'silos' that weren't integrated, but now integration is our chairman's top priority."

Steering Committees

Most companies use steering committees to align business and IT and provide guidance and governance for enterprise IT initiatives, including performance dashboards. Most companies have both a steering committee and a working committee.

The steering committee is comprised of high-level business representatives from various departments; it sets strategy, prioritizes projects, and allocates funds. The working committee, which is comprised of end-users and members of the technical team, gathers requirements, discusses enhancements, resolves data definitions, and addresses technical issues.

Some companies have even more layers of committees to guide an enterprise-scale project. A major insurance company, for example, has the following committees guide its enterprise data warehousing and BI effort:

- **Data Warehousing Advocacy Team.** Represents the executive steering committee, which sets the strategic direction for the data warehouse. Serves as a liaison to the Business Advisory Team.
- **Business Advisory Team.** Owns the data warehousing strategy and prioritizes projects. Is comprised of business representatives from all functional areas and meets every three weeks.
- **Data Governance Team.** Defines definitions and rules for data elements and enforces policies about data ownership, changes to data, and user training. Is comprised of 20 end-users representing every functional area.
- **BI Solutions Team.** The technical team that translates the decisions of the Business Advisory and Data Governance team into the system. Trains users.

Research from The Data Warehousing Institute (TDWI) shows that companies with successful BI solutions are more likely to employ BI steering committees,

EXHIBIT 14.6   ALIGNMENT STRATEGIES

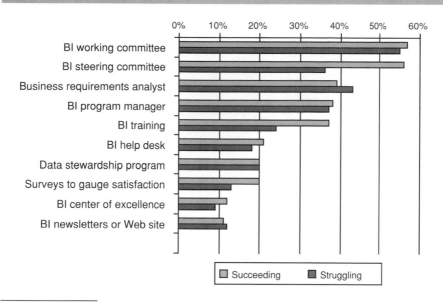

Companies use a variety of strategies to align business and IT and keep BI projects on track. Steering committees, training, and surveys show the most correlation with successful projects.

Source: Wayne Eckerson, "Smart Companies in the 21st Century: The Secrets of Creating Successful Business Intelligence Solutions" (*TDWI Report Series*, 2003).

provide adequate training, and use surveys to gauge user satisfaction (see Exhibit 14.6).

Information Management Groups

One of the best ways to align business and IT is to create a separate business unit that sits between the two groups and is charged with meeting business requirements in a timely fashion. These groups go by many names—Information Center, Information Management, or Business Intelligence Competency Center—and are a relatively new phenomenon. Those who run these organizations feel they are delivering significant value.

Absa Bank

For example, Absa Bank Ltd. in South Africa established its Information Management (IM) group in 2001, originally spinning components out of IT and marketing (i.e. customer information management) so it could focus on managing customer information, which corporate executives deemed was "essential to

EXHIBIT 14.7   INFORMATION MANAGEMENT GROUP AT ABSA BANK

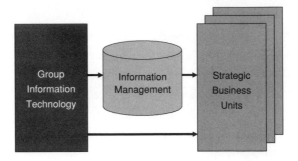

Absa Bank in South Africa created an Information Management (IM) group in 2001 to improve information delivery to business units. Spun off from corporate IT and marketing, the group is responsible for developing and managing the bank's overall information architecture as well as its data warehouse, BI tools and applications, data mining programs, and geographic information systems. It works closely with corporate IT, which manages the bank's operational systems, hardware, servers, and databases.

Source: Courtesy of Absa Bank.

the future success of the organization," according to Dave Donkin, group executive of Information Management at the bank. Today, the IM group's charter is to: 1) allow information- and knowledge-based strategy formulation and decision making, and 2) leverage information to improve business performance.

Absa's IM group is a shared service that is positioned between corporate IT and the strategic business units (see Exhibit 14.7). Corporate IT is responsible for managing the bank's 400+ operational applications, hardware, servers, databases, and the technology and applications architecture. On the other hand, the IM group is responsible for the data warehouse, BI tools and applications, data mining, and geographic information systems. IM also develops the bank's information strategy and architecture that defines how the bank stores and manipulates information in a cost-efficient and effective manner. IM oversees information governance activities, development methodologies, and end-user tools, among other things.

Close Cooperation

Although this division of responsibility seems clear-cut—corporate IT handles operational systems and IM manages analytical systems—there are many areas in which the two groups need to work closely together, such as defining the overall enterprise architecture for the bank. Also, whereas IM designs the data warehouse and analytical systems, corporate IT manages data warehousing operations (including extracting data from source systems) and builds and maintains the systems that run IM's analytical applications.

When the IM group was formed four years ago, Absa's data warehouse was "sub-optimized: not customer centric, operationally unstable, and not business directed," according to Donkin. Today, Absa's 20+ terabyte data warehouse is more stable (99 percent uptime) and more responsive to changing business needs. Also, it offers a slew of relevant business applications, such as scorecards, fraud detection, risk management, and customer analytics, which drive cross-sell, up-sell, retention, customer segmentation, and lifetime value scores.

One way that the IM group stays in touch with the information requirements of the business units is to assign a "business development manager" to each unit. The business development managers, who are business managers with substantial information and technology experience, meet regularly with their counterparts in the business units to discuss ways the units can better leverage information to meet their strategic objectives and address business problems.

The business development managers have been so effective in delivering value back to the business units that the IM group has added eight business development representatives in the past two years. "The best part is that the business units are so eager to get business development managers that some of them have transferred staff over to the IM division to enable establishment of the role," says Donkin.

Deutsche Börse

Similarly, Deutsche Börse, one of the leading international exchange organizations, several years ago established the Information Center, a technical group that is charged with turning data into information products requested by the business. To make this happen, the Information Center is responsible for data warehousing, ETL, data marts, reporting and analysis tools, data quality, job scheduling, and metadata management. The group is supported by corporate IT, which provides server support, database administration, and custom programming using Java, C, and other languages for components not available as commercial tools. This division of responsibility enables IT to focus solely on managing technology instead of trying to empower the business with information, which is not its strong suit, according to Dr. Klaus Detemple, director of information operations at the stock exchange.

A key to the success of IM groups is having individuals who combine a knowledge of the business and IT and are equally comfortable operating in either environment. Although rare today, these types of individuals are the future of IT. They know how to communicate with the business because they come from the business but they also have a strong technical background or experience managing IT projects.

IM groups take the pressure off the IT department from having to play a role it is not comfortable playing. The IM group enables technologists to focus on technology instead of the business. It gives them a separate career track and an organizational structure designed to maximize their capabilities. It is a win–win situation for both the business and IT.

SUMMARY

For years, business and IT have been locked in a cycle of mistrust. The business does not trust the IT department to place its interests above technical requirements. The IT department does not trust the business to stick to its priorities and provide adequate resources to meet technical requirements.

This cold war can begin to thaw if both sides take steps to understand each other's predicament and find new ways of working together. The IT department must learn the business, and think and talk in business terms. It also needs to develop infrastructure incrementally and create a BI portfolio that shows the business how it will generate valuable analytical applications over an extended period. It needs to establish an IM group that sits between IT and the business and mediates information requirements using individuals who combine a knowledge of both business and technology issues.

At the same time, the business needs to understand that Rome was not built in a day. They need to give IT time to develop a standard infrastructure that, once built, can accelerate development while reducing costs. And, while business units may be tempted to build their own applications, they need to work with the IT or IM group to transfer these early successes into valuable enterprise resources built on a common technology platform.

The good news is that during the past decade both sides have acknowledged the problem and seem earnest to address the issues that divide them. While this is a good first step, there is still much work to do to align business and IT.

CHAPTER 15

How to Ensure Adoption and Manage Performance

You have spent a lot of time and effort creating a performance dashboard. You have sold the idea, secured funding, and created a team. You have worked diligently with the business to define metrics and targets, standardize rules, and locate data, and you have worked with the technical team to create an appropriate business intelligence (BI) infrastructure. Now you are ready to launch and watch the performance dashboard do its magic.

But will it?

If you have done a good job selling the performance dashboard, expectations are high. Executives see it as a powerful tool to communicate strategy and change the behaviors of individuals and groups. They want employees to work more proactively, using timely information to fix problems, streamline processes, and make more effective decisions and plans. They want the performance dashboard to foster better collaboration between managers and staff and improve coordination among departments. They view the system as a way to manage performance, not just measure it. To them, the performance dashboard is like a steering wheel that they can turn right and left to keep the organization headed in the right direction.

TWO TASKS

1. Ensure Adoption

To meet these expectations, you still have two tasks to accomplish; the first is obvious: make sure people use the system! If people do not log in and view the data, the performance dashboard will not have any impact on the organization.

Nothing will change except your career prospects, which will plummet along with next year's performance dashboard budget.

2. Change the Culture

The second task is more formidable: use the performance dashboard to change the culture and optimize performance. A performance dashboard is an instrument of organizational change with a hairline trigger. Aim it in the right direction and performance will skyrocket; aim it in wrong direction and results will plummet along with worker morale (see Spotlight 15.1). Before rolling out a performance dashboard, executives and managers need to learn how to use it correctly to get the results they want.

SPOTLIGHT 15.1   EIGHT WAYS TO UNDERMINE A PERFORMANCE DASHBOARD

Performance dashboards are powerful agents of organizational change, but they can easily backfire and cause performance to decline or stall instead of climb. Below are eight cardinal sins that can turn a Performance Dashboard into a performance quagmire.

1. **Display too many metrics.** This scatters people's energy and attention and makes them less efficient and effective than before.

2. **Fail to get user buy-in.** Users resent when performance dashboards are imposed on them without their approval or input, and their productivity declines.

3. **Do not assign accountability.** People will not change their habits unless they are held accountable for the results.

4. **Create metrics that are too abstract.** Users cannot improve results if they do not understand what a metric means or what steps they can take to influence the outcome.

5. **Create metrics that undermine each another.** Employees work hard, but their efforts cancel each other out, sub-optimizing processes and demoralizing the staff.

6. **Use metrics to punish, not empower.** Managers who view metrics as a way to control rather than coach their staff cause morale and productivity to plummet.

7. **Attach compensation to metrics too soon.** This causes workers to spend too much time debating the reliability of a metric rather than doing their jobs.

8. **Fixating on measures, not management.** Managers who fixate on measures reward short-term spikes in performance, change plans too quickly, and fail to see larger trends driving performance.

STRATEGIES TO ENSURE ADOPTION

There is truth to the adage, "You can bring a horse to water, but you can't make it drink." Once you build a performance dashboard, will workers use it? Asking that question at the end of the development process is not a good sign! To ensure rapid uptake of the system, you need to develop a strategy to ensure end-user adoption at the very start of the project. Below are several techniques to guarantee end-user adoption and make the project a success.

1. Make the Business Drive It

The performance dashboard is a technical solution to a business imperative—the need to measure, monitor, and manage performance. To succeed, however, the technical solution must be driven by the business, not a technical team or the IT department. The head of a business unit or department must initiate the project, secure its funding, oversee its direction, sell it to mid-level managers, evangelize its use, and assume responsibility for its outcome. Chapter 4 showed that there is a strong correlation between an actively involved and committed business sponsor and a successful project with strong end-user adoption.

Too often the project team takes too much responsibility for driving a project, allowing the business to become a dispassionate observer instead of an actively involved leader. Or the IT department tries to meet the requirements of too many groups at once, which dilutes sponsorship. Without a clearly identifiable business sponsor driving the solution, the project gets mired down in bureaucracy, political infighting, and conflicting motivations. In both cases, the project gets a tepid response from target users, if it is deployed at all.

2. Make the Business Own It

This is a corollary to "make the business drive it" above. It is one thing for business sponsors to drive a project and quite another for them to put their reputations and careers on the line and assume responsibility for its outcome. When this happens, they will make time to attend meetings, provide guidance, and evangelize its importance to ensure that the project succeeds. Once a sponsor is committed to the project, the person has vested interest in getting users to adopt the system.

Business ownership also trickles down to lower levels of the organization, where the project gains traction as a resource that end-users find valuable. Here, representatives from various groups sit on governance committees that guide the project and oversee the information infrastructure. Also, subject matter experts from the business "own" the metrics in the performance dashboard and certify the accuracy of data on a daily basis, among other things.

Having the business involved at all levels in the design and administration of a performance dashboard creates considerable momentum for the system. The business has a vested interest in making sure the project succeeds. Business "owners" will identify problems and bring them to the attention of the governance committees or technical teams rather than let the problems fester into major impediments to system usage.

3. Make the Business Evangelize It

Active sponsors and drivers evangelize the performance dashboard every chance they get. They discuss the system at company and departmental meetings, and they write about it in company newsletters and on the corporate intranet. This communication continually emphasizes the importance of the project to the group's strategy and plans.

Sponsors also work with the project team to establish a marketing plan to promote the performance dashboard. The plan targets the various constituencies that either will use the system or whose support is required to build it. It defines the appropriate message for each constituency and the appropriate channels and frequency with which to deliver the information. The sponsor and project team work especially hard to sell the system to mid-level managers, who can make or break end-user adoption.

To promote the system, many organizations link articles to the performance dashboard that outline recent enhancements, answer frequently asked questions, and highlight testimonials of individuals who have had a major success with the system. They also provide links that enable users to provide feedback on the system, contact the help desk, request training, and search for help documents. Some organizations place this information on a corporate portal that users must go through to access the performance dashboard so it's hard to miss.

4. Make the Business Use It

Actions speak louder than words. Business sponsors and drivers may spend considerable time evangelizing the system, but if they do not use it, neither will anyone else. Workers pay close attention to verbal and visual cues from their managers about how much time and energy they should invest in learning a new system. When sponsors continue to rely on analysts to create reports or managers continue to use their spreadmarts, workers get the message loud and clear: do not go out on a limb when your boss is not. However, when executives and managers start using the output of a performance dashboard (whether directly or indirectly), the trickle-down effect is powerful.

"The tip of the iceberg that got this thing going was when executives had our reports all over the boardroom table and began asking 'Where's the data to back up this decision?'" says Deb Masdea, former director of business information and analysis at The Scotts Miracle-Gro Company.

To build awareness among top executives about the power of the information now available to them, Masdea met one-on-one with many of them to demonstrate the system and get them comfortable with the output, even if they would never directly use the system. To ensure penetration at lower levels of the organization, Masdea established a network of "super users" who create custom reports for colleagues in their department. "To get people to use [the system], we created super users, not because IT couldn't create reports, but because we needed people in the business who know how to get data and get others feeling comfortable with the system," says Masdea.

5. Prove the Validity of the Data

No matter how good the system looks, if users do not trust the data, they will not use it. Validating that data in a new performance dashboard is accurate is painstaking. Users tend to distrust data that they have not seen before. Even though data in the performance dashboard may be more accurate than in the reports or spreadmarts that employees currently use, they will reject the data unless you prove to them beyond a shadow of doubt that the new data can be reconciled with their own.

For example, Masdea's team also worked hard to convince executives, managers, and analysts that the data was accurate and trustworthy. "Once you automate [the delivery of information], they don't trust it. Their secretary didn't give it to them so they're suspicious. Once you get them to the point where they have looked at data in enough different ways that they are comfortable with it, they quickly get dependent on it. Now, our users can't live without logging on [to the system] in the morning!" says Masdea.

6. Add Personal Data to the Dashboard

There is nothing that gets users to use a performance dashboard faster than displaying information that lets them calculate what their bonus or commissions will be. This helped drive initial usage of the dashboards at Quicken Loans and Hewlett Packard TSG. Once users access the performance dashboard, they quickly realize that there is other content there that can help them perform their jobs more effectively and they're hooked. In addition, allowing users to personalize the dashboard gives them added motivation to visit the site. The ability to change colors, add Web links, and select which metrics, reports, and other documents they want on the home page, gives users a feeling of ownership that prompts them to return on a regular basis.

7. Train Users

Training is critical to the successful roll-out of a performance dashboard. Chapter 14 showed a correlation between training and BI success (see Exhibit 14.6). Ironically, however, most users do not want to attend training classes. This requires project teams to get creative in the way they deliver training. Organizations need to provide a mix of training options to cater to everyone's preferences and needs. Here are some of the more common methods to train workers and increase their proficiency using the performance dashboard:

- **One-on-One Training.** Reserved primarily for top executives and their administrative assistants. Also, "super users" (described previously in no. 4) can provide one-on-one training to colleagues in their departments.

- **Classroom Training.** Usually offered to employees that have not had any experience with the system. To encourage attendance, some organizations provide continuing education credits, keep class sizes small, and offer the course on a regular basis in a professional training center. Most courses run two to three hours in length.

- **Virtual Classrooms.** Because it is expensive and time consuming for people to travel to a training facility, many organizations provide virtual training using Web conferencing or online courseware. Web conferencing sessions are live events scheduled periodically in which users can see a demo of the system and ask questions. Most sessions can be archived for later viewing. Online learning software steps users through a series of learning objectives and uses quizzes to reinforce concepts and track users' progress. Online courseware can be delivered via the Web or CD-ROM.

- **Online Help.** Most companies provide various forms of "right-time" training through which users can learn about different metrics, features, and functions as they go along. Online help may consist of documents and user manuals housed on the corporate intranet or dynamic links embedded in the software that present users with context-sensitive help. Some organizations let users request one-on-one help via Web conferencing or NetMeeting utilities.

- **Release Updates.** Many companies are getting creative in the way they inform and train employees about the functionality contained in new releases of software. Some offer classroom training, but most inform users about the enhancements through e-mail, newsletters, online help, or intranet updates. Some build mini-online courses or animations that pop up when users log into the system, providing users with a painless way to stay current with the system if they desire.

- **Rotating Tips.** Many companies publish "Did You Know?" tips in e-newsletters and when users log in to the performance dashboard. These tips highlight high-value features, provide answers to commonly asked questions, and alert users to new content in the system. Some companies use these tips or show interesting facts other users have gleaned from the system. "These tidbits of facts and figures pique users' interest," says Dave Donkin, group leader of Information Management at Absa Bank Ltd. in South Africa.

- **Help Desk.** Most companies also let users call the company's help desk to get answers to questions, instead of just report problems. Help desk personnel keep a record of the most frequently asked questions and create a link to them from the corporate intranet and the performance dashboard.

8. Track Usage

The best way to judge the effectiveness of a new release and training programs is to monitor its usage. Some companies closely monitor usage statistics, using them as an early warning signal of problems with the software or its training. For example, International Truck and Engine Corporation tracks usage even during the pilot phase of a new release. "If only three people out of ten are using the system, we meet with the other seven to find out the problems they have with it and make changes before we roll out the release," says Jim Rappé.

Rappé's group has tracked usage statistics so closely that it now knows what the uptake rate should be after issuing a new release of the software. If adoption rates are lower than normal, the team jumps into action. "If usage is below the norm, we book a 30-minute presentation during a departmental meeting to provide additional education and answer questions. We try to be proactive," says Rappé.

9. Review Satisfaction

It is important to ask users periodically what they think of the system and to get their feedback. This helps in evaluating the overall effectiveness of the system and how it can improve in future releases. Hewlett Packard TSG conducts a customer satisfaction survey every six months. International Truck and Engine issues a survey once a year that lets users express requirements for future upgrades.

PERFORMANCE MANAGEMENT STRATEGIES

Once user adoption is ensured, the next task is more challenging: using the performance dashboard to change organizational culture and improve performance. Dr. Bob Frost, principal of Measurements International Inc., describes the impact that measuring performance has on individuals:

> There's something about performance charts. When most of us see a chart depicting our efforts, we immediately feel something—positive or negative. This feeling may be about the past or the future, but it's almost always motivational and emotional….If your employees know that you value metrics and track the entire organization's performance, an amazing thing happens: the culture changes. Whether mentally or on paper, employees begin to track how their own performance contributes to enterprise performance. And a 'results-tracking culture' is one of the most powerful competitive advantages your enterprise can have.[1]

The trick with a performance dashboard is to harness this emotional reaction to drive behavior in the direction that delivers the most value to the organization. This is not easy. Workers can react negatively to metrics that are improperly designed or circumvent them for personal gain. Or performance metrics and targets can push and pull individuals and the organization in potentially different directions. The following are recommendations about how to use metrics and performance dashboards to drive performance in the right direction.

Test Assumptions

This book earlier discussed the importance of strategy maps to define linkages among objectives and metrics. However, strategy maps are not just a design tool; executives should used them continuously to test assumptions about what drives performance and make adjustments. By fine-tuning strategy, metrics, targets, and initiatives, executives can use a performance dashboard to literally "steer" the organization in the right direction.

Ideally, each linkage correlates objectives and metrics using a mathematical relationship. For example, executives believe that if customer loyalty increases by 5 percent, revenues go up by 1 percent. A performance dashboard then enables executives to evaluate the validity of their assumptions about these linkages. Perhaps customer loyalty does not affect revenue growth as much as they thought, but product quality—which they did not specify as a revenue driver—correlates very strongly. They then add this new metric to the strategy map and recalibrate the linkages to create a more accurate model.

In the past, executives kept these assumptions and models of how the business operates in their heads. Often, they never formally expressed or tested these assumptions, sometimes with disastrous consequences. Many executives have launched multi-million-dollar initiatives based on false assumptions about what drives profits, revenues, or shareholder growth.

Focus on Management not Measurement

The temptation with performance dashboards is to focus too much on measures and results and not enough on process and strategy. When this happens, executives fail to see the "forest for the trees." They are so focused on measures that they fail to see the bigger picture of what is going on and what they need to do to move the organization in the right direction.

Whipsawing

One symptom of this problem is when executives reward or punish managers for short-term spikes in performance. When performance is evaluated every day or week, there is a tendency to overemphasize short-term fluctuations and miss emerging trends.

"Just like the temperature, metrics swing significantly. You need a process to balance that. You can't throw your planning away if you don't make your numbers one week. It is very counterproductive to overfocus and overdrive on specific elements. You may drive one metric up but the means you use to get there may not overall satisfy the needs of the business," says John Lochrie, senior vice president at Direct Energy Essential Home Services.

Achieving Balance

Lochrie recommends creating a set of metrics that balance the key drivers of the business, which for Direct Energy are operational efficiency, customer satisfaction, and employee satisfaction. "You should evaluate each metric by how good it is for employees, customers, and the business. If a customer likes it, but you kill your employees in the process, then you're ultimately going to fail," says Lochrie.

Examine the Business Context

It is also important to understand what is really driving the measures and continually reevaluate your assumptions. For instance, a performance decline may not mean employees are slacking off—even though this was the case in the past—something else may be going on that you have not anticipated. For instance, staff may be saddled with additional work or requirements that did not exist before. In many instances, the current metrics may no longer be a valid way to assess performance in a changing or more complex environment.

"What I've learned is don't just tend to the numbers. Think more about what is driving the numbers. Are people making the effort but just not getting there, or are people not making the effort any more because they can't overcome the challenges out there? You have to continually pause to take a breath, every 6 to 12 months, and assess the overall climate in which you are operating and ask whether the current metrics are still relevant," says Lochrie.

The important thing, he adds, is to make sure employees have the resources and training they need to be successful. This includes training their managers to provide them with assistance and guidance in the field. Ultimately, the goal is to make employees and, by extension, the organization successful.

Law of Diminishing Returns

Also, it is important to know when you become a victim of the law of diminishing returns. This is when the effort and cost to increase performance outweigh the returns. When a company first introduces a metric, performance usually increases rapidly but then it gradually tapers off. For instance, a company that starts tracking customer satisfaction sees scores increase from 50 percent to 70 percent in one year, but then can barely get the scores to nudge above 72 percent for the next three years no matter how much effort it expends. When you have reached the point of diminishing returns, it is better to expend the company's energies elsewhere.

Get User Buy-In

Avoid "Us versus Them"

Performance management is not something you impose on workers or do to them. Such heavy-handedness always backfires. When workers see performance metrics as a stick rather than a carrot, their enthusiasm and motivation will wane. To avoid an "us versus them" mentality, it is important to get users' feedback on the validity and reasonableness of metrics and targets before applying them. This can be done in group meetings, surveys, or comment forms.

Respond to All Input

However, do not make the mistake of taking feedback and not responding to it. Every comment should be recorded and a response delivered in person or in writing. This takes time but it demonstrates to workers that you have received their input, acknowledged their ideas, and taken them under consideration. It would also be helpful to schedule "open door" sessions in which workers can call, e-mail, or visit to discuss their concerns.

Expect Pushback

Workers often get nervous about the impact performance metrics will have on their jobs and compensation. So, expect users to push back, but do not be alarmed; this is part of the process. "The first thing that happens when you hold people accountable for metrics is that they say it isn't tracking them right. That's a healthy feedback loop. If you are not getting that pushback, you are probably not challenging the staff enough," says Ripley Maddock of Direct Energy Essential Home Services.

Explain the Data

If a worker has a serious issue with a metric or a performance result, the first thing to do is explain how the data were collected and calculated so the person understands the mechanics. Then work backward from individual events—a sale, a repair, a work order—to the aggregated data to see whether the system tracked the event correctly. "Too many times people will say, 'I don't think that metric is right.' We try to get them down to factual examples. Let's look at this sales order and see how it was measured. If they don't think the business should measure it this way, we'll bring that back up to management for review," says Direct Energy's Maddock (see Spotlight 15.2).

SPOTLIGHT 15.2   A TACTICAL DASHBOARD IN RETAIL SERVICES

In 1999, Direct Energy Essential Home Services, North America's largest competitive energy and home services retailer, was founded as a result of deregulation of the natural gas industry in Canada. To compete effectively in the open market, Direct Energy developed a tactical dashboard to monitor the execution of its new business strategy (see Exhibit 15.1).

"We knew we couldn't do business like we had previously," said Ripley Maddock, director of customer management at the company. "We now had to be driven by ROI, shareholder value, and customer needs. To make this transition, we needed a way to measure our performance against these new metrics and hold everyone in the organization—from executives to field technicians—accountable for the results."

Today, more than 400 personnel, including 300 field technicians, view their performance against budget contained in an easy-to-use Web-based dashboard that costs less than $100,000 a year to maintain. District managers use the dashboard to compare their district's and staff's performance against other districts. They review the results with field technicians on a regular basis and showcase individuals who have exceeded targets.

In the two years after Direct Energy implemented the dashboard, the firm reduced the number of repair calls by 2.82%, saving the company $1.3 million while improving customer service. Most of this reduction was driven by a *repeat call* metric on the dashboard, which tracks how many times a technician visits a household to fix a problem. Direct Energy believes this metric offers a good indicator of customer satisfaction and service efficiency, among other things.

Perhaps the most important benefit of the dashboard is that it has changed the entire tenor of discussions about performance at the company. According to Larry Ryan, the group's former general manager, the dashboard is a communications vehicle designed to bring managers and staff together to discuss how to meet or exceed performance expectations and fix outstanding problems, not to dwell on excuses for underachievement.

EXHIBIT 15.1   A SIMPLE TACTICAL DASHBOARD

STEM Corporate	Week Ending 6-Mar				March 2004			December 2003		2004 Year to Date		
STEM CORPORATE	28-Feb	6-Mar	Last Week Budget	Last Week Variance	Actual	Budget	Variance	Actual	Variance	Actual	Budget	Variance
Sales Management												
Measure A	337	154	217	-63	154	217	-63	0	0	2,505	2,432	73
Measure B	29.35%	29.07%	30.00%	-0.03%	29.07%	30.00%	-0.03%	0.00%	0.00%	29.36%	30.00%	-0.64%
Measure C	22.68%	16.03%	30.00%	-14.07%	16.03%	30.00%	-14.07%	0.00%	0.00%	28.29%	30.00%	-1.71%
Measure D	$4,159.87	$3,779.22	$3,350.00	$429.22	$3,779.22	$3,350.00	$429.22	$0.00	$0.00	$3,753.90	$3,350.00	$403.10
Measure E	58.68%	56.70%	48.00%	8.70%	56.70%	48.00%	8.70%	0.00%	0.00%	58.68%	48.00%	10.68%
Measure F	248	229	0	229	229	0	229	0	0	2524	0	2524
Product Holdings												
Measure A	809	-1,979	807	-2,786	-1,979	807	-2,786	0	0	6,426	-350	6,826
Measure B	607	480	0	480	480	0	480	0	0	6,509	0	6,509
Customer Satisfaction												
Measure A	89.26%	89.86%	90.00%	-0.14%	89.86%	90.00%	-0.14%	0.00%	0.00%	86.20%	90.00%	-3.80%
Measure B	0.00%	0.00%	75.00%	0.00%	0.00%	75.00%	0.00%	0.00%	0.00%	67.46%	75.00%	17.54%
Technician Efficiency												
Measure A	88.41%	87.70%	85.00%	2.70%	87.70%	85.00%	2.70%	0.00%	0.00%	85.90%	85.00%	0.90%
Measure B	6.3	5.2	5.7	-0.5	5.2	5.7	-0.5	0	0	5.9	5.7	0.2
Measure C	11.33%	9.87%	9.50%	0.37%	9.87%	9.50%	0.37%	0.00%	0.00%	11.72%	9.50%	2.22%
Workload												
Measure A	10,349	7,229	6,855	372	7,229	6,855	372	0	0	96,844	83,320	13,524
Measure B	2,808	1,906	3,008	-1,102	1,906	3,008	-1,102	0	0	21,207	27,542	-6,335

Legend for MTD and YTD figures
Actual/Budget >= .98
Actual/Budget >= .9499 & < .98
Actual/Budget < .9499
NA

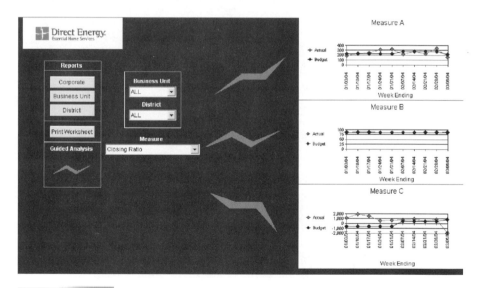

This tactical dashboard from Direct Energy Essential Home Services keeps things simple, which is often best. The dashboard (top image) lets users define three key metrics to view by selecting from a list of measures, such as closing ratio, that appear in a drop-down box. Users then choose the business unit and district they want to see data for using the drop-down boxes above the measures drop-down box. If users want more detailed data, they cannot yet drill down into the charts or select other dimensions or filters. However, the dashboard does provides a button to view a list of color-coded corporate, business unit, or district reports, which they can display on the screen or print as Excel spreadsheets (bottom image). If they are not sure which report to view, they can click on the "guided analysis" button, which steps them through a series of "yes/no" questions to narrow down their choices.

Source: Copyright © 2005 Direct Energy–Essential Home Services. Reprinted with Permission.

Let Users Focus

A performance dashboard uses metrics to focus workers on high-value tasks that drive performance in the right direction. The fewer the metrics, the more focused workers can be. Thus, a critical factor in using dashboards to optimize performance is to select the right number of metrics to display on the screen for each user. Unfortunately, no one agrees on a single number. However, most believe it is counterproductive to overwhelm workers with too many metrics.

As a rule of thumb, workers managing operational processes should track fewer metrics, probably less than a handful, whereas executives responsible for setting strategic direction should view many more metrics, perhaps a dozen or more, each with multiple levels of drill-down to lower level metrics. The more areas and activities someone manages and oversees, the more metrics that person will need to monitor.

Hold Users Accountable

It is important that there is an individual or group accountable for the outcome of each metric. This puts teeth into the measures and galvanizes the organization. It lets everyone know in a very personal way that executives are serious about using the dashboard to improve performance and change the culture.

It is best to hold individuals accountable for results. This is true even when performance is a shared responsibility among many people and groups, such as customer loyalty. However, the accountable individual must be given certain authority to allocate resources, make decisions, delegate responsibility, and reward performance to achieve the objectives.

Another way to galvanize the organization around performance metrics and reinforce accountabilities is to publicize the results broadly. Allow people to see how their performance compares with that of their peers. This fosters a competitive environment in which few people want to be seen as laggards or slackers in the organization.

Empower Users

If you are going to hold people accountable, you have to empower them to act. You need to give them more leeway to make decisions and not force them to adhere to prescribed processes or procedures. You also need to make it clear how they can affect the measures. This means creating measures that are easy to understand and appropriate to each level in the organization. For example, you cannot expect assembly floor managers to know how to improve net profits, but they probably have a good idea about how to reduce scrap and quality problems.

"For metrics to be motivational, people must be able to see what to do. There must be a *line of sight* between the actions employees can take and the changes that occur in the measure," writes Frost.[2]

Train Managers to Coach

The problem with individual performance reviews is that they rarely happen. Often, the reason is because managers are too busy to compile the relevant information and write up the results. However, a performance dashboard collects a lot of the information for managers. It becomes an effective tool to help managers conduct performance reviews on a regular, or even continuous basis as needed.

The key to using a performance dashboard for performance reviews is not to punish workers for poor performance, but help them see how they can improve. Managers need to know how to provide workers with the resources, tools, and knowledge to help their staff succeed. This requires training, not just education, says Lochrie. "You can educate managers by going through the process and telling them what's good and bad, and then they go out and do their own thing. By training, you physically witness what the managers do and make sure they do the right things and behave in the right way. Then you coach and re-coach them."

Reinforce with Monetary Incentives

A major way to focus workers' attention on the metrics is to pay for performance. It has been said that "What gets measured, gets done." However, it is also true that "What gets done is what you pay people to do."

None of the companies mentioned in this book use performance dashboard as the exclusive vehicle for calculating bonus payments or total compensation. However, most have a few metrics in the dashboard that affect compensation, and some are slowly moving to adopt the performance dashboard as the primary tool for determining bonus payouts.

It is important not to attach compensation to metrics and targets until they become stable. It is not easy to change metrics once people's compensation is based on them. Even the smallest change can cause people's income to rise or fall dramatically, and they will protest vehemently. If a change or restatement of results is required, it is best if it works in favor of the staff, to avoid dissension.

Another reason to postpone attaching pay to metrics is that it takes time to close all the loopholes that might allow staff to jury-rig the results or take unwarranted shortcuts to boost their performance scores. In a similar vein, you should not let executives design metrics that are used to calculate their bonus payments. They will surely shape the metrics to ensure that they can meet their numbers and earn a sizable bonus.

SUMMARY

End-User Adoption. A performance dashboard is a powerful agent of organizational change. However, if employees do not use the system, the dashboard will not have any impact at all. Thus, the first task of any business performance manager is to ensure that employees use the system and see it as an integral part of how they do their jobs.

Ensuring end-user adoption starts at the beginning of the project when business sponsors and drivers are being recruited. Business sponsors must provide the organization with the right visual and verbal cues that the system is worth the time and effort to learn and use. Sponsors need to sell and evangelize the project, accept responsibility for its outcome, and, most importantly, use the system. Sponsors must also ensure that lower levels of the organization step into "ownership" roles, such as serving on stewardship committees and taking responsibility for defining, updating, and certifying key metrics and data elements.

Another key element to ensuring end-user adoption is to get users to trust the data in the new system. This requires the project team to reconcile data in the new system with data in the old systems. Other techniques to ensure a fast uptake of the performance dashboard include flexible training, usage tracking, and regular surveys of end-user satisfaction.

Performance Management. A performance dashboard is a tool to help the organization achieve its strategic objectives. To do that, the performance dashboard needs to motivate individuals and groups to work on the right tasks that move the organization in the right direction. However, it is not easy to ensure that every metric has its intended effect on its target audience. This requires executives to constantly fine-tune their assumptions about what is really driving performance.

A strategy map is a good way for executives to document and test their assumptions about the relationships between metrics. They also need to beware of fixating on short-term results without considering larger trends driving performance, which may require new or revised metrics to track accurately. Most importantly, executives need to ensure that managers and staff have the appropriate knowledge and resources to succeed. Managers, in particular, need to be trained how to use the performance dashboard to empower staff, not punish them.

Metrics and performance dashboards naturally get users' competitive juices flowing. To sustain motivation, organizations can publicize performance results so workers can compare their performance against that of their peers. They can also attach bonus payments to performance results, which really ups the ante. However, before mixing pay with performance, executives need to make sure the metrics are stable, reliable, and tamperproof.

NOTES

1. Dr. Bob Frost, "Measuring Performance" (Ogdensburg, NY: Measurements International Inc., 2000), p. 43.
2. Ibid.

Criteria for Evaluating Performance Dashboards

Whether you plan to build or buy a performance dashboard, you can use these criteria to evaluate potential products or solutions and determine whether it is a good fit for your organization.

DESIGN

- **Web-Based.** Simplifies user access and centralizes data management and administration, making it easier to support thousands of users. Also avoids downloading large volumes of data to user desktops across potentially low-speed networks.
- **End-User Design.** Lets authorized end-users define objectives, metrics, targets, thresholds, initiatives, and alerts quickly without coding.
- **Associations.** Lets authorized end-users associate objectives, metrics, targets, and initiatives with each other.
- **Multiple Targets.** Lets users apply two or more targets and associated thresholds to each metric, including forecasts, budgets, prior actuals, and external benchmarks, among others.
- **Groupings.** Lets authorized end-users categorize objectives, metrics, and initiatives by different perspectives.
- **Layouts.** Provides various ways to group related metrics, scorecards, and other objects on the screen, such as tabs, folders, tables, columns, and custom designs.
- **Strategy Maps.** Lets executives visually map linkages between metrics and estimate and test the degree of correlation.

- **Personalizable.** Lets end-users select metrics, alerts, and other objects from authorized lists and arrange them on the screen to suit their preferences without coding.

- **Flexible Graphs.** Provides various types of graphs, symbols, and color-coding that let users quickly evaluate performance state, trends, and variance for critical metrics.

- **Multiple Disciplines.** Supports multiple methodologies for measuring and managing performance: Balanced Scorecards, Six Sigma, Total Quality Management, Economic Value Add, European Foundation of Quality Management, and ISO 9000.

ANALYSIS

- **Layered.** Arranges information in layers, with each successive layer providing additional detail and perspectives about a metric, process, or event.

- **Tables and Charts.** Plots data using tables and a wide selection of chart types. Lets users toggle between a table and a chart or different chart types or lets them view both a table and chart on a single page.

- **Comparisons.** Tables and charts compare data with targets and thresholds by applying rules against a repository of performance data to ensure fast response times.

- **Drill Down/Up.** Lets users drill down from summary level views of metrics to detailed views with a single click of the mouse on the object they want to view in more detail.

- **Drill Across.** Lets users switch views of a metric by changing dimensions (i.e., customer, geography, channel) using a drop-down list box or some other graphical control.

- **Drill Through.** Lets users drill through to transaction details stored in a remote system (e.g., a data warehouse, operational system, or external database) or online reports created in other applications.

- **Interactive Reports.** Lets users sort, rank, filter, regroup, or format the data, and insert or delete columns, modify calculations, and drill to more detail if available.

- **Landmarks.** Visually shows users where they are in the data using a path metaphor or decision tree. Lets them return to any previous location with a single click.

- **Guided.** Uses steps to guide less experienced users through the data or analysis by limiting the drill down/across paths and providing context-sensitive recommendations for next steps (i.e., reports to see or actions to take).

- **Dynamic Views.** Lets users define and subscribe to new views of "right-time" data coming from one or more operational systems.
- **Advanced Analysis.** Lets users perform "what if" analysis to model scenarios and perform regressions to improve the accuracy of forecasts, among other things.

DELIVERY

- **Access.** Lets managers access different scorecards at various levels of the organization.
- **Publishing.** Lets users publish custom views of the data to the Web for their own use or for others to view. The views are automatically updated with the latest data when users next access them.
- **Custom Output.** Lets users schedule and publish views in a variety of formats (i.e., Web, Excel, PDF, and so on) to a variety of channels (e.g., Web, e-mail, printer, wireless device).
- **Custom Access.** Lets users view and interact with the dashboard via wireless devices and access published views via Excel and PowerPoint.
- **Portable.** Lets users disconnect from the network and take the dashboard with them on the road. This can be done by exporting to Excel or creating a replica of the original view or report.
- **Printable.** Lets users print one or more views in the dashboard with proper page breaks and headings, in any order they prefer, such as from most to least below target.
- **Annotations.** Lets users attach comments to individual metrics and respond to comments made by others.
- **Workflow.** Lets users set up a workflow that routes their published view of data to designated people for review and/or approval.
- **Data Entry.** Provides forms that let users enter performance data manually and automatically reminds them to fill out the forms.
- **Properties.** Lets end-users right-click on any object to examine its properties, such as its owner, when it was last refreshed, how it was derived, and so on.
- **Multi-Source Queries.** Dynamically populates different elements on a dashboard screen with data from different sources, or merges data from multiple sources into a single element on the fly.

ADMINISTRATION

- **Metadata.** Stores definitions and rules about metrics, dimensions, hierarchies, user roles, preferences, and system configuration, among other things, for static lookup, auditing, and dynamic runtime invocation.

- **Customizable.** Lets administrators customize the screens by roles and users, displaying only the tabs, metrics, reports, and data that users are authorized to see.

- **Role-Based Security.** Dynamically displays only the objectives, metrics, initiatives, and other objects that users are authorized to see based on their role in the organization.

- **Row-and-Column Security.** An extra level of security provided at the database level that prevents users from seeing specific rows or columns based on their security profile.

- **Audit Trails.** The software records every change made to the system and by whom and when for control and auditing purposes.

- **Lock-Outs.** Keeps users from changing manually entered data and comments after a certain date to prevent tampering.

- **Usage Statistics.** Tracks usage by users and objects. Used to monitor uptake of the software by target users and for chargebacks.

- **Configuration.** Lets administrators configure the software to run against various data sources, design multidimensional models for analysis, set up drill paths and prompts, customize layouts, manage security, and tune the software for performance, among other things.

- **Responsive.** Lets developers deliver new capabilities within days or weeks, not months or years.

- **Intelligent Agents.** Lets administrators create rules that trigger a series of context-sensitive actions in response to an exception condition, such as sending different types of alerts (i.e., Web, pager, e-mail) based on the nature of the exception; lets administrators issue queries to locate the right person to call or perform other functions.

INFRASTRUCTURE

- **Compatibility.** Works with existing hardware, software, database, network, and storage systems.

- **Alignment.** Works within your organization's existing information architecture that specifies how data flow from operational systems to end-users for reporting and analysis purposes.

- **Standards.** Supports industry standard interfaces, technologies, and frameworks, such as Web Services, XML, LDAP, services-oriented architectures, and so on.

- **Data Management.** Stores historical performance data in a data mart or data warehouse; stores "right-time" data in an operational data store or online cache; and accesses "real-time" data via middleware (i.e., EAI) or dynamic queries against operational systems (i.e., EII).

- **Application Integration.** Integrates with third-party applications, such as portals, budgeting, planning, forecast, project management, and operational applications. Integration can be done via an import/export mechanism, exchanging data and metadata via a synchronization mechanism, or programmatically using application programming interfaces and middleware.

- **Data Integration.** Reads any data type (e.g., Excel files, Web pages, text, XML, relational data) from any system (e.g., mainframe, minicomputer, file server) and stores it to an intermediary server where the data can be scrubbed, transformed, and joined as needed and loaded into the performance dashboard.

- **Multidimensional Views.** Supports multidimensional views of data, usually delivered via an OLAP tool that either stores data in a specialized multidimensional database or maps relational data into a multidimensional view on the fly.

- **Security.** Integrates with an organization's existing security system and supports security standards, such as LDAP.

- **Software Customization.** Lets developers customize the look and feel or functionality of the software using application programming interfaces and custom code, preferably in an industry standard language, such as XML or Java.

- **Fast.** Provides fast response times to user clicks and requests for data, measured in seconds not minutes.

- **Scalable.** Performance doesn't degrade no matter how many users are on the system at any given time or how much data are stored or requested at a given time.

- **Reliable.** The system is continuously available, even when new data are being loaded into the system or updated, and suffers few, if any, outages.

VENDORS

- **Type.** Does the vendor offer a best of breed or integrated solution? If the former, does it focus solely on delivering Balanced Scorecards or some other type of dashboard (i.e., operational or tactical)? Does it sell dashboards exclusively or broader BI solutions? If it sells an integrated solution, does the vendor focus solely on business performance management (i.e., budgeting, planning, dashboarding, reporting, and analysis software) or does it sell an enterprise suite of applications including BPM? Best of breed solutions offer greater functionality but don't integrate as well as packaged solutions or enterprise suites.

- **Viability.** Is the vendor a startup or established player? If your organization is a leading-edge adopter of technology, a startup might be better, to gain a competitive advantage. If not, selecting an established player is the better route.

- **Partnering.** How much is the vendor willing to partner with your organization to ensure its success? Does it leave consulting to a third party or provide such services itself? How high do you have to escalate a problem within the vendor organization before you get a satisfactory response? Observing vendors during scripted demos, proofs of concept, and negotiations provides clues to their commitment to your success later on.

- **Service and Support.** Check references to find out the quality of the vendor's service and support. The vendor help desk can bail you out of tight situations, so they had better be good.

- **Pricing.** How flexible is the vendor pricing? Does it offer named user, concurrent user, role-based, or server-based pricing or variants of all three? Does it charge by server, CPU, or CPU clockspeed? The latter can be expensive if you upgrade your hardware. Are maintenance charges based on list price or net price? Does maintenance include all new releases and versions or just point upgrades?

- **Technology.** Does the established vendor need to upgrade its architecture to keep pace with advances in technology? If the industry spawns more than one startup with modern architectures and substantially lower prices, the vendor may soon get squeezed by its legacy technology.

Glossary

Active data warehousing. A hybrid data warehousing platform espoused by Teradata, a division of NCR, that supports both analytical and operational queries.

Agents. A rule-based engine that triggers a flexible set of actions in response to an event or exception condition, such as sending different types of alerts, querying data, or creating a workflow process to resolve a situation.

Alerts. Notifications sent by users or administrators that let users know when a metric exceeds predefined thresholds.

Balanced Scorecard. A strategic dashboard methodology defined by Professor Robert S. Kaplan and consultant David P. Norton using a balanced set of metrics across all facets of an organization that focus employees on the activities and tasks that will achieve strategic objectives and deliver lasting business value.

Business performance management. A series of organizational processes and applications designed to optimize the execution of business strategy. Includes Performance Dashboards as well as financial consolidation and reporting, forecasting, planning, and budgeting, among other things.

Business process management. Technology designed to automate and optimize business processes using modelling, work flow and middleware tools.

Corporate portal. A personalized Web interface to business content that people need to do their jobs. (Courtesy of Colin White.)

Dashboard. A visual display mechanism used in an operationally oriented performance management system that measures performance against targets and thresholds using right-time data.

Data. The output of source systems and applications, i.e., transaction data or text data.

Data mining. Also known as knowledge discovery in databases (KDD), data mining lets statisticians and skilled business analysts create models that automatically "mine" or discover patterns in the data and generate statistical models and rules.

Data mart. A data warehouse that focuses on a single subject area and is targeted to a specific homogeneous group of users.

Data model. The logical representation of how the business operates and its physical instantiation within a database management system.

Data warehouse. A repository of clean, integrated information culled from multiple systems that delivers information to end-users or downstream data marts.

Enterprise application integration (EAI). Middleware that integrates applications by transmitting events among applications in near real time.

Enterprise information integration (EII). Tools that query multiple, distributed data sources and join the results on the fly for display to end-users.

Extraction, transformation, and loading (ETL). Tools that extract, transform, and load data from source systems into a data warehouse or data mart.

Graph. A visual display of quantitative data that includes a scale, visible or suggested, along an axis of some sort. Examples of graphs are charts (e.g., bar, pie, line, scatterplots, and so on), histograms, sparklines, empire graphs, meters, gauges, and dials. (Courtesy of Stephen Few.)

Information. Transactional data that have been integrated or aggregated for analysis.

Key Performance Indicator (KPI). A metric measuring how well the organization or individual performs an operational, tactical, or strategic activity that is critical for the current and future success of the organization.

Lagging indicator. A KPI that measures the output of past activities, such as most financial metrics.

Leading indicator. A KPI that measures activities that have a significant effect on future performance.

Measurement. The result or output of measuring an object or activity.

Metric. The standard measurement of a known object or activity. For example, a company has a metric to calculate customer profitability and another that calculates customer loyalty.

Online analytical processing (OLAP). Gives users the ability to slice and dice information dimensionally. OLAP databases (also called multidimensional databases) store information dimensionally, whereas OLAP tools let users access and analyze those data.

Operational dashboard. A performance management system that delivers right-time information about core operational processes and emphasizes monitoring more than analysis or management capabilities in a performance dashboard framework.

Operational data store (ODS). A slimmed-down data warehouse designed to deliver rapid responses to short, operational queries, such as a request by a telemarketer for a profile of a customer who just called in.

Parameterized report. A report offering users pick lists or prompts that let users filter a report dynamically. Mimics OLAP and ad hoc querying to a certain degree.

Performance dashboard. A multilayered application built on a business intelligence and data integration infrastructure that lets users monitor, analyze, and manage performance using a dashboard or scorecard interface. Also called a performance management system.

Performance management system. An information system built on a business intelligence and data integration infrastructure that lets users monitor, analyze, and manage performance using a dashboard or scorecard interface. Also, a performance dashboard.

Query and reporting tools. Tools used by end-users to create their own reports.

Real time. The delivery of information about events as soon as they occur versus right time, which delivers information to users when they need it to make proactive decisions.

Report design tools. Tools used by professional developers or business authors to create custom reports.

Right time. The delivery of information to users when they need it to make proactive decisions. Right-time data delivery ranges from seconds to days or weeks, depending on user requirements.

Scorecard. A visual display mechanism used in a strategically oriented performance management system that charts progress towards achieving strategic objectives by comparing performance against targets and thresholds.

Spreadmart. A spreadsheet or desktop database created by a business user that functions like a surrogate data mart, containing unique terms, definitions, and rules that are not consistent with those used in other systems throughout the enterprise.

Strategic dashboard. A performance management system that focuses employees on the activities and tasks that will achieve strategic objectives and deliver lasting business value. It emphasizes management more than analysis or monitoring capabilities in a performance dashboard framework.

Strategy map. A tool used in a strategic dashboard or Balanced Scorecard to define linkages between strategic objectives and the measures that represent them. Used to both create and refine the organizational strategy and help executives test their assumptions about causal linkages between objectives and metrics.

Symbol. An image or shape that refers to something else. Common dashboard examples are colored circles, arrows, icons, and traffic lights.

Tactical dashboard. A performance management system that lets managers and analysts track the progress of departmental initiatives and projects and analyze trends and issues. It emphasizes analysis more than monitoring or management capabilities in a performance dashboard framework.

Index